Empty Without You

Other Books by Rodger Streitmatter

Mightier than the Sword:
How the News Media Have Shaped
American History

Unspeakable:
The Rise of the Gay and Lesbian
Press in America

Raising Her Voice:
African-American Women Journalists
Who Changed History

THE WHITE HOUSE
WASHINGTON

"Sunday night, March 5th: Hick, my dearest, I cannot go to bed to-night without a word to you. I felt a little as though a part of me was leaving to-night, you have grown so much to be a part of my life that it is empty without you even though I'm busy every minute.

These are strange days & very odd to me but I'll remember the joys & try to plan pleasant things & count the days between our times to-gether!"

Empty Without You

THE INTIMATE LETTERS of ELEANOR ROOSEVELT and LORENA HICKOK

Edited by

RODGER STREITMATTER

DA CAPO PRESS

Quote on page ix from Virginia Woolf, A Room of One's Own, *New York: Harcourt, Brace & World, 1957 [1929].*
All illustrations from the Franklin D. Roosevelt Library.

A CIP catalog record for this book is available from the Library of Congress
ISBN 0-306-80998-2

First Da Capo Press Edition 2000

Published by Da Capo Press
A Member of the Perseus Books Group
http://www.dacapopress.com

1 2 3 4 5 6 7 8 9 10——04 03 02 01 00

To Tom

When a subject is highly controversial—and any question about sex is that—one cannot hope to tell the truth. One can only show how one came to hold whatever opinion one does hold.

VIRGINIA WOOLF

Contents

Introduction

Anna Eleanor Roosevelt Roosevelt was, by birth as well as marriage, a patrician—descended from one of the fifty-six men who signed the Declaration of Independence and married to a president of the United States. At fifteen, Eleanor was sent off to England to a proper finishing school where she learned to speak French and comport herself as an aristocratic lady. She returned to America, married her handsome and ebullient fifth cousin, and proceeded to fill the role for which she had been born and bred: producing the next generation of Roosevelts and standing dutifully beside her husband as his political fortunes lifted him to the pinnacle of American statesmanship. It was a pinnacle not unfamiliar to Eleanor, who had often visited her Uncle Teddy when he had resided in the White House some thirty years earlier. By 1933 when Eleanor became first lady, her five-foot-eleven-inch frame and bolt-upright posture made her the epitome of stately grace. She was not a natural beauty, but she was most definitely a lady.

The most that Lorena Hickok could claim in the way of lineage was that her great-granddaddy, according to family legend, *might* have been frontiersman Wild Bill Hickok. When Lorena was fourteen, her tyrannical father—an itinerant day worker—threw her out of the house; she then worked a succession of back-breaking jobs as a dishwasher and domestic. But through luck, pluck, and the ability to turn a graceful phrase, Lorena found her way into the rough-and-tumble world of 1920s journalism. A demon for work, she rose from sob sister to sports writer to news reporter. By 1932, Lorena—everyone who knew her called her "Hick"—was covering the top political stories in the country for the sprawling Associated Press while cutting a wide swath not only because of her hard-drinking, cigar-smoking, ribald-talking demeanor, but also because her 200-pound bulk carried on a five-foot-eight-inch frame commanded attention, even though her shoulders slumped forward and she tended not to walk so much as to trudge.

Unlikely friends, to be sure.

But in 1978 when the Franklin D. Roosevelt Library opened eighteen cardboard boxes filled with Eleanor Roosevelt and Lorena Hickok's personal correspondence to each other, no longer did the two women—by that time Eleanor had been dead sixteen years, Lorena ten—merely make a couple that oldtimers remembered as a bit odd; they also provided the fodder for a vociferous historical debate. For the 3,500 letters that Eleanor and Hick had written during their thirty-year friendship—the first lady sometimes writing two letters in a single day—documented that these women had shared a relationship that was not only intense and intimate, but also passionate and physical.

When journalists learned that the correspondence contained dozens of erotic passages written both to and by Eleanor Roosevelt, they dutifully recorded—and helped provoke—the nation's collective gasp. The *National Enquirer* headlined one front-page scorcher "Secret Romance of President Roosevelt's Wife—The Untold Story"; the *New York Post* announced "The truth about Eleanor Roosevelt!" The nation's more august news organizations lifted an eyebrow and stuck to what they considered to be the obvious facts. The *Washington Post* reported that the letters revealed "clear implications of lesbianism," *Newsweek* labeled the relationship "a lesbian love affair," and the *Los Angeles Times* called the evidence of a same-sex relationship "incontrovertible."

Even the *New York Times* felt duty-bound to acknowledge that the facts did, indeed, point to Eleanor having been involved in a "homosexual affair."[1]

Such straightforward assessments prompted denials from several quarters. Eleanor had been "an emotionally dependent woman whose entire life was characterized by a hunger for affection," wrote historian Arthur M. Schlesinger Jr., insisting that the letters reflected Eleanor's Victorian upbringing when women who had been denied the love of men wrote romantically to each other, even though their relationships were entirely platonic. Rhoda Lerman, who wrote a novel based on Eleanor's life, offered a modern parallel: "I suspect it is more a case of girl scout camp stuff—you know, where they all have names like 'P.J.'"[2]

Since the debate took fire twenty years ago, a few scholars have mined the most titillating nuggets from the letters, each offering what he or she purported to be the definitive interpretation of the letters. In 1980, Lorena's biographer, Doris Faber, announced to the world—in a decidedly defensive tone—that the romantic language in the letters "does not mean what it appears to mean"; early this decade, Eleanor's most recent biographer, Blanche Wiesen Cook, tipped the balance in the other direction, quoting one of the most graphic letters in the correspondence to insist that Eleanor and Lorena most certainly had engaged in a fervent love affair—"A cigar may not always be a cigar, but the 'northeast corner of your mouth against my lips' is always the northeast corner."[3]

Despite the passage of two full decades since the provocative correspondence became public, however, neither journalists nor scholars have offered the reader more than bits and pieces that have been quoted,

---

[1] Edward Sigall, "Secret Romance of President Roosevelt's Wife—The Untold Story," *National Enquirer,* 13 November 1979, 1; Harriet Van Horne, "The truth about Eleanor Roosevelt!," *New York Post,* 24 October 1979, 29; Haynes Johnson, "Spotlighting the Offstage Lives of Onstage People," *Washington Post,* 28 October 1979, A-3; Dennis A. Williams, "The Letters of Mrs. FDR," *Newsweek,* 5 November 1979, 50; Carolyn See, "Lorena Hickok: journalist with a friend in high places," *Los Angeles Times Book Review,* 10 February 1980, 1; Christopher Lehmann-Haupt, "Books of The Times," *New York Times,* 5 February 1980, C-9.

[2] Arthur M. Schlesinger Jr., "Eleanor Roosevelt and the Styles of Friendship," *Washington Post,* 23 October 1979, C-1; Lerman quoted in Henry Mitchell and Megan Rosenfeld, "Eleanor Roosevelt and the Styles of Friendship," *Washington Post,* 23 October 1979, C-4.

[3] Doris Faber, *The Life of Lorena Hickok, E.R.'s Friend* (New York: Morrow, 1980), 176; Blanche Wiesen Cook, *Eleanor Roosevelt, Volume One: 1884-1933* (New York: Viking, 1992), 479.

requoted, and re-requoted. None has allowed Eleanor and Lorena to speak with their own voices and in the full context of their lives.

This book contains more than 300 of the letters that Eleanor and Lorena wrote to each other between March 1933, when Eleanor became first lady, and September 1962, two months before she died. It is an attempt to reproduce the rich and highly textured conversation as the two authors created it—letter by letter, day by day, year by year. It is necessarily only a portion of their total correspondence, which runs in its entirety to some 16,000 pages. I have concentrated on the years 1933 and 1934 when the relationship was at its most intense, and on 1935 when the relationship went through an important transition. I also have omitted letters in these years if they were not particularly substantive in content or vivid in presentation. Each decision I made while choosing and annotating the letters was guided by a single intent: to provide readers with the closest approximation possible to an unobstructed window into the lives and minds and hearts—perhaps, on occasion, even the souls—of the two women.

Eleanor and Lorena were both extraordinary. In the early 1930s, Eleanor was evolving into a woman who, before the phrase *women's liberation* had even entered the language, insisted on her right to self-identity. She became a woman of consummate power and courageous vision who today stands tall—with precious few, if any, peers—as a symbol of integrity and humanity. Lorena, also a woman before her time, became one of the first to succeed in the competitive, male-dominated endeavor of political reporting, while also daring to create her own unique style—wearing bright red lipstick and colorful silk scarves on the job, switching to flannel shirts and work boots on her own time.

Also remarkable was the world in which these women lived. Their most intense letters were written between 1933 and 1935, against the backdrop of three of the most monumental events in American history: the Great Depression, the New Deal, the first rumblings that ultimately led to World War II. During these days of unprecedented crisis, Eleanor and Hick were in the very eye of the storm, as both women were living at the White House. (In the summer of 1933, Lorena quit the Associated Press and became the federal government's chief investigator of relief programs. Between trips around the country, she slept on a daybed in a room adjoining Eleanor's bedroom.) So Eleanor and Lorena both had daily contact with FDR—who called Hick his wife's "she-man"—as he altered forever how the world's greatest democracy serves its citizens.

The letters are written with a degree of candor and introspection comparable to a private diary, allowing the reader to gaze into the innermost thoughts and feelings, fears and joys, insecurities and motivations of their authors. In those pre-television and pre-videotape days, the letters offer the single best way we have to gain a sense of the private side of these two women and their relationship.

Lorena was not the only person Eleanor wrote with ardor and affection. After their correspondence became public, ER biographer Joseph P. Lash was so appalled at the suggestion that the first lady may have engaged in a lesbian affair that he published two volumes of her most effusive letters. Lash reproduced more than 1,000 pages of letters—hundreds of them beginning with "Dearest" and ending with "Devotedly"—that Eleanor wrote to male as well as female friends—including Lash.[4] None of those letters, however, approaches the emotional intensity found in Eleanor and Hick's correspondence; only these two women spoke of lying down together and kissing each other on the mouth.

One of the most intriguing themes in the correspondence is the glimpses it gives of an Eleanor Roosevelt who is strikingly different from the icon she has become. Many of her sentences ramble on and on and on with many twists and turns, comma splices, misspelled words, and challenges to coherence. More fundamentally, the figure who emerges from between the lines is not a paragon of virtue but a woman who could be not only sarcastic and funny, but also catty and judgmental, snide and petty. Of course this should not diminish Eleanor's stature, but rather should serve to reassure us that she was, like all of us, *human*. The first lady of the world had feet of clay.

The letters also reinforce the positive legends about this venerated figure. The daunting list of activities that she participated in day after day testifies to an incredible level of energy. The enormous number of African-American women and men whose careers and agendas she boosted—sometimes inviting musicians to the East Room to perform

---

[4] Joseph P. Lash, *Love, Eleanor: Eleanor Roosevelt and Her Friends* (Garden City, N.Y.: Doubleday, 1982); *A World of Love: Eleanor Roosevelt and Her Friends, 1943-1962* (Garden City, N.Y.: Doubleday, 1984). Lash also wrote *Eleanor and Franklin* (New York: Norton, 1971) and *Eleanor: The Years Alone* (New York: Norton, 1972).

publicly, other times inviting political leaders upstairs at the White House to plan political strategies in private—speaks to her courage as a civil rights activist. The parade of political, intellectual, and artistic luminaries that Eleanor invited for weekends at the White House— Joseph and Rose Kennedy, Albert Einstein, Helen Hayes, Will Rogers— reminds the reader of the first lady's enormous breadth of interests and commitments. Her casual references to joining FDR and his top advisers to discuss political strategy demonstrate that her political acumen had gained her a level of respect that was unparalleled for a first lady—or any woman, for that matter—in the history of the presidency up to that point. In July 1936, for instance, Eleanor wrote Lorena, "I spent 2 hours with F.D.R., Jim Farley, [Charlie] Michelson, Stanley High & Forbes Morgan." During that session, on the heels of the Democratic National Convention where FDR had been nominated for a second term, the president developed the strategy for his re-election campaign. The letter shows us that FDR relied not only on four men to help him craft that strategy—but also on one woman.[5]

Although the goal of this book is not to impose a particular interpretation of the nature of the relationship between the first lady and her first friend, I feel that I would be shirking some implicit duty as the editor of their letters—which I have become intimately familiar with during the last three years—if I did not share at least a few thoughts on the subject.

Regardless of the boundaries of Eleanor and Lorena's own relationship, there is no question that they both spent enormous quantities of time with women who loved women. Most Americans living in the early years of this century considered lesbians—or women living in "Boston marriages," as they were called then—to be loathsome creatures; Eleanor and Lorena did not. Throughout the 1920s, Eleanor spent at least one night a week, sometimes several, in the Greenwich Village home of Elizabeth Read, an attorney and scholar of international affairs, and her life partner Esther Lape, a college professor and successful publicist—having dinner, reading poetry out loud to each other, and talking about the world they dreamed of creating through the progressive social ideals the three women championed.

[5] Eleanor to Lorena, 2 July 1936.

Eleanor's innermost circle of friends also included Nan Cook and Marion Dickerman, another couple who lived in the Village. ER's involvement with Nan and Marion evolved into a variety of interconnected activities. In 1924, they built a retreat together on the Roosevelt family estate at Hyde Park. Although FDR donated the land for the fieldstone cottage and built a swimming pool beside it primarily for his own physical therapy, he viewed Val-Kill—which he referred to as the "love nest" and "Honeymoon Cottage"—as the private domain of Eleanor, Nan, and Marion. When Nan crafted furniture for the house, she carved the initials "E.N.M." into the wood, and when Eleanor embroidered towels and bed linens for it, she stitched in that same monogram. In 1925, the three women founded the newsletter *Women's Democratic News* to galvanize the Democratic women of New York state. In 1926, they bought the Todhunter School for Girls in New York City, with Marion as principal and Eleanor as teacher. In 1927, they opened a factory at Val-Kill, with Nan as manager and Eleanor as sales agent for their hand-crafted reproductions of early American furniture.

These intense friendships with Elizabeth and Esther, Nan and Marion show that love between women was definitely not an alien concept for Eleanor. She was a professed believer in sexual freedom—including people acting on homosexual desires. In 1925, she wrote in her personal journal: "No form of love is to be despised."[6]

Hick, meanwhile, had embraced her love of women unequivocally. In 1918, soon after she had begun reporting for the *Minneapolis Tribune*, she met Ellie Morse and entered into a same-sex relationship with her. Ellie, two years older and from one of the wealthiest families in the state, had dropped out of Wellesley College to take a lowly job at the *Tribune*. For eight years, Lorena and Ellie shared a one-bedroom apartment in the Leamington Hotel and became a classic butch/femme couple. Lorena—Ellie called her "Hickey Doodles"—was a head taller and sixty pounds heavier than the waif-like Ellie, whose feet were so tiny she had to have her shoes custom made. Lorena spent as little time as possible on personal grooming; Ellie had her hair curled and wore make-up even when she stayed in the apartment. Lorena covered her bulky body in shapeless shirtwaists; Ellie shopped for stylish fashions that empha-

<hr>

[6] Cook, *Eleanor Roosevelt,* 318.

sized her tiny waist. Lorena loved reporting so much that she spent far more than forty hours a week on the job; Ellie preferred to wile away her days reading poetry.[7]

Eleanor and Hick's correspondence shows that these earlier friendships continued throughout their own relationship—Eleanor mentions Elizabeth and Esther as well as Nan and Marion dozens of times; Lorena does the same with Ellie. In her memoirs, Eleanor wrote of Elizabeth and Esther, "I have for years thought that Providence was particularly wise and farseeing when it threw these two women together, for their gifts complement each other in a most extraordinary way."[8]

Another relevant point is that, by the time Eleanor and Lorena began the intense period of their relationship, they were worldly wise adults. In 1933, Eleanor turned forty-nine, Lorena forty. Fifteen years earlier, Eleanor had discovered that her husband was having an affair and had agreed to continue the marriage—but not sexual relations with her husband. Hick had felt the sting of betrayal as well; she and Ellie Morse had lived together as a loving couple for eight years until the day in 1926 when Ellie, frightened by Lorena's chronic depression and emotional flare-ups, had walked out. By 1933, Eleanor and Lorena both had loved—and both had lost.

The first two years of Eleanor and Lorena's relationship were the most intense. In one of the first letters in the collection, Eleanor showed that the friendship was too intimate to share even with members of her own family. Eleanor wrote that her son Jimmy, then twenty-five years old, had been near her during the telephone conversation she had just had with Lorena, so "I couldn't say *je t'aime et je t'adore*[9] as I longed to do, but always remember I am saying it and that I go to sleep thinking of you and repeating our little saying." At some level, Eleanor and Lorena knew that theirs was a forbidden love.[10]

Six months later, in November 1933, Eleanor wrote that the capital city was abuzz with gossip about her daughter Anna's affair with John Boettiger. Anna and John were both married at the time—but not to each other—and Eleanor told Hick that Washington wags were taking

[7] On Lorena and Ellie, see Faber, *Lorena Hickok*, 61–69.
[8] Eleanor Roosevelt, *This Is My Story* (New York: Harper & Brothers, 1937), 325.
[9] The words are French for "I love you and I adore you."
[10] Eleanor to Lorena, 6 March 1933.

bets on exactly how soon after John's divorce became final that Anna would begin the proceedings for hers. The first lady noted, "One cannot hide things in this world, can one?" And then: "How lucky you are not a man!" If Lorena was not a woman, Eleanor clearly was saying, those same wags would have been gossiping about her relationship with her first friend.[11]

Later that same month, Eleanor made clear her longing for physical intimacy. Eleanor and her friend Tiny Chaney had been cleaning and decorating a mutual friend's new home in upstate New York. "Sunday morning we worked till 1 a.m. but slept well. Tiny & I in her big double bed which was comfortable in the guest room only I wished it was you."[12]

Additional evidence that the relationship was far more than a casual friendship came from a series of references that Eleanor and Lorena made to their plans to unite, at some point in the future, to blend their separate lives into one. Some of the comments came from Lorena; consoling herself about being hundreds of miles away from the first lady, she wrote, "We'll have our time together later on." But more often the comments came from Eleanor. After they weren't able to spend as much time alone together during a visit as they had hoped, Eleanor wrote, "We'll have years of happy times so bad times will be forgotten." On another occasion, this time after visiting an aging friend, she said, "It is sad to be helpless & poor & old, isn't it? I hope you & I to-gether have enough to make it gracious & attractive!" The most concrete of the references came in the spring of 1934, when Eleanor was in New York City and had just returned from looking at the models for the new pieces of furniture coming from the Val-Kill factory. "One corner cupboard I long to have for our camp or cottage or house, which is it to be? I've always thought of it in the country but I don't think we ever decided on the variety of abode nor the furniture. We probably won't argue!"[13]

Other testimony to the intimate nature of the relationship comes from looking at how Hick altered the correspondence that creates the core of this book. In 1936, she began retrieving the letters she had written to

---

[11] Eleanor to Lorena, 22 November 1933.
[12] Eleanor to Lorena, 25 November 1933.
[13] Lorena to Eleanor, 31 August 1934; Eleanor to Lorena, 23 May 1934; Eleanor to Lorena, 25 April 1934; Eleanor to Lorena, 18 April 1934.

Eleanor; between that year and 1968 when Lorena died (having stipu-
lated that the Roosevelt Library could not open the letters until ten
years after her death), she purposely destroyed hundreds of letters. In
1966, Lorena confided in Anna why she had done so: "Your Mother
wasn't always so very *discreet* in her letters to me." Lorena burned the
most explicit of the letters, dramatically dropping them, one by one,
into the flames of a fireplace.[14]

We can only imagine what has been lost. Because Lorena destroyed
all of her own letters and most of Eleanor's from the first half of 1933,
for example, the reader is left with only eight letters—all from Eleanor
and one of them incomplete—from that crucial period. In addition,
whenever Eleanor and Lorena spent time together—sometimes for long
weekends, other times for vacations that extended for several weeks—
they obviously had no reason to write letters. What's more, they often
talked to each other by telephone. So the correspondence contains myriad statements of eager anticipation (even the counting down of days)
before a particular rendezvous, followed only by vague references to
what they did during their precious days together. On three occasions,
these times together had such significant impact on their relationship
that I have supplemented the letters with material from other sources in
an attempt to fill these gaps. These summaries, like the letters, allow
Eleanor and Lorena to speak for themselves, as they draw heavily from
Reluctant First Lady, the biography of Eleanor that Lorena wrote in
1962, as well as Eleanor's own autobiography.[15]

The biography that Lorena wrote about Eleanor is a major source for
the prologue that describes how Eleanor and Hick crossed paths for the
first time in 1928 and how their friendship escalated when Lorena was
assigned to cover the soon-to-be first lady during the 1932 presidential
campaign. That prologue carries the reader up to the day the correspondence begins in March 1933.

While I acknowledge that the question of whether the first lady and
first friend's relationship was a sexual one is highly titillating, I believe

---

[14] Lorena to Anna Roosevelt Halsted, 9 June 1966. Lorena and Esther Lape burned the letters at Esther's estate in Connecticut after Eleanor died.

[15] Lorena A. Hickok, *Eleanor Roosevelt: Reluctant First Lady* (New York: Dodd, Mead,
1962); Roosevelt, *This Is My Story;* Eleanor Roosevelt, *This I Remember* (New York: Harper
& Brothers, 1949). *Reluctant First Lady* was not a comprehensive biography of Eleanor's
entire life, focusing only on the late 1920s and early 1930s.

that ultimately the far more important question is: What *impact* did the relationship have on each woman?

By the time Eleanor and Lorena began corresponding, they both had recognized that their emotional similarities, no matter the differences in their backgrounds, were striking. Eleanor and Hick were both strong-willed and built of sturdy intellectual timber, both possessed a zealous and passionate nature, both were endowed with enormous physical vitality (though Lorena squandered much of hers by smoking, drinking, and eating too much, while the abstemious Eleanor resolutely did not), both were intuitively compassionate and responsive to the moods and sorrows of others, both had been deeply scarred by past betrayals of male sexuality and yet still longed to give and receive a totality of emotional and physical commitment. For all these reasons, by the spring of 1933 Eleanor and Lorena's bond had grown so strong that it would stand firm for the rest of their lives.

At the time that their correspondence began, Eleanor was at one of the lowest points in her life. Although detached observers assumed that any woman would be delighted to become first lady, Eleanor was, in reality, deeply depressed. She feared, and with good reason, that moving into the White House would force her to abandon the social and political agenda that she had committed her energies to for the last fifteen years and, instead, to accept the frightfully limited role of the demure hostess whose most momentous decision of the day was whether lunch would consist of sandwiches filled with cucumbers—or watercress.

Lorena not only empathized with Eleanor's fears in a way that most people could not, but she also was a self-made woman who possessed the stunning combination of innate drive, professional expertise, and political sophistication. That combination enabled her to help Eleanor transform an ineffectual role that ER detested into a position of influence and impact far beyond anything that the thirty-three first ladies before her had ever imagined it could be. Lorena recognized that ER was poised to do great things, for herself as well as for American women writ large, so the hard-driving reporter became the behind-the-scenes catalyst helping to shape ER's decisions and activities that ultimately revolutionized the relationship between the first lady and the public. In matters of media coverage as in so many others that would evolve in the next several years, Lorena was, in short, the woman behind the woman.

When Eleanor wrote Lorena that her life would be "empty without you," the most eminent American woman of the twentieth century was speaking not only of an emotional void but also of a substantive one.

It was Lorena who, much like the White House handlers who earn six-figure salaries for creating positive public images of their candidates today, introduced Eleanor to the American public by writing stories in decidedly rose-colored hues. Hick painted that flattering portrait while she was still on the Associated Press payroll, thereby violating journalistic standards of professionalism.

It was Lorena who persuaded Eleanor to become the only first lady in history to conduct weekly press conferences. Those sessions provided ER with a public venue to promote the social and political agenda that she had feared she would have to abandon. During a daunting 348 press conferences, Eleanor championed everything from establishing a minimum wage to capping the number of hours in a workweek and from enlarging the role of women to expending public funds for housing, education, and programs for the handicapped.

It was Lorena who suggested a way that Eleanor could finally achieve the sense of personal fulfillment and financial independence that she had desperately craved for many years; ER could attain that elusive goal, Lorena counseled, by writing magazine articles (which the former reporter spent hours on end editing before Eleanor actually submitted them) for the country's largest and best-paying magazines.

It was Lorena who helped Eleanor grow into one of history's most legendary humanitarians by giving this woman born to wealth and privilege a close-up view of the plight of the poor and the powerless; Lorena took ER to the West Virginia coal mines in the fall of 1933, propelling the first lady to become the point person for the government's subsistence homestead project that soon evolved into "Eleanor's Baby."

It was Lorena who suggested that Eleanor publish a syndicated newspaper column to communicate her vision for humanity to the entire country on a daily basis. "My Day" began in 1935 and continued until Eleanor died in 1962, allowing her to speak her mind in the form of a phenomenal 8,000 columns published in scores of American newspapers.

More important than all of these tangible contributions combined, it was Lorena who provided unflagging emotional support. Early in their relationship, Lorena offered Eleanor a love that was complete and absolute. Never before and never again would Eleanor, despite her social stature and her myriad accomplishments, feel the sense of being loved *exclusively*. On the strength of that love, Eleanor blossomed and thrived, grew and flourished—took flight. "Every woman wants to be first to someone in her life," Eleanor would later write. For Eleanor, being first in Lorena's life allowed her to transform the conventional role of president's wife into a public figure in her own right. Lorena's love allowed Eleanor to construct the kind of life she wanted even while living in the public fishbowl known as the White House. "Believe me," she wrote Lorena at Christmas 1933, "you've taught me more and meant more to me than you know." The next year, Eleanor expanded that sentiment, "You've made of me so much more of a person just to be worthy of you—*Je t'aime et je t'adore.*"[16]

For the remaining thirty years of her remarkable life, Eleanor lived according to a code of her own design, following the rhythms of her own needs and desires. She reinvented herself, she established a new paradigm for the American woman, and she stepped boldly onto the world stage to confront the most controversial issues of the day with a sense of honor and principle that has remained a model for the generations that have come after her. But if it had not been for the unconditional love and steadfast emotional support that Lorena had bestowed on Eleanor in those early months of her tenure at the White House, none of it may have happened.

Unfortunately, the profound role that the relationship played in *Lorena's* life proved not to be nearly so enriching. The euphoria that her relationship with Eleanor had initially brought soon turned to anguish. Soon after Eleanor moved to the White House, Lorena realized she could not abide the constant activity and public nature of living close to the first lady—Hick was an independent soul, an appendage to no one. So she accepted a job, which Eleanor secured for her, as chief investigator for the Federal Emergency Relief Administration, traversing the country to gauge the effectiveness of the nation's relief programs and then writing detailed reports on her findings. The major advantage of

---

[16] Lash, *A World of Love*, 116; Eleanor to Lorena, 23 December 1933; Eleanor to Lorena, undated 1934 letter the content of which indicates it was written in the fall.

the job was that, between trips, it allowed Lorena to return to Eleanor and sleep in the White House within a matter of feet from the first lady. Still, the nomadic lifestyle was far from ideal. As Hick's letters from one lonely hotel room after another testify, when she was not with Eleanor, she felt restless and unhappy; the government work failed to give her the personal gratification that journalism had. Unwittingly, Lorena had allowed herself to slip into a role where she lost her sense of self, becoming emotionally (and eventually financially) dependent on Eleanor. No longer a successful journalist herself, she found it degrading when reporters described her solely in relation to the first lady, as if she were some pathetic sycophant. "I'm so fed up with publicity I want to kick every reporter I see," she raged in February 1934. "Why the Hell CAN'T they leave me alone?"[17]

Ironically, as Eleanor was growing into the new type of first lady that Hick had helped her envision, the intensity of their relationship diminished. Because Eleanor now was embraced by the love and admiration of thousands, she no longer needed the private reassurance and emotional nourishment from Lorena that had sustained her in the anxious days before and immediately after she moved to the White House. Early in the relationship, it had been Eleanor who desperately needed support and encouragement from Lorena, a successful career woman who had accomplished so much in the world. But as Eleanor took flight, Lorena began to become not so much an inspiration as an albatross.

Sensing that she had sacrificed a career that she loved for a woman who was, each day, drifting further and further from her, Lorena became increasingly moody and sullen, demanding time alone with Eleanor away from the first lady's family, friends, and commitments. The loyal Eleanor tried to accommodate her first friend, but she repeatedly found herself apologizing to Lorena for including other people in their plans. "Anna said to-day she might want to go with us [to Puerto Rico]. I'd rather go alone with you but I can't hurt her feelings." Besides ER's daughter to consider, there were her many friends such as the women reporters who gathered adoringly around her each Monday morning for the weekly press conferences and the lunches that often fol-

---

[17] Lorena to Kathryn Godwin (secretary to Federal Emergency Relief Administration director Harry Hopkins), 18 February 1934.

lowed, plus several feminist friends the querulous Hick refused to be in the same room with, and all the people the first lady worked with on her various social issues and political campaigns, plus her four sons—not to mention the president, who increasingly relied upon Eleanor's political instincts and affable nature to further his agenda. "You told me once it was hard to let go," Eleanor wrote Lorena, "but I found it was harder to let go & yet hold on. Love as much & yet share." Still, each time that the first lady disappointed Lorena, she felt guilty. "I went to sleep saying a little prayer, 'God give me depth enough not to hurt Hick again.' Darling, I know I'm not up to you in many ways but I love you dearly." By 1934, whenever either woman wrote of her love for the other, it seemed to be in the context of pain rather than pleasure. In February, Eleanor wrote, "Love is a queer thing, it hurts one but it gives one so much more in return!"[18]

During the three remaining decades that the first lady and first friend would continue to correspond, they would experience many more ups and downs in their relationship—including a disastrous holiday on the West Coast in July 1934. But throughout those years, both women remained steadfastly concerned about the other's well-being, offering constant support and reassurance—a safe harbor whenever outside forces threatened them. Eleanor sometimes used Lorena to blow off steam, especially about her husband; when an incident with one of their sons angered the first lady to the point that she, at least momentarily, considered leaving her husband, she expressed her rage to Hick but then, in her next letter, acknowledged that divorce was out of the question—"I know I've got to stick. I know I'll never make an open break." For Lorena, the correspondence provided a venue for her to complain about her job—actually, a series of jobs, none of which came anywhere close to providing her with the sense of fulfillment she had known as a pioneering newswoman.[19]

In the final years, the only point on which Eleanor and Lorena consistently seemed to disagree involved whose fault it was that the intensity of their relationship had not been sustained; each woman insisted on

[18] Eleanor to Lorena, 24 January 1934; Eleanor to Lorena, undated 1934 note the content of which indicates it was written the first week of October; Eleanor to Lorena, 23 December 1933; Eleanor to Lorena, 4 February 1934.
[19] Eleanor to Lorena, 2 May 1935.

blaming *herself*. Eleanor wrote, "I never meant to hurt you in any way, but that is no excuse for having done it. Such cruelty & stupidity is unpardonable when you reach my age." Hick countered, "It would be so much better, wouldn't it, if I didn't love you so much." Perhaps the best coda to the relationship was written by Lorena in a letter in late 1940. "I'd never have believed it possible for a woman to develop after 50 as you have in the last six years," she said. "My trouble, I suspect, has always been that I've been so much more interested in the *person* than in the *personage*. I still prefer the person, but I admire and respect the personage with all my heart!"[20]

---

[20] Eleanor to Lorena, 19 January 1938; Lorena to Eleanor, 1 November 1939; Lorena to Eleanor, 11 November 1940.

The Lady and the Reporter

For Eleanor, a crucial step on the path that ultimately led to her relationship with Lorena can be traced to September of 1918. It was then—
ten years before she laid eyes on the hard-driving reporter and fifteen
years before they began corresponding—that Eleanor suddenly veered
from the course of dutiful wife that, until that moment, had defined her
life. For when Eleanor stumbled upon a packet of lightly scented letters
that documented her husband of thirteen years had been having an affair with the very young and very beautiful Lucy Page Mercer, the bottom dropped out of her life. The man she had loved, trusted, obeyed,
and honored had betrayed her, had made love to her very own social
secretary. Even though Eleanor was concerned about her five small children (then aged two to twelve) growing up without their father in the
house, she was so opposed to a loveless marriage that she offered her
husband a divorce. But Franklin quickly informed her that he didn't
want the marriage to end. (FDR's widowed mother, Sara Delano Roosevelt, told her only child that if he left his wife and children, he'd never

see another cent of the Roosevelt fortune; FDR's political mentor, Louis Howe, warned that if he kissed his marriage goodbye, he'd be doing the same to his political career.) So Eleanor agreed to continue the marriage because she didn't want her children to endure life without a father, as she had. Franklin promised never to see Lucy Mercer again (a promise he would later break repeatedly) and acquiesced to his wife's demand that their marriage no longer include a sexual dimension.

Eleanor's discovery of her husband's infidelity signaled, after a severe bout with depression followed by a long and painful process of introspection, a turning point in her life. No longer willing to define herself solely in terms of the needs of an unfaithful husband, she began to reassess exactly what Eleanor Roosevelt might make of her life.

In 1920, FDR was nominated for vice president, propelling the Roosevelts into the national spotlight for the first time. On the Democratic ticket behind Governor James M. Cox of Ohio, Franklin added youthful vitality to the ticket that, from the outset, was clearly the underdog to a Warren G. Harding/Calvin Coolidge pairing that promised to end international involvement and "Let business be business." On Election Day, the Republicans won a decisive victory.

Franklin's political career suffered a far more serious setback a year later when he contracted polio. While FDR devoted his energies to the challenge of relearning how to function without the use of his legs and to develop a physical rehabilitation center in Warm Springs, Georgia, Eleanor was free to redefine herself, at least to some degree, as an entity separate from her husband.

Her initial step was to develop a network of independent women friends to provide the stimulus she craved. First among them were Elizabeth Read and Esther Lape; second, Nan Cook and Marion Dickerman. Although ER's close friendships with these two same-sex couples inevitably led to gossip—her acid-tongued cousin Alice Roosevelt Longworth remarked loudly in a fashionable Washington restaurant, "I don't care *what* they say, I simply cannot *believe* that Eleanor Roosevelt is a lesbian."[1]—they served as the conduit through which Eleanor moved into the community of politically astute women who were effecting so-

---

[1] Ralph G. Martin, *Cissy: The Extraordinary Life of Eleanor Medill Patterson* (New York: Simon & Schuster, 1979), 360.

cial reform. ER began devoting her considerable talent and energy to organizing conferences, serving on committees, and raising money for the Democratic Party.

In 1928, the party asked her to help lead Al Smith's campaign for president. Although the land-rush prosperity of the Republican administration virtually guaranteed that Herbert Hoover would win the White House, Eleanor worked diligently behind the scenes as co-director of the party's National Women's Committee, keeping things running smoothly at the Democratic National Committee headquarters in New York City.

Lorena Hickok's route to that very same location had begun in South Dakota and then had taken her to newspaper jobs in Michigan and Wisconsin before she arrived at the *Minneapolis Tribune* in 1918. Along the way, Lorena matured into a first-rate reporter while also adopting the unseemly habits of the newsroom—smoking too many Camel cigarettes, eating too many rich foods, drinking too many whiskeys straight up. Hick efficiently wrote the trial and government meeting stories that are the bread and butter of daily journalism, while also spotting the occasional off-beat feature for page one. She scored on the sports page as well, securing the coveted job of covering college football in a state that considered what happened on the gridiron to be serious business.

It was also during her Minnesota years that Lorena lived in a relatively stable same-sex relationship with Ellie Morse. The one problem they struggled with was Hick's emotional volatility. A perfectionist in her work, Lorena erupted whenever she thought she had either made a mistake in a story or committed a violation of journalistic ethics. Whenever Lorena got either idea in her head, she flailed herself unmercifully for days on end, as Ellie tried everything she could to pull her temperamental partner back onto an even keel.

In 1926 when Ellie finally persuaded Lorena to consult a doctor, he discovered high blood sugar and diagnosed an early stage of diabetes, recommending that Hick not work so hard. When Ellie's father died, leaving her the family fortune, she proposed that she and Lorena move to San Francisco, with Lorena shifting from the frenetic pace of chasing the news to the slower one of writing fiction. Lorena agreed, and the couple headed west.

The move was a disaster. Quickly discovering that her talent for news didn't translate into fiction, Lorena spent days on end at the typewriter

crumpling up page after page of turgid prose while cursing her work—
and herself. No longer having daily bylines to bolster her spirits, she ca-
reened out of control—blowing up at minor problems, becoming so
depressed that she slept two and three days straight. Eager to escape
Lorena's emotional turmoil, Ellie renewed her acquaintance with a
childhood friend from a Minneapolis dance class twenty years earlier
and then eloped with him.

Lorena, with both her career and her relationship in shambles,
boarded a train for New York, the huge city so many people turn to in
times of despair. After a brief stint reporting crime news tabloid-style for
William Randolph Hearst's *Daily Mirror,* Lorena joined the handful of
women working for the Associated Press, the largest news network in
the country. Once again driven not merely to achieve but to overachieve,
she threw every ounce of her energy into getting her stories first and
best—ignoring the doctor's warning not to overwork. The only other
woman working in the AP office in New York, Kay Beebe, later recalled,
"She was a big sort of masculine type, and she could play poker and
swear and smoke and drink with the best of 'em." Being resolutely determined did not mean, however, that Lorena was unpopular with her
co-workers, as Beebe said flatly, "*Everybody* liked Lorena."[2]

Now that Lorena was writing major stories every day—one of them
even won her the distinction of being the first woman to have her byline
appear on the front page of the *New York Times*—she decided the time
was right to move into the news beat she had always coveted but that
the male reporters who dominated the Fourth Estate had continued to
hold tight in their grip: politics. Lorena's strategy was to focus on the
Democratic National Committee headquarters a few blocks from AP's
New York office. It was the fall of 1928 and the Democrats were finally
giving Al Smith, despite his Catholic background and New York accent,
a shot at the White House. The timing, Lorena figured, was perfect.[3]

In September 1928, the lady met the reporter.

[2] Interview with Katherine Beebe Pinkham Harris by Shirley Biagi, Women in Journalism
oral history project of the Washington Press Club Foundation, 22 September 1989 to 19 September 1990, Oral History Collection, Columbia University, New York City, 56, 114.
[3] Lorena A. Hickok, "Drifted 22 Hours with Woman in Sea," *New York Times,* 15 November 1928, 1. The story was an interview with a survivor of the cruise ship Vestris that ran into
a storm and sank in the Atlantic, killing 100 passengers and crew members.

By no means, though, was it love at first sight. Lorena later wrote in *Reluctant First Lady* that she was unimpressed with ER's physical appearance. For although Hick was no beauty herself, she had the reporter's critical eye for assessing others: "She was very plain," she wrote of Eleanor. Lorena also was determined to hold fast to her rule, as a woman news reporter, to avoid what she derisively called "women's page stuff," such as stories about the wife of the Democratic candidate for governor of New York, that would push her off the front page. So throughout the campaign, Lorena steadfastly avoided writing stories about Eleanor.[4]

When the votes were counted in November, on the national level the Democrats, as expected, got trounced. FDR bucked the trend, however, and won his race for the Governor's Mansion in Albany.

From 1928 to 1932, Hick covered Governor Roosevelt whenever he visited New York City, but she continued to keep her distance from the missus. Lorena's refusal to write about Eleanor was not easy, as New York's first lady was a highly newsworthy subject. Having broken free of many of the shackles that previously had constrained her, ER was working hard not to allow her husband's success in public life to push her back into subjugation. Each Sunday afternoon she left Albany and traveled to New York City to teach at Todhunter School for the next three days, spending the evenings with one of the couples who had grown so important in her life, either Elizabeth and Esther or Nan and Marion. Each Wednesday afternoon, ER returned to Albany just in time to preside over midweek tea, the beginning of the non-stop whirl of social events that composed the second half of her week.

In the meantime, Lorena's social life was virtually nonexistent. Because she enjoyed her work, she didn't mind the long days and demanding pace. But still, when she came home at night and when she had a free weekend, she longed for someone to share her life. In an effort to fill the void, Hick acquired a German shepherd puppy. Prinz then became her constant companion, even accompanying his mistress to the office on the Sundays that it was her turn to make sure the Associated Press didn't miss any breaking news. Lorena became so attached to Prinz, in

[4] Hickok, *Reluctant First Lady,* 10–11; 16.

fact, that some of her friends and colleagues began describing the relationship as "weird" or "eccentric"—some even mentioned the adjective "unnatural." One year Lorena's Christmas card featured a photo of Prinz in the way parents showcase their children; under the photo, Lorena wrote "Merry Christmas to You and Yours from Me and Mine." Lorena also stunned her friends when she began arriving at dinner parties with Prinz in tow, calling him her date.[5]

But Hick's most desperate effort to find companionship involved not a dog, but a female co-worker. In early 1932, Lorena and Kay Beebe were among several reporters sent out of town on a big story. Being the only two women in the group, they shared a hotel room. Late that night, Kay recalled fifty years later, Lorena made unwelcome and uninvited physical advances: "She made for me." More specifically, Lorena lunged for Kay and tried to embrace her in the manner that a lesbian would embrace another lesbian. "She wanted to hug me, and it wasn't good." After Kay pulled back, Lorena apologized and never tried to touch her co-worker again.[6]

On a professional level, Hick avoided contact with Eleanor until June 1932. That was the month that the Democratic Party decided that FDR was the man who, after the stock market crash in 1929 on the Republican watch, could retake the White House. Lorena recognized that ER could be a major story; never before had the wife of a presidential nominee been not merely an appendage to her husband, but a woman with her own career (as a teacher and furniture plant owner) and political track record (as a national campaign staff member). When Lorena recommended that a reporter be assigned, for the first time, to a candidate's wife, her editors agreed. Still leery of having her stories land in the women's page ghetto, though, Lorena turned down the new beat that was then passed to Kay Beebe. Lorena, meanwhile, won a plum assignment as one of three AP reporters covering FDR's national campaign— the only woman in the country on that prestigious beat.

Part of Lorena's job was to report changes in the Roosevelt campaign strategy, and that meant talking to Eleanor, because the candidate's wife

[5] Jeannette Brice letter to Doris Faber, 7 November 1978, Doris Faber Papers, Franklin D. Roosevelt Library.
[6] Doris Faber notes from 15 November 1978 interview with Katherine Beebe, Box 3, Doris Faber Papers; Beebe oral history, 115.

also had evolved into one of his most trusted political advisers. The first time Hick interviewed Eleanor, the usually hard-boiled reporter was bedazzled. When she returned from the session, one of her male colleagues had to remind her, for the first time in her twenty years as a reporter, "Don't get too close to your sources."[7]

Lorena no longer had the option of distancing herself from Eleanor. By early fall, Lorena's role had changed from a reporter *pursuing* a source to a reporter *being pursued by* a source. Time and time again, Eleanor plucked Hick from the gaggle of reporters. During a stop in Arizona, Eleanor invited Lorena to accompany her on a social call to see her childhood friend Isabella Selmes Greenway. Another time, Eleanor asked Lorena—and Lorena only—to ride alone with her in a private car as she inspected the site of a proposed dam on the St. Lawrence River. ER next made a point of coming to talk to Lorena—just the two of them—in a parked car, and, soon after that, playfully challenging Lorena to keep up with her as she maneuvered through an Iowa cornfield (Eleanor glided gracefully through the stalks; Hick got tangled up in a barbed wire fence). In upstate New York, Eleanor even invited Lorena to have breakfast alone with her in her hotel room.[8]

Then the fates took a hand. During the summer and early fall, Kay Beebe had written only a couple stories about Eleanor—Beebe wasn't really interested in politics. Then in October 1932, Beebe transferred from AP's New York office to the one in San Francisco to get married. Because it had been Hick's idea to assign a reporter to Eleanor in the first place and now she was the only woman left on the AP news staff in New York, she was automatically assigned the beat. City editor Bill Chaplin was unknowingly prescient when he launched Lorena on her new assignment to cover the would-be first lady—"She's all yours, Hickok. Have fun!"[9]

By this point, both women were, in fact, delighted to share each other's company. And on a political level, Eleanor also was getting a major boost from the relationship that was gradually shifting from professional to personal. Lorena was presenting the American public with a resolutely flattering portrait of their soon-to-be first lady. Lorena was

---

[7] Warner B. Ragsdale letter to Doris Faber, 13 December 1978, Doris Faber Papers.
[8] Hickok, *Reluctant First Lady,* 38; 48; 38; 39; Eleanor to Lorena, 26 October 1932.
[9] Hickok, *Reluctant First Lady,* 43.

still the only reporter in the country paying attention to the woman who, she told her readers, had "the energy of a dynamo" and was "an outstanding civic and welfare leader." At the same time, the adroit reporter made sure Eleanor came across as modest and frugal, describing her as a woman who was "embarrassed when she is recognized" and who lived "a truly Spartan life"—wearing ten-dollar dresses, eschewing taxis for city buses, eating lunch at drug store soda fountains. In short, after Eleanor had been buffed, fluffed, and puffed through the magic of Hick's typewriter, she appeared before the public as a 1930s version of the modern-day Superwoman.[10]

That Lorena was by this stage infatuated with Eleanor also was clear from her willingness to violate the ethical standards of her profession. Specifically, Lorena sent her articles to her editors in New York only after they passed inspection by Louis Howe, the former newsman who was running the Roosevelt campaign. Allowing Howe to see her dispatches was such a blatant breach of journalistic tenets that if her editors had known about it, Lorena would have been fired on the spot. Earlier in her career, Lorena had done all she could to succeed in the male-dominated world of journalism—working untold hours without overtime pay, even though the pace endangered her health. As the presidential campaign moved into its final laps, a new agenda had taken precedence over her long-standing desire to see her byline on page one: She wanted to help the woman she loved.

Two weeks before the election, the campaign train was passing through Albany when the mother of FDR's personal secretary, Missy LeHand, died in far northern New York state. Concerned that the distraught young woman was in no condition to travel by herself, Eleanor offered to accompany Missy on her trip home. They would both take the train to Potsdam for the funeral, then Missy would stay with her family while Eleanor returned to Albany. Not eager to make the return trip alone, Eleanor asked Lorena to join her, and Lorena readily agreed.

On the cold and rainy evening of October 30, 1932, the two women left Potsdam on the overnight train that sped southward into the frosty

---

[10] Hickok Associated Press copy, September 1932, Hickok Papers; Hickok, *Minneapolis Tribune*, "'First Lady' Won't Give Statement," 9 November 1932, 1; "She'll Be Just Mrs. Roosevelt," 10 November 1932, 8; "New First Lady Even Tempered," 12 November 1932, 7.

night. Eleanor had booked a private drawing room with only a lower berth and a long, narrow couch across from it. After they closed the drawing room door and with the funeral still weighing heavily on Eleanor's mind, the two women began to share childhood memories. Eleanor spoke of her mother's death when she was only eight, followed the next year by her younger brother's death, then her father's. Hick shared details of her life that were no less tragic; her mother died when she was thirteen, and a year later when her father remarried, he threw her into the street.

Eleanor and Lorena talked well into the night, and their conversation proved to be an epiphany as to just how much, on an emotional level, the refined lady and the streetwise reporter had in common—losing their mothers at an early age, growing up too quickly, being betrayed by the men in their lives, considering themselves unattractive and unloved, trying to compensate for their low self-esteem by overachieving in their careers. In the most poignant moment of the conversation, Lorena told Eleanor of a childhood trauma that she had suppressed tight inside herself for many years. For Lorena's cruel and tyrannical father had not only psychologically abused and physically beaten his adolescent daughter, but he also had performed the ungodly act of raping her.

When Eleanor Roosevelt, a woman of infinite sensitivity and compassion, heard that shocking revelation, she instinctively reached out to the poor, unfortunate victim who, twenty-five years later, was sharing the same tiny room with her. Eleanor's long, graceful arms embraced and comforted Lorena—assuring her that she was safe, showing her that she was loved. Neither woman got much sleep that night, Lorena later wrote, but by the next morning their relationship had reached what the reporter called a new level of intimacy.[11]

After FDR's landslide victory, Eleanor and Lorena grew ever closer. With both of them now in New York (the Roosevelts had kept a townhouse there throughout their marriage), several nights a week they attended plays, concerts, and operas before dining late either in one of Manhattan's out-of-the way restaurants—one favorite was an Armenian cafe far downtown—or, more likely, in the privacy of Hick's one-room

---

[11] Hickok, *Reluctant First Lady,* 47–49.

apartment in midtown. Lorena usually did the cooking; her specialty was thick steaks slathered with catsup and baked in the oven. And on the mornings that the two women didn't wake up in the same room, Eleanor dialed Hick's telephone number—WI2-6131—first thing.

Christmas of 1932 was a special time, as it was the occasion when Lorena presented Eleanor with an extravagant sapphire and diamond ring. The gift was far too expensive for a news reporter to have purchased; Madame Ernestine Schumann-Heink had pressed the magnificent piece of jewelry into Lorena's hand in 1916 after the young reporter had written a flattering story about the grand diva. Eleanor protested that the gift was too precious for Lorena to part with, but eventually she slipped the ring onto her left hand where it would remain for the next four years.

During the first two months of 1933, Eleanor and Lorena continued to spend as many hours together as possible. Hick asked to be transferred to the Associated Press bureau in Washington when the new first lady took up residence in the White House, but her editors said AP already had one woman in Washington, Bess Furman, who could cover the woman's angle. In a note to Furman, Lorena only hinted at how disappointed she was that she would no longer be covering ER—"I shall miss her terribly."[12]

Eleanor and Hick's most enjoyable getaways were to the Dutch colonial cottage at Val-Kill. They spent the daylight hours meandering through the woods thick with red pines and sugar maples, their evenings close to the stone fireplace in the cozy living room with its knotty pine walls and overstuffed furniture. One of their favorite activities during these serene times together, outdoors or in, was reading poetry and historical biographies; they took turns reading out loud to each other so they could share the experience.

The resourceful couple also managed to transform one of the traditional duties of a new first lady into a holiday. Following White House tradition, Eleanor scheduled a meeting with Lou Henry Hoover to see the private quarters and make decisions about how she would use the

---

[12] Lorena to Bess Furman, undated, Box 27, Bess Furman Papers, Library of Congress, Washington, D.C.

various rooms. Unlike the other presidential wives who had come before her, however, ER made the trek to Washington accompanied by the woman who was about to fill an entirely new position: first friend. Eleanor even treated Hick to the grandeur of the Mayflower Hotel's presidential suite—not the last time she would trade her austere ways for lavish ones on Lorena's account. After spending the night and having breakfast in their room, the two women traveled the five blocks to the White House on foot.

Only when Eleanor and Lorena arrived at the iron gates outside the mansion did they separate, Eleanor striding forward to meet the departing first lady while Lorena waited outside for what she later described as the longest hour of her life, knowing that this brief separation foreshadowed the much longer one that would soon place the women in two different cities. On the walk back to the hotel, Eleanor talked about how she would change the living quarters on the second floor. She decided she would occupy the suite in the southwest corner with its large sitting room, bedroom, and bath—the same suite where Grover Cleveland consummated his marriage to Frances Folsom, twenty-eight years his junior, following their June 1886 White House wedding—exclusively for herself and any guest she might choose to have sleep near her. Lorena nodded her approval.

Eleanor and Lorena did not always agree. When the reporter first suggested that Eleanor hold weekly news conferences, ER shook her head. Not only did she have no news worthy of conferring, Eleanor argued, but why should she subject herself to a mob of rowdy reporters constantly criticizing her every move? Lorena persisted, promising to guide ER on how she could win the reporters—Lorena suggested the conferences be limited to women only—over to her side so they would write supportive stories. Still skeptical, Eleanor agreed at least to broach the possibility with her husband.

FDR loved it. A master at finding new ways to manipulate public opinion, he immediately saw the benefits of his wife generating a continuous stream of news targeted at women voters. Besides, Franklin had the highest respect for Lorena's judgment. During the campaign, he had told his wife that Lorena was a reporter worth paying attention to. "Franklin used to tease me about you," ER told Lorena. "He'd say,

'You'd better watch out for that Hickok woman. She's smart.'" Concerned that Hick might be offended by her husband's remarks, Eleanor
quickly added, "He likes you a great deal."[13]

So with the double-barreled endorsement of both Lorena and
Franklin, then the two most influential people in Eleanor's life, she
agreed to conduct her own press conferences on a regular basis. The sessions would become the signature element in Eleanor's legendary success at redefining the role of the first lady as a public figure as well as a
newsmaker independent of her husband. Lorena worked behind the
scenes to help ER plan the details for the first session—such as Eleanor
serving the women candied grapefruit peels so they would feel like personal friends rather than journalistic adversaries—and Eleanor would
call Lorena immediately after that first session to report that all had
gone well.

Just how devoted the soon-to-be first friend was to the soon-to-be
first lady became dramatically clear on March 3, 1933, the day Lorena
committed her most egregious journalistic breach. She had again accompanied ER on the Baltimore & Ohio train to Washington, but this
time, because it was the official journey of the president and his family
for the inauguration the next day, Lorena had to ride in a separate car—
holding Eleanor's Scottish terrier Meggie on her lap. On that last night
before the inauguration, the ascending first lady planned a quiet dinner
and evening for herself and Hick in the privacy of the presidential suite
at the Mayflower; they knew it was their last night together.

The evening was stressful not just for Eleanor and Lorena, but for the
entire nation. For people everywhere—from bankrupt investors on Wall
Street to unemployed factory workers in the beleaguered Midwest—
were turning their eyes toward Franklin D. Roosevelt in the desperate
hope that the buoyant new president held the secret formula that would
somehow pull the nation out of the worst economic crisis it had ever
suffered. In an effort to answer that call, FDR worked late into the night
on the final draft of his inaugural address. When he finished, he sent a
copy down the hall to Eleanor's room, and she read it out loud to
Lorena.

[13] Hickok, *Reluctant First Lady,* 49.

Thirty years later, Lorena wrote, "There I was, right in the middle of what, that night, was the biggest story in the world. And I did nothing about it. It did not even occur to me at the time, but I could have slipped out to a telephone after she read the inaugural address to me and could have given the AP the gist of it, with a few quotations. If I had, it would have been the biggest scoop of my career." Indeed. For that was the speech that contained the single statement that, more than any other, would come to symbolize FDR's approach to the Great Depression: "The only thing we have to fear is fear itself." Hick's priorities clearly were no longer on her professional career.[14]

What was important to *Eleanor* during those momentous days jumped off the page of her personal engagement book. On the page for March 4, 1933, Eleanor wrote at the top "inauguration day" and then made a cursory list of the various public events—"Capitol," "parade," "tea." The only entry that suggested any personal attachment whatsoever—or sufficient significance even to merit a complete sentence—was the one that recorded a private moment inside Eleanor's suite. Beside the time block for 6:30 p.m., she wrote: "Said good-bye to Hick." The following night, Eleanor commenced the extraordinary exchange of letters that would continue for the next thirty years.[15]

[14] Hickok, *Reluctant First Lady*, 95–96.
[15] Eleanor Roosevelt Engagement Book, Eleanor Roosevelt Papers, Franklin D. Roosevelt Library.

One

MARCH 1933

The Pain of Separation

The eight letters in this chapter were all written by Eleanor, most of them in the days immediately after the inauguration while the nation's thirty-fourth first lady was settling into her new home and her new role. Unfortunately Lorena destroyed all of her letters to Eleanor written prior to November 26, 1933 (see p. 41).

Eleanor generally wrote her letters at the end of the day, often writing in bed by propping herself up on her down pillows. She used a fountain pen and elegant, creamy white stationery with "The White House" embossed in rich gold letters across the top.

The first paragraph of Eleanor's first letter provided the phrase that ultimately has become the title of this collection of letters: *"Empty Without You."*

With this first letter, Eleanor established the three-part organization that she would repeat hundreds of times. First came personal words to Lorena. Then came a recitation of the events that had occurred that particular day, almost as though she were copying them straight from her engagement calendar. And last came more personal words to Lorena. In this particular letter, the first lady ended with several lines of verse.

March 5th

Ṫʜᴇ Wʜɪᴛᴇ Hᴏᴜsᴇ

Washington

Hick my dearest, I cannot go to bed to-night without a word to you. I felt a little as though a part of me was leaving to-night, you have grown so much to be a part of my life that it is empty without you even though I'm busy every minute.

These are strange days & very odd to me but I'll remember the joys & try to plan pleasant things & count the days between our times together!

To begin my diary, after you left I went to supper taking Fjr. [Franklin Jr., Eleanor and Franklin's third son] & John [Eleanor and Franklin's youngest son], Mama [FDR's mother, Sara Delano Roosevelt] & Betsey [the wife of James, Eleanor and Franklin's oldest son] & we were followed by F.D.R. & James just before the boys left. I went to the station with them & left the Secret Service man at home. (1st assertion of *independence*!) Saw the boys onto the train. Returned, had a short talk with F.D.R. James & Betsey. Tommy [Malvina Thompson, Eleanor's secretary] came & we arranged to-morrow's work. At ten Meggie & I took her to the gate & I thought of you & "Prinz" [Lorena's German shepherd]. She [Tommy] seemed very happy & said everyone had a grand time, also that you looked "*stunning*" dressed up! I then went back & devoted 3/4 of an hour to talking to Mama, then listened to F.D.R. broadcast,[1] sorted mail & am now preparing for bed. So endeth my first Sunday.

---

[1] During this nationwide radio broadcast, FDR announced that every bank in the country would be closed for the next four days as the first step in his effort to bring the country's banking crisis under control.

I'll call you to-morrow night & this should reach you Tuesday a.m.

Oh! darling, I hope on the whole you will be happier for my friendship. I felt I had brought you so much discomfort & hardship to-day & almost more heartache than you could bear & I don't want to make you unhappy. All my love & I shall be saying to you over thought waves in a few minutes—

> Good night my dear one
> Angels guard thee
> God protect thee
> My love enfold thee
> All the night through.

Always yours,
E.R.

[March 6]

THE WHITE HOUSE
Washington

Hick darling, Oh! how good it was to hear your voice, it was so inadequate to try & tell you what it meant, Jimmy[2] was near & I couldn't say *"je t'aime et je t'adore"* as I longed to do but always remember I am saying it & that I go to sleep thinking of you & repeating our little saying.

Well, now for the diary! Got up 7:15, walk with Meggie, breakfast in my room at 8 & suddenly Missy [LeHand, Franklin's personal secretary] appeared half asleep to announce [Chicago Mayor Anton] Cermak's death.[3] Then she had breakfast in my room & I began to unpack & move furniture. Tommy & Nan [Cook, Eleanor's close friend and business associate] came about nine and I left them in charge and went

---

[2] Eleanor often referred to her son James as Jimmy.

[3] Cermak had been injured during an attempted assassination of President-elect Roosevelt in Miami in February; on March 6, 1933, Cermak died of the wounds he had sustained in that incident.

off with F.D.R. & James at 9:45 to Sen. [Thomas] Walsh's funeral.[4] I sat in the Senate Gallery & the coffin with the candles & lovely flowers looked impressive but I thought the service very *un*impressive & the people in the gallery seemed to have come to a show rather than to mourn someone they cared about. I stopped to talk to the widow & daughter, saw [Secretary of Labor] Frances Perkins[5] for a minute. She is a little startled to find how many purely social people write her for purely exhibition purposes.

Back by 11 & moved furniture till 12. Then press conference of which I told you.[6] 1 p.m., all governors at conference [with FDR] & their wives to lunch [with ER], then a little more furniture moved & at 4:20 National Women's Press Association tea, then home to find a mixture [of people] at tea with Mama. 7:30 Isabella [Selmes Greenway][7] came to dine & we had a short talk about her children & Congress & Anna [Dall, Eleanor and Franklin's oldest child and only daughter] & Elliott [Eleanor and Franklin's second son]. At last 12:10, bed & a talk with you—the nicest time of the day. A week from to-morrow[8] I came back from the telephone & began marking my calendar, Tuesday week is so much better than Thursday![9]

My room is nearly in order & my bed is in the little room[10] & I can see the [Washington] monument from it—a great comfort the monument has always been to me. Why, I wonder?

Give Jean [Dixon][11] my love she is a swell person. No one is like you though. Hick—I love you & good night.

Devotedly,

E.R.

[4] FDR had designated Montana Senator Thomas Walsh his Attorney General, but Walsh died suddenly on his way to the inauguration.

[5] FDR had appointed Frances Perkins the first woman to serve in a presidential cabinet.

[6] Eleanor had telephoned Lorena immediately after her first press conference, to report that it had gone well.

[7] Isabella Selmes Greenway, a childhood friend of Eleanor's who had been a bridesmaid at her wedding, had been elected to the U.S. House of Representatives from Arizona in 1932.

[8] Eleanor was planning to see Lorena during a trip to New York the next week.

[9] Eleanor originally had planned her trip to New York for the next Thursday but now had rescheduled it for two days earlier.

[10] Previous occupants of the suite on the southwest corner of the White House where Eleanor was sleeping had used the larger room as their bedroom and the smaller one as a sitting room, but Eleanor reversed the two uses.

[11] Jean Dixon was a long-time friend of Lorena's.

On the day that Eleanor wrote this letter, Lorena turned forty. The letter includes the first of Eleanor's many references to wanting to hold Lorena in her arms, as well as a clear statement about the importance that the first lady attached to the sapphire and diamond ring that Lorena had given her.

[March 7]

The White House
Washington

Hick darling, All day I've thought of you & another birthday [when] I *will* be with you, & yet to-night you sounded so far away & formal, oh! I want to put my arms around you, I ache to hold you close. Your ring is a great comfort, I look at it & think she does love me, or I wouldn't be wearing it!

Well here goes for the diary (let me know when you get bored!) Breakfast downstairs Nan [Cook] & I, joined very late by James. Then E.R. interviews Mrs. [Henrietta] Nesbitt[12] & begins at the top of the house, meets all the domestics & talks over work, then with Tommy to meet secretarial force & 11:30 received [delegation of] Sioux Indians, at 11:45 the executive secretary of the "Girl Scouts" & must go to meeting (minus uniform) on Saturday at four. Then lunch & tour the White House, then take Mama to the train[13] & had tea & took a party to the concert.[14] There I thought only of you & wanted you even more than I do as a rule. Home at seven & Tommy & I worked till 11:15 & then I put all my children to bed. Elliott & Ralph Hitchcock [a friend of Elliott's] go west to-morrow a.m.[15] Louis [Howe] moved in & Mary Howe [Louis's daughter] came to stay to-day—Missy [LeHand] moves in to-morrow.[16]

[12] Henrietta Nesbitt was the Hyde Park neighbor Eleanor had brought with her to the White House as head housekeeper.

[13] Sara Delano Roosevelt was returning to Hyde Park.

[14] The inauguration concert at Constitution Hall featured the New York Philharmonic Symphony Orchestra with Arturo Toscanini conducting.

[15] Elliott Roosevelt, after failing the entrance exam to Harvard, continued to have trouble getting his feet on the ground. He was planning to travel West in hopes of finding a career that suited him.

[16] Louis Howe and his family as well as Missy LeHand all lived on the second floor of the White House with the Roosevelts.

By Saturday I hope to begin to read, & write, & think & feel again. What shall we read Hick?[17] You choose first.

It is late 1:15 & I am very weary, so goodnight my dearest one. A world of love & how happy I will be to see you Tuesday.

Ever Yours,
E.R.

Tuesday night or rather Wed. a.m. March 8th—Hick dearest I know just how unhappy you are & I'm glad you'll be with Jean [Dixon] tomorrow night & so glad you have Prinz. Give him my love—my thoughts are around you!

[March] 8th

THE WHITE HOUSE
Washington

Dearest, Your two letters this morning were such a joy & I loved your letter to Miss [Bess] Furman.[18] She was outside Justice [Oliver Wendell] Holmes'[19] when we went there to-day & I walked Meggie home so she walked along with me & told me she was sending me your letter & you were coming on the 20th!

Just telephoned you, oh! it is good to hear your voice, when it sounds right no one can make me so happy!

Diary. 8:30 a.m. breakfast & saw Elliott & Ralph Hitchcock off for the West in a Plymouth roadster packed with bags so the top couldn't close! What a gamble it is,[20] I wish I felt surer of Elliott. Saw the housekeeper 9:30 then about accounts at 10. Was presented by a California man named Staley with a box of dates at 10:45 in the red room & 11 the Cabinet ladies came. We agreed on no entertaining till autumn except for children's eggrolling at Easter & veterans garden party. I told

---

[17] Eleanor and Lorena had agreed to read books simultaneously so they could discuss them by letter or, when possible, in person.

[18] Bess Furman was the Associated Press reporter covering the first lady.

[19] Oliver Wendell Holmes had been a justice on the U.S. Supreme Court until he retired in 1932.

[20] Elliott Roosevelt had no job or solid prospects in the West.

them I would receive at tea once a week (Sat. p.m. we meet the diplomats) & otherwise we would only have people in informally & Mrs. [Etta] Garner [wife of Vice President John Nance Garner] was much relieved. At 2:45 Nan [Cook] & I went to Sloane's to choose some lamps [for the Roosevelt living quarters], then toured the town & back here for tea. At 5:30 Franklin, James & I went to Justice Holmes'. He is a fine old man with flashes of his old wit & incisiveness. We got back about the same time, though I walked Meggie & was almost rude to Miss Furman! She's nice though & likes you which melted my heart! We dined [at] 8 "en famille" between conferences & it is now 12 & I am going in soon to find out if F. is staying up all night or not! I think when things settle I'll have some privacy & leisure & I have better hopes than I had of getting away & of cutting red tape & pomp & ceremony! Perhaps we'll be almost human by the time you come!

I miss you so much & love you so much & please never apologize. I always know & understand, one does if one cares enough.

My dear, love to you,
E.R.

At the end of the first paragraph of this letter appears Eleanor's first recognition of the fact that she can expand the role of the first lady in ways that could be meaningful and satisfying to her. In the third paragraph, Eleanor describes placing Lorena's photo in a strategic position where she not only can be reminded of Hick throughout the day but also can kiss the first friend's image as her first activity each morning and her last activity each night.

[March 9]

THE WHITE HOUSE
Washington

Hick dearest, It was good to talk to you & you sounded a bit happier. I hated to have Nan go to-night & yet it is rather nice to have a few hours alone, so I know how you feel but I shall miss Nan to-morrow. She has been such a help & apparently enjoyed herself. The one thing which reconciles me to this job is the fact that I think I can give a great many people pleasure & I begin to think there may be ways in which I can be useful. I am getting some ideas which I want to talk over with you—

Life is pretty strenuous—one or two a.m. last night & 12:15 now & people still with F.D.R. but this should settle things more or less.

My pictures are nearly all up & I have you in my sitting room where I can look at you most of my waking hours! I can't kiss you [in person] so I kiss your *picture* good night & good morning! This is the first day I've had no letter & I missed it sadly but it is good discipline.

Now for the diary! Out with Meggie as usual. Breakfast 8:30, 9:30 housekeeper, 10:30 got splint for my finger[21] & went to kitchen. Put books ornaments etc. around left at 11:40 for Capitol, back at 1:40 for lunch & James brought a California congressman making us 10 instead of 8 at last minute which was good training in our ways for the staff! After lunch some went back to Capitol. I took Nan to Mt. Vernon, back 4:40 saw 2 ladies for 5 minutes each, one brought gifts, one wanted to reorganize all government cafeterias! Tea, took Louis [Howe] to garage to see his car back, dressed for dinner & to-night dictated to Tommy, signed oodles of mail, took Nan to train & Tommy home. Gus [Gennerich][22] paid me a long visit while I signed & now 12:35 & to bed!

Anna & the children[23] left to-day at 2. So I have asked John [Boettiger][24] to go for a drive with me to-morrow a.m. Remind me to show you a note he wrote me, he is pretty sweet & I am so sorry for them [because they had to keep their love a secret]. James left at 3:30 by plane for Boston & returns with Betsey & Sara Saturday night. Betsey wired that Elliott has reached Little Rock! Here is the chronicle of my family, a bit varied, isn't it?

One more day marked off my dear. My dear if you meet me [in public] may I forget there are other reporters present or must I behave? I shall want to hug you to death. I can hardly wait!

---

[21] Eleanor had sprained her finger while moving furniture.

[22] Gus Gennerich was a New York state trooper who had been one of Governor Roosevelt's bodyguards in Albany; the president brought him to the White House.

[23] Anna's daughter Eleanor, nicknamed Sisty, was six; her son Curtis, nicknamed Buzzie, was three.

[24] John Boettiger was a *Chicago Tribune* reporter who was romantically involved with Eleanor's daughter, even though Anna was still married to Curtis Dall.

A world of love to you & good night & God bless you "light of my life,"

                                                                        E.R.

The first paragraph of this letter contains one of Eleanor's many cryptic messages about her relationship with Lorena.

                                                              [March 10]

                           THE WHITE HOUSE
                              Washington

Hick darling, The air mail, special delivery letter has never come, but the next one came this morning & my dear I was glad. Remember one thing always, no one is just what you are to me. I'd rather be writing this minute than anything else & yet I love many other people & some often can do things for me probably better than you could, but I've never enjoyed being with anyone the way I enjoy being with you.

Diary March 10th 8:30 a.m. out with Meggie. A cold, clear, beautiful day. Breakfast in the west sitting room (hall) much brighter than downstairs, Louis & Missy & I. 9:30 Mrs. [Henrietta] Nesbitt, 10:10 Mr. [Ike] Hoover,[25] 10:30 picture hangers & furniture movers. 11:25 went off from back door in my car & picked John [Boettiger] up at the Washington [Hotel]. He drove out to Elton Fay's for me as I wanted to leave some candy & tangerines.[26] Back in time for lunch. Then Tommy & I moved books & furniture till four when we drove to the Congressional Club to meet the new Congressmen's wives & then I dashed in to see Elinor Morgenthau.[27] Back here at five. F.D.R. appeared about 5:30.

---

[25] Ike Hoover was the long-time chief usher at the White House who had known Eleanor when she visited her Uncle Teddy there.

[26] Elton Fay, chief political reporter for the Associated Press, and his wife had a new baby.

[27] Elinor Morgenthau was a close friend of Eleanor's and the wife of newly designated Treasury Secretary Henry Morgenthau.

The rooms begin to look homelike! 6:30 dressed & dined 7:30 just ourselves & had a movie of F.D.R. . . .

The preserved copy of this letter ends abruptly in mid-sentence.

The second from the last paragraph of this letter contains one of the many sensual passages that Eleanor wrote to Lorena.

[March 11]

THE WHITE HOUSE
Washington

Hick my dear, The missing letter is still missing but I rejoiced over the Thursday evening one this morning. It is hard to decide what we shall read but let's try the essays. You can give them to me Wednesday.

We could lunch at the house Tuesday if Anna is out or if you don't mind having her with us but I thought you'd rather be alone in a crowd than have anyone else to talk to. It shall be just as you say dear. Stick to your diet, lose twenty pounds more & you'll forget you are forty & please go see the doctor next week.[28]

Last night after I finished writing they called about Los Angeles[29] & I woke & F.D.R., Louis [Howe] & finally poor Steve Early [Franklin's press secretary]. What a bad time the West Coast does have!

Diary. 8:30 Missy [LeHand] & I out with Meggie. A note announcing Forbes Amory & his brother[30] downstairs so I reluctantly order 2 more places for breakfast making us five when the table only holds 4 comfortably. It finally is disclosed that Harry Amory wants to be an assistant Sec. of Commerce & I undertake to hide F.D.R. & get him out of seeing

---

[28] Lorena had been feeling unusually fatigued since returning to New York City to resume her job as a news reporter.

[29] On March 10, a major earthquake had shaken Southern California, killing 100 people and injuring 4,000.

[30] Businessmen Forbes and Harry Amory had made large financial contributions to the Roosevelt presidential election campaign.

them! 9:30 Mrs. [Henrietta] Nesbitt. 10 Ike Hoover, then got most of
F.D.R.'s pictures hung. 11 hair & nails done,[31] signed old mail. Missy &
I alone at lunch, more pictures hung, signed mail till 3, dressed, went to
see Sen. [Thomas] Walsh's widow. She's much more composed & I like
her. She told me all about this "romance," poor things![32] Four p.m. arrived at D.A.R. [Daughters of the American Revolution] building for my
first go at the Girl Scouts (E.R. not in uniform!). Said a few words,
lighted their cake, was photographed & left, got back at 4:20 to find numerous carriages already lined up [for the diplomatic dinner at the White
House that night]. Then all Ambassadors & ministers being lined up according to precedence in the East Room. We were notified—Tommy &
Missy rushed down & sat at their seats to pour tea & chocolate in the
big dining room & we stood in the Blue Room F.D.R., E.R., the Sec. of
State [Cordell Hull], Mrs. Hull, William Phillips, who is undersecretary.
They shook hands & went on in for tea & then we went in & F.D.R. sat
down & every ambassador was taken up to talk to him & the ministers
& I walked all around the room & said sweet nothings to them. I think
they enjoyed it, though it was stiff. You can't be anything else with complete strangers, can you? Tommy came through with flying colours [sic]!
At six I was back in my room writing to you when Louis & Steve Early
appeared, so I sat down & knit & chatted for an hour & now Tommy &
I are dining alone by my fire. F.D.R. & Louis go to the newspaper corre-
spondents dinner. I shall sign mail all evening or dictate to Tommy.

I miss you greatly dear. The nicest time of the day is when I write to
you. You have a stormier time than I do but I miss you as much, I think. I
couldn't bear to think of you crying yourself to sleep. Oh! how I wanted
to put my arms around you in reality instead of in spirit. I went & kissed
your photograph instead & the tears were in my eyes. Please keep most of
your heart in Washington as long as I'm here for most of mine is with you!

A world of love & good night my dear one,

E.R.

---

[31] Eleanor had her hair shampooed and set as well as her fingernails manicured once a week
throughout her years in the White House.

[32] Senator Walsh, seventy-three, had married the much younger Nieves Perez Chaumont de
Truffin in her native Cuba only five days before his death; they had known each other less than
a month.

Eleanor and Tommy had flown to New York City on March 15 and had
seen Lorena while they were there.

[March 16]

THE WHITE HOUSE
Washington

Hick Darling, I've just said "goodnight" & you are right we should not
do it [talk on the telephone] every night. So I'll put a "special" on this
[letter] & not call you to-morrow in the hope that I won't mind not
hearing your voice when I know I'm going to hear it on Saturday. Oh!
dear, I can hardly wait!

Well, we had a very bumpy trip but I was fine & poor Tommy suffered all day.

I had [Secretary of Labor] Frances Perkins, Elinor Morgenthau &
Mary Miller[33] to lunch. Saw a man about the welfare of mountain children, took Maude [Gray, Eleanor's aunt] to the Senate & heard some dull
speeches on beer & listened to F's message on farm relief. It's not very
profitable for me to go to the Senate or Congress as I hear so badly. Got
home, dressed & received the Supreme Court & I think they enjoyed
their tea. Had a talk with John Boettiger on the telephone, did some mail,
dressed for dinner. Fred Hale (Senator from Maine [a Republican] & an
old friend of Maude's) and Steve Early [came] to dinner and then were
given a private showing of the movie "Gabriel Over the White House."[34]
Some of it is raw & silly but oh! some of it is swell & I have so much more
faith in the people than the Fred Hale type [does]. He'd have the soldiers
out if a million unemployed marched on Washington & I'd do what the
President does in the picture![35] Some agreed & I finally took the dogs for
their evening walk & we are going to bed after a good night to you.

I love you & seeing you again [yesterday] was such a joy. Bless you
my dearest,

E.R.

---

[33] Mary Miller was a long-time friend of Eleanor's whose husband Adolph Miller was a
member of the Federal Reserve Board.

[34] Based on the satirical novel that Thomas F. Tweed published in 1933, the movie *Gabriel
Over the White House* told the story of an easy-going president who was knocked on the head
in an auto accident and suddenly enacted an extraordinary program of reform.

[35] The president depicted in the film welcomed unemployed protesters into the White House
and listened to their concerns.

A Perfect Holiday

After living in separate cities from March to June 1933, Eleanor and Lorena arranged their schedules so they could go on a road trip together in July. They had no reason to write to each other during their shared holiday, but the biography the first friend later wrote about the first lady included detailed descriptions of the remarkable holiday. The adjective *remarkable* applies not because of any particular event that occurred during those three weeks but because *absolutely no* major events occurred; just two middle-aged women motoring through the northern United States and French Canada—unaccompanied and (even though one of them was by this time one of the most-photographed women in the world) unrecognized. Their vehicle was well beyond the ordinary, too, because Eleanor had selected as her personal automobile not a somber black Cadillac or Lincoln, like Grace Coolidge and Lou Henry Hoover before her, but a sporty light blue Buick roadster with a white convertible top. Complete with chrome headlights, chrome bumper, and chrome grill in the front and a jaunty rumble seat on the back, the car raised (with the Depression still holding the country tight in its grip) many a Washington eyebrow.

After spending the Fourth of July weekend at Val-Kill, the two women drove north and spent several leisurely days in the secluded woods of Vermont and New Hampshire. Eleanor next spoiled Lorena by picking up the tab for four glorious nights at the Chateau Frontenac, the majestic castellated hotel inside the old stone city of Quebec. After indulging in manicures, facials, and massages by the hotel staff and exquisite meals of escargot, vichyssoise, chateaubriand, and crepes from the hotel's world-class chef—this was a vacation, price be damned!—they proceeded north along the banks of the St. Lawrence. Finally they reached their destination proper: the rugged Gaspé Peninsula that juts out into the Atlantic beyond the northern tip of Maine. For the next week, they meandered along the 500-mile coastline with its breathtaking scenery and charming French villages. Then they stopped at the Roosevelt summer home on Campobello Island in New Brunswick before spending a few final days along the Maine coastline—where, for the only time on the trip, the first lady drew a crowd.

It wasn't the landmarks along the way or the number of days spent at each stop that the women remembered most, though, but a series of magical moments that blended humor and pathos and romance that they would treasure for the next thirty years. The first of the moments erupted the instant that Eleanor announced that she and Lorena were taking an extended motor trip—by themselves. When the head of the Secret Service, Bill Moran, got wind of the plan, he exploded. "The Lindbergh baby was kidnapped only a little more than a year ago," Moran barked. "I will not allow such a thing to happen to the president's wife—not on my watch." But ER barked back: "*We're* not infants." And then, without taking a breath, she adeptly turned the whole idea of an abduction into a joke. "If someone tried to kidnap us, where could they possibly hide us? They certainly couldn't cram us into the trunk of a car!" Lorena quickly chimed in. "The idea of anyone trying to *kid*nap two grown women, one nearly six feet tall and the other weighing almost 200 pounds, is ludicrous."[1]

With ER and Moran at loggerheads, the issue was passed on to higher authority. And in this case, that meant high authority indeed. FDR ultimately was swayed neither by his wife nor the head of his security network, but by Lorena. For in addition to trusting and enjoying the company of the woman who had become the first lady's intimate friend, he had complete faith in the robust woman's ability to protect his wife as well as any bodyguard could. Case closed.

Though Bill Moran had no choice but to accept FDR's decision, he persuaded Eleanor at least to carry a revolver along with her. Details about that gun, however, would remain Eleanor and Lorena's secret. For Lorena admitted years later that, throughout the entire trip, the gun remained locked in its case "which in turn was locked in the glove compartment," unloaded and with no bullets anywhere in the car. If Moran

[1] Hickok, *Reluctant First Lady*, 120.

had known exactly where ER kept the gun and that without bullets it offered her no protection whatsoever, he would have been furious—but probably not surprised.[2]

Another memorable moment played out as the women were driving through the picturesque Adirondack Mountains in upper New York state. The resolutely disciplined Eleanor had decided, because this was a holiday, to give herself permission to adopt a trait that she previously had only read about; she was going to be *impetuous*. She'd been totally responsible for forty-nine years—why not? So even though her plan for the first day of the trip was to drive to Lake Placid and spend the night in a proper hotel there, when dusk came and she passed a cottage in the woods with a sign on the fence stating "Tourists Welcome," she slammed on the brakes. "Let's go back and try it. I've always wanted to stay in one of those places." For a woman accustomed to the finest accommodations that America and Europe had to offer, the novelty of spending a night in a private house by the side of the road was seductive.[3]

The young couple who owned the cottage immediately admitted to their guests that the plumbing wasn't fully installed yet so there would only be enough hot water for one bath. It didn't matter, the travelers assured them. In her book, Lorena recalled telling Eleanor, after they retired to their tiny bedroom with its lone double bed, "You're the first lady, so you get the bath." Lorena then described a playful scene that readers familiar only with the public persona of Eleanor Roosevelt may have trouble envisioning. "Mrs. Roosevelt started thrusting her long, slender fingers in my direction. I was so ticklish that all she had to do to reduce me to a quivering mass of pulp was to point her fingers at me." A few moments later, the first lady, still in an impetuous mood, had Lorena "writhing out of control" among the pillows and blankets.[4]

Another memorable moment evolved when Eleanor and Lorena stopped at the Shrine of Sainte Anne de Beaupré, the Roman Catholic memorial known for the mountain of crutches and canes left behind by the legions of pilgrims who have gone there in search of healing miracles. But when Eleanor and Lorena tried to enter the church, they hit a

[2] Hickok, *Reluctant First Lady*, 121.
[3] Hickok, *Reluctant First Lady*, 121.
[4] Hickok, *Reluctant First Lady*, 122.

snag. To enter the Romanesque basilica, women had to have their heads covered; Eleanor happened to have wrapped a white silk scarf around her hair that day, but Lorena was bareheaded. Hick had a hat in the roadster, but they were a mile away from the parking lot and none too eager to walk that distance, and back again, just to get a hat. When she couldn't think of an immediate solution, Lorena became frustrated— this was precisely the kind of incident that could send her into an emotional tailspin. Fortunately, Eleanor reacted very differently. Like a magician, the first lady—with a playfully theatrical flair—extracted a white lace handkerchief from the depths of her huge pocket book and adroitly tied knots in each of the four corners and, with a fanciful flourish of her hands and a coquettish grin on her face, produced a few hairpins to secure the makeshift *hat* on the top of Lorena's head. *Voila!* Problem solved. In addition to getting the women into the church, ER's whimsical creation also produced a memorable image that neither woman would soon forget; Lorena finished her telling of the anecdote by focusing on Eleanor: "I must have looked funny, for I can still see her, laughing until she cried!"[5]

When the roadster reached the Gaspé Peninsula, looped by a scenic highway where beetling precipices alternate with craggy beaches, the motorists felt like they'd stepped halfway around the world. "The whole landscape and atmosphere were those of a French countryside," Eleanor wrote in her memoirs. "The only road was dirt, frequented by comparatively few people." Neither woman had any complaints about the sense of isolation, though, as they both were pleased to have a respite from the crowds they were used to in New York and Washington. Basking in their temporary freedom, they picnicked in the woods, swam on secluded beaches, and took walks in the twilight. Another of their daily rituals was to lie in bed reading aloud from the books they had brought along.[6]

Just how remote the peninsula was came home to them when they stopped to admire a tiny church along the road and accepted the parish priest's invitation to join him for lunch. It was only after they had consumed the freshly caught trout that the generous cleric asked his guests

---

[5] Hickok, *Reluctant First Lady,* 125.
[6] Roosevelt, *This I Remember,* 121–22; Hickok, *Reluctant First Lady,* 122, 130.

their names. The first lady later wrote, "When I gave my name as Eleanor Roosevelt, he asked: 'Are you relation to *Theodore* Roosevelt? I was a great admirer of his.'" Eleanor smiled and said, "'Yes, I am his niece.'" The fact that another Roosevelt was now residing in the White House—and that he had quite an adventurous wife—had not yet penetrated this part of the continent, and ER saw no need to inform him of that fact.[7]

In several French Canadian villages, indeed it was not Eleanor who attracted attention, but her car. "My Buick convertible was so much admired that when I came out of church one Sunday," Eleanor later wrote, "most of the male population of the village was patting it and even the old curé came up and asked me about it and seemed awed at the idea that any woman should own anything so expensive and beautiful." The men were so eager to examine and admire the car, in fact, that none of them bothered to ask just who that female car owner might be—or who she was married to.[8]

Only when Eleanor and Lorena crossed the border into Maine at Presque Isle did their idyllic getaway come to an end. ER wrote that, "To our horror, word of our coming had preceded us." For two travelers intent upon maintaining their privacy, that afternoon's "horror" came in the form of the townspeople putting together an impromptu parade. For as the roadster—with its convertible top down—entered town and moved unwittingly down the main street with a sunburned Eleanor behind the wheel and an equally sunburned Lorena sitting next to her, crowds of children suddenly appeared on the sidewalks, waving flags and cheering as if the women were conquering heroines returning from the Crusades.[9]

So much for anonymity.

As soon as the roadster pulled inside the White House gates on July 28, Franklin immediately scheduled a private dinner with Eleanor and Hick so he, in his wife's words, "could hear the whole story while it was fresh and not dulled by repetition." It's hard to say who enjoyed that reunion dinner more—the returning adventurers or the president himself.

[7] Roosevelt, *This I Remember,* 122–23.
[8] Mrs. Franklin D. Roosevelt, untitled article written for the North American Newspaper Alliance, August 1933, Box 3026, Eleanor Roosevelt Papers.
[9] Roosevelt, *This I Remember,* 124.

Certainly Eleanor and Lorena relished reliving the magical moments of their carefree holiday. Eleanor's favorite anecdote was about the priest not knowing the name of America's new president; Lorena's was the first lady getting such a kick out of spending the night in a private "tourist home." That latter tale became FDR's anecdote of choice as well, Lorena writing, "Oh, how he enjoyed that story!" That wasn't the only time that evening that FDR threw back his great leonine head and laughed uproariously; Lorena wrote, "Several times the president's great, booming laugh filled the dining room."[10]

Although the amusing moments were sheer delight that the women savored for the rest of their lives, the aspect of their escapade that elevated it from a pleasurable getaway to a personal triumph was the anonymity that the secluded northern woods and isolated beaches had offered them. For Eleanor, the trip proved her contention that she still could, with some thought and planning (she had replaced her District of Columbia license tags with New York ones for the trip), remain independent and even preserve a measure of true privacy; for Lorena, the enormous value she placed on their successfully evading both the public and the press was poignantly captured in how she chose to title the chapter that she wrote about the holiday: "Incognito."

---

[10] Roosevelt, *This I Remember,* 125; Hickok, *Reluctant First Lady,* 128.

Two

SEPTEMBER–DECEMBER 1933

"Deeply & Tenderly"

After the Roosevelt administration was in place, editors at the Associated Press continually pressed Lorena to provide them with inside information about the first lady and the president, even though she was no longer assigned to cover Washington. Not willing to jeopardize her friendship with Eleanor, Lorena refused to produce the information that her editors demanded. When Eleanor saw the pressure that Lorena was under (and realizing it would grow even more intense when Anna's troubled marriage and romantic relationship with John Boettiger became public knowledge), she contacted her close friend Harry Hopkins, head of the Federal Emergency Relief Administration, and persuaded him to offer Lorena a job as chief investigator for the agency.

Lorena then made a decision that ultimately would prove to be the biggest miscalculation of her life: She resigned from the Associated Press.

That decision meant that Hick was forfeiting her identity as a pioneering newswoman and her daily bylines that had, for twenty years, provided the sustenance that had given meaning to her life. In 1933, however, career sacrifices were irrelevant to Lorena; Eleanor's well-being was paramount in her life. Lorena officially left the world of journalism in June and began her new job as soon as she and Eleanor returned from French Canada in late July. In that job, Lorena was to traverse the country to gauge the effectiveness of the nation's relief programs and then write detailed reports on her findings for Hopkins, identifying which programs were working and which were not. Hoping that Lorena's vivid snapshots of America's suffering multitudes would touch the hearts of even the most recalcitrant of New Deal opponents, Hopkins sent copies to the senators and congressmen whose support the Roosevelt administration so desperately needed in this era of social revolution. Lorena also sent copies of her reports to Eleanor, who often showed them to Franklin. After seeing how compelling Lorena's reports were, FDR read them out loud at Cabinet meetings.

Regarding ER and Hick's relationship, Lorena's new job kept them apart for weeks—sometimes months—at a time. Between her fact-finding trips, though, Lorena lived at the White House. During those respites, which varied from a few days to several weeks, she slept on a maple daybed—a Val-Kill piece Eleanor gave her—in the room adjoining the first lady's bedroom.

This chapter contains the earliest correspondence from Lorena. As did Eleanor, Lorena wrote her letters at the end of the day and often while lying in bed.

When Eleanor wrote this letter, she was vacationing on Cape Cod with Anna, Anna's children, and Louis Howe. The first paragraph filled with references to John Boettiger and his public activities with Anna and her children suggests that Eleanor fully accepted and supported her daughter's relationship with Boettiger, even though Anna was still married to Curtis Dall.

[September 6]

[Cape Cod]

Dearest, It was nice to find your letter here. I started the day by signing mail from 7-8 then Tommy came from 9-9:20 & then Nan [Cook] & drove up & saw "Sisty" [Eleanor Dall, Anna's daughter] drive her pony in the show and win a red ribbon—was she proud? She fairly beamed. I stayed to see John show New Deal [Boettiger's horse] but he won nothing so 1 blue for New Deal & a 4th for John & Anna riding as a pair is all they have won so far. There is a different kind of beauty here from any we have seen this summer & sometime you & I must go up the Cape to-gether.

How funny you are about your reports, of course they are good, absorbingly interesting. F.D.R. told me he wished your letters could be published! He is hard to please and always asks if I've anything to read from you.

I am glad I took this jaunt tho' I wasn't keen to do it, it would have been easy to stay put but I think it is a pleasure to Louis [Howe].

Only Friday, Sat. Sun. & Mon. & we will be to-gether! I can hardly wait—A world of love—

E.R.

ER's comments about Missy LeHand in this letter provide an example of Eleanor being catty about the vivacious and handsome woman who had been Franklin's personal secretary since 1920. Eleanor surely recognized that Missy was in love with the president, as she was completely immersed in aspects of his life in ways that ER refused to be—sharing his hobbies, reading the same books that he did, even adopting his characteristic accent and patterns of speech.

November 17th

THE WHITE HOUSE
Washington

Hick darling, In ten minutes I go down to supper & then Betsey & I leave on the Federal to Boston. I'm glad I'm not motoring. I'd miss you too much![1] No letter from you to-day so I hope for one to-morrow.

It was a busy and rather fruitless day. Henry Morgenthau wanted a ceremony to swear him in [as Treasury Secretary] so by 12 [when] that took place it was too late to ride. Well, Russia is recognized,[2] [William] Bullitt[3] goes as ambassador. I wonder if that is why F.D.R. has been so content to let Missy play with him![4] She'll have another embassy to visit next summer anyway!

I'm holding a meeting here on Monday on the [problem of] unemployed women—17 for lunch, tea for F.D.R. entourage, packed[5] & now must go to supper.

A world of love to you, darling, take care of yourself. I'm getting so hungry to see you.

Devotedly,
E.R.

---

[1] Eleanor is saying that driving by car from New York to Washington with Betsey, James's wife, would have been a painful reminder of how much she missed Hick and their road trip of the previous summer.

[2] For the first time, the United States had recognized the Soviet Union that had come into existence after 1917's Russian Revolution.

[3] William Bullitt was a wealthy businessman who had made major financial contributions to FDR's presidential campaign.

[4] William Bullitt had begun dating Missy LeHand.

[5] Eleanor was leaving for Hyde Park.

[November 18]

Val-Kill Cottage

Dearest one, It was so good to see your letter this morning & to find you comfortable & happy with the Dillons.[6]

"Time" has a dreadful cover picture of me & pages *on* me, not too scathing I'm told.[7]

Does it ever occur to you that it would be pleasant if no one ever wrote about me? Mrs. Doaks would like a little privacy now & then![8]

I'm back writing to you & wishing you were here. We've had such good times here [at the Val-Kill cottage] to-gether & I would have enjoyed every minute on the train too with you. We do have such good times to-gether but I'm not unhappy for I like to think of our times here & hope we'll be here again!

Dear, I shouldn't have told you so often I was tired for while I've kept rather late hours I am very well & not really tired only a little sleepy & temporarily tired now & then!

How quietly everyone takes resumption of intercourse with Russia.

The 18th, less than a month till you return.

Bless you & keep well & remember I love you,

E.R.

---

[6] While investigating the relief programs in Minnesota, Lorena was staying with her journalistic mentor Thomas Dillon, editor of the *Minneapolis Tribune,* and his wife Clarissa.

[7] The photo on the cover of the November 20 issue of *Time* magazine showed Eleanor wearing a somber expression, but the story inside praised her as the most active first lady in history.

[8] "Mrs. Doaks" was the fictitious name that Eleanor and Lorena used to refer to the ordinary and inconspicuous private citizen that both women often wished that Eleanor could be.

[November 20]

THE WHITE HOUSE
Washington

Dearest one, A feast of letters, 3 to-day, your report & a road map![9]

Got home here late for dinner having Mrs. [Margaret] Fayer-weather[10] talk a steady stream & found it rather restful, fell into my clothes & dined, went & spoke a few words for TB [tuberculosis] stamps & went to [the play] "Alice in Wonderland," entirely delightful & why didn't we go to-gether? I loved it till I got sleepy towards the end. Fjr. wires he & another boy come to-morrow to go to Warm Springs[11] as the Dr. thinks he needs to get over his cold. Of course all he needs is sleep but he says he can't get it in college! What is one to do to teach one's children backbone?

Dear one, I'm tired but very well. I can't bear to get no letters Friday or Saturday so I'm wiring you my addresses and from the 29th-3rd I'll be in Warm Springs. I would give a good deal to put my arms around you and to feel yours around me. I love you deeply & tenderly.

Devotedly,
E.R.

November 21st

THE WHITE HOUSE
Washington

Hick darling, For some strange reason no letter to-day but I expect I got two yesterday! Busy till twenty minutes before twelve on entertainments, mail & routine, had Eva LeGallienne,[12] Frances Perkins & Isabella [Selmes Greenway] to lunch, much talk on a national theatre & she [LeGallienne]'s anxious of course to be subsidized. I asked her to write out her ideas & I'd try to arrange a meeting with F.D.R. on his re-

[9] Lorena sent Eleanor road maps marked with the cities she was planning to visit, along with the names and addresses of the hotels where she would be staying.

[10] Margaret Fayerweather had been a friend of Eleanor's since FDR's days as governor.

[11] Franklin Jr. was a student at Harvard. Each year the Roosevelt family spent the Thanksgiving holiday at Warm Springs, Georgia.

[12] Eva LeGallienne was a Broadway producer.

turn.[13] I like her, she has charm. I've just had one tea & in fifteen minutes there is another & Tommy & I work to-night. Anna telephoned she wouldn't be here to-morrow. John [Boettiger] has his divorce.

I hope Earl [Miller]'s annulment goes off as quietly & smoothly next Saturday![14]

Dear one I think of you always with tender love & every day that passes brings you nearer. I don't know just how I shall behave! A hug goes to you.

Devotedly,

E.R.

When Lorena traveled to the coal mining region near Morgantown, West Virginia, to investigate the relief programs there, she found the living conditions so appalling that she telephoned Eleanor, who then came to see for herself—the first time Eleanor had ever seen poverty close up. When ER returned to Washington, she lobbied her husband to make the area the site of the pilot project for the subsistence homestead program that he had proposed and that Congress had approved but had not yet actually started. The concept was for the government to move unemployed workers to houses that the government built but that the residents gradually purchased. The program then began on a 1,200-acre farm previously owned by the Arthur family, so the homestead commu-

---

[13] LeGallienne was lobbying for a national theater that would hire unemployed actors to present quality plays at low prices. Her theater ultimately was established as part of the New Deal, although Congress killed the project in 1939.

[14] Earl Miller was a New York state trooper assigned to protect FDR when he was governor. A tall, handsome former Olympic gymnast with a flirtatious manner, Earl spent a great deal of time with Eleanor, and several scholars (as well as Eleanor's son James) have speculated that they were romantically involved, even though Earl was twelve years Eleanor's junior. In 1947, Earl's third wife, Simone, named Eleanor co-respondent in divorce proceedings. After the court documents were sealed, Simone won a hefty financial settlement as well as custody of their two children, Earl and Anna Eleanor—ER was godmother to both children. No correspondence between Eleanor and Earl has been preserved, however, to document the depth of their relationship. Earl later admitted that he married his first wife (the ceremony took place on the Roosevelt estate) as well as Simone to quell rumors about his relationship with Eleanor. After FDR chose to take a trooper other than Earl with him to Washington, Earl took a job with the New York Department of Corrections. When Earl's first marriage ended in the fall of 1933 (after less than a year), Earl moved to Glens Falls, New York, and often visited Hyde Park when Eleanor was there.

nity became known as Arthurdale. In this letter, Eleanor makes her first of many references to the project that informally became known as "Eleanor's Baby." It is also in this letter that Eleanor makes her revealing statement about the Washington wags not gossiping about her relationship with Lorena because they both were women.

November 22d

THE WHITE HOUSE
Washington

Hick darling, I found your two letters of the 19th & 20th here to-night with all the enclosures & your excellent report. I wish you had looked Elliott up. I imagine that Ruth is having a baby. I have a letter from her thanking me for their dining room furniture, very sweet but I feel pretty distant![15]

Dear me, how I laughed over your reminiscences. Well, if I have stopped your drinking of too much corn liquor I probably have increased your chances for health in the next few years[16] & as hangovers can't have added much to the job of life perhaps this last year's changes aren't all bad! For me they've been all good & I hope you are going to find that so also as time goes on!

The day at "Arthurdale" was interesting. We had breakfast with the workers & everyone asked about you. Little Pabywork[17] kissed me when I got there this morning & asked for you! The village is going to be nice. Left at 2 & got in at 8. Anna has gone to meet John [Boettiger]. Louis [Howe] tells me one of the newspaper men casually mentioned the other day to a group of them "now that John Boettiger has his divorce I suppose we'll soon hear of Mrs. Dall's getting hers"! One cannot hide things in this world, can one? How lucky you are not a man!

---

[15] While traveling from Iowa to Minnesota, Lorena had passed near Chicago where Eleanor's son Elliott was living with his second wife, Ruth Googins Roosevelt. A gulf had developed between Elliott and his parents because Eleanor and Franklin were not in favor of him marrying so quickly after his divorce from his first wife. Because of this gulf, Elliott had not yet informed his parents that Ruth was, in fact, expecting their first child.

[16] Eleanor's abstinence from liquor had encouraged Lorena to reduce the amount of alcohol that she drank.

[17] "Little Pabywork" was the child of one of the miners who was homesteading at Arthurdale.

My dear one I love you devotedly. Take care of yourself & goodnight. Sleep sweetly—

E.R.

This letter refers to President Roosevelt's support of the United States departing from the gold standard as a major step in the country's effort to regain economic stability. Al Smith, the 1928 Democratic presidential candidate whom Eleanor had worked to try to elect, publicly disagreed with FDR and insisted that the country should remain on the gold standard.

[November 24]
49 East 65th Street
New York City
[the Roosevelt townhouse]

Darling, Well, how do you feel about Al [Smith]'s pronouncement on sound money! He certainly feels no obligation to loyalty but I don't think it will hurt.

Dear one, I always want you here in this room with me. Somehow you visualize easily here because we've been here to-gether so much.[18] Well perhaps you'll come up & spend the night of Dec. 21st here with me. It is sentimental & I didn't mean to tell you but I'd like to have you here that night & celebrate a little X-mas of our own! Probably you can't do it but perhaps—who knows!

A world of love to you dear one.

Devotedly,
E.R.

This letter is the earliest of Lorena's letters to Eleanor that has been preserved, as well as one of her earliest reports on the status of the coun-

---

[18] Between November 1932 and March 1933 when Eleanor and Lorena were both living in New York City, they often had found privacy in Eleanor's bedroom at the Roosevelt townhouse.

*try's relief programs. Lorena wrote her letters on the stationery pro-
vided by whatever hotel she was staying in that particular night. She
ended her letters with "H" for Hick. Regarding writing style, Lorena
wrote in a much more flowing narrative form than Eleanor did.*

November 26th

The Ottumwa

Ottumwa, Iowa

My dear:

I've slept most of the day. I left Des Moines at 11 a.m. and arrived in
Ottumwa at 2. Flopped on the bed the moment I landed in this room
and just woke up, at 5 o'clock. After I've finished this and have done my
expense accounts for the last two weeks, I think I'll dine early and perhaps go to a movie, and then I'll go to bed early tonight—by 10 o'clock
or so. *Should* work—see people. But the week *has* been strenuous, and I
seem to be about at the end of my rope. So I think I'd better get some
rest and a little relaxation. Probably I'll work all the better for it tomorrow. I think probably "the curse" is imminent, and that's perhaps what's
the matter with me. I feel so gloomy and "uncertain"—unstable ner-
vously and emotionally—the way I felt a couple of times last summer.
Remember? I'll be alright in a day or two.

Well, no matter how they may be pounding the president in the
East,[19] Iowa and Nebraska seem quiet and contented enough. I mean
people generally. And, although I've been moving so rapidly that I
haven't been so aware of it as I might have been had I remained in one
locality—Sioux City, for instance—I believe that in the month since I
came out here there has been a remarkably swift and strong change in
the current of public opinion in the "Farm Belt"—sweeping back
toward the administration. They never were really against the president.
NRA is not at all popular, to be sure.[20] Well, how *could* it be? Their
prices *did* go up faster than their incomes. And practically every city and

[19] FDR was being criticized because recovery was not occurring as fast as he had promised
voters that it would.
[20] The National Recovery Administration approved codes for various industries that provided, among other things, for price fixing. The result was that already-destitute American
farmers were having to pay higher prices for many consumer items.

town in Iowa, from Des Moines down, is almost wholly dependent on agriculture.

Sioux Falls, South Dakota, interested me. Its population, in figures, hasn't changed since the depression—which is 10 or 12 years old out here, remember. But in the *character* of its population there has been a change most disastrous from an economic standpoint. It's the largest city in the state. It's always been purely a trading center, and many, many traveling salesmen working out through the Dakotas, Montana, Wyoming, and down into Western Nebraska have their homes there. There are darned few traveling salesmen on the road out there any more—and, if you could have overheard, as I did the other day, an oil-burner salesman trying to sell an oil-burner to a small town restaurant proprietor, you'd understand why. Only the man selling the absolute necessities of life can get by, even take a commodity like paint, for example, why, there obviously hasn't been a paint brush on those farm buildings in years. And that's true of Iowa, too. What chance has a paint salesman had out here? And the condition is the same this year—what with closed banks, low prices, and crop failures.

Well, the result, they tell me, has been that most of those traveling men and their families—good, solid, paying customers—have left Sioux Falls or have been forced on to the relief rolls, and their places have been taken by farmers and their families who lost their farms and moved to town, hoping they'd be able to get work there.

And yet, despite NRA, things are beginning to look up—in Iowa and Nebraska at any rate. Wheat allotments have come in, corn loans are arriving, the corn-hog program is getting under way. Henry Morgenthau is apparently going to kick some of the "Tories" out of the credit picture, and the farm strike died on its feet.[21]

I think I shall have to quit reading the Chicago Tribune.[22] Their latest was to run—*today*—two weeks after it was all over—pages of farm strike pictures. Battles! They looked to me as though they'd been posed, by the scrub football teams of Northwestern and Chicago universities! They *do* make me so *damned* mad!

---

[21] The Great Depression had pushed American farmers into a state of economic crisis and deprivation so catastrophic that they had been preparing, both psychologically and through organized action, to undertake the nation's first large-scale farm strike.

[22] The *Chicago Tribune* was one of the leading Republican newspapers in the country.

I must go and eat.

Darling—only eighteen more days!

H

Eleanor's comments in this letter show that Lorena was concerned that people were gossiping about the closeness of their relationship. Eleanor's response suggests a cavalier attitude on her part, which provides evidence that, as Lorena later would write, Eleanor was not "discreet" in her letters to Lorena—the reason Lorena ultimately destroyed so many of them.

November 27th

THE WHITE HOUSE
Washington

Hick dear, I found two letters & a road map to-day & did I devour them!

I forgot [to] write you that after 10:30 a.m. on Dec. 15th I will be free to meet you & I will have nothing to do so come as early as you can. Why don't we, if the weather is nice[,] take our lunch & go off each day to neighboring places? If we think we'll be tempted to stay the night we could take a bag & telephone [back to the White House] what we decided to do. There may be people staying here so I think one night anyway we'll stay away as otherwise we might have to be polite a while in the evening unless the guests all dine out which is quite unlikely!

There's a bit about you & a picture in the Literary Digest. It's nice! Tommy is mailing it to you.[23]

Press conference at 11 this morning then 2 women to see, had five of the girls [the women reporters who attended Eleanor's weekly press conferences] to lunch & worked all the rest of the time on accumulated mail but I'm fairly caught up tho' I won't be able to ride to-morrow.

[23] The November 18 article described Lorena as "an experienced newspaperwoman who is a close friend of Mrs. Roosevelt's" and reported that it was Lorena who had prompted the first lady to visit the West Virginia coal mining region and take the lead in the subsistence homestead project.

John [Boettiger] came in to-night & dined with us. I do like him. They sat on my sofa all evening & seemed to have a swell time while I worked!

Dear one, & so you think they gossip about us. Well they must at least think we stand separation rather well! I am always so much more optimistic than you are. I suppose because I care so little what "they" say!

I rather think some of the girls [woman reporters] are getting [to be] pretty good champions! There have been one or two inaccurate stories & I spoke about them this morning [at the press conference] & I trusted the majority of them were with me![24]

Dear heart I would like to be with you when this letter reaches you. If I were free I would meet you in Minneapolis Wed. only my sense of duty keeps me from doing it! I'll call you anyway about one on Thanksgiving day.

A world of love & my thoughts are always with you,

E.R.

The letterhead for this hotel included a drawing of the building. At the top of the first page of her letter, Lorena drew an arrow pointing to a room on the second floor. Beneath the arrow she wrote: My room—for Two Dollars! And I suspect *bed bugs!*

November 28th

Hotel Hildreth
Charles City, Iowa

Madame!

Now will you please tell me what in the world one is going to do about cases like these?

---

[24] One reason the women championed the first lady was that several of them owed their jobs to her. The *New York Times, New York Herald Tribune,* and United Press were among the organizations that had not employed any woman reporters in Washington until Lorena's suggestion to create the news conferences forced them to—or get scooped every week.

I just came in from a long talk with the chairman of the county relief committee. He put them up to me—and I pass them on to you, *not* expecting or asking you for anything except ideas.

But what *can* be done about these, please?

No. 1 consists of an old carpenter and his wife, both about 70. They'd starve—and almost did—rather than be on relief. Furthermore, they're not strictly eligible, since they own their home, unencumbered save for $25 or $30 in back taxes. I think they'd probably rather starve *in* that home than give it up, too. The relief chairman told me the county would probably be willing to take a deed to the home & give them $20 a month to live on the rest of their lives. But that, to them, would mean "being on the county." It's probably stubborn of them, and all that, but—dammit, I think it's outrageous that an old couple, who have worked hard all their lives, should be obliged to have their pride, their self-respect, broken down that way. The relief chairman said he'd known this old man for years, and he has always been a hard-working, respected citizen.

Today the old man, much too frail to work outdoors in winter weather, came in and begged for a job with a shovel or wheelbarrow in a stone quarry, on the roads—anywhere there was a CWA[25] job for him. There *isn't* any job for him. He couldn't stand the work. It's too heavy.

The old man wanted the job to earn the money to pay up his back taxes—about $25 or $30—on his home. He's had an extension, but that runs out March 1, and theoretically at least, if they aren't paid by then, he'll lose his home. He was really frantic.

The relief chairman asked him how he'd managed to live these last few years. He knew the old man had been working in a small grocery store up until nearly two years ago, when the proprietors died, and he lost his job.

The old man told him that when he lost his job he had $126 saved up.

"We've been living on that ever since," he said.

Two old people—living nearly two years on $126! And he refused to make an application for relief.

---

[25] The Civil Works Administration created government jobs for unemployed workers.

Now what *are* you going to do with a couple like that? I say it's a crime to force them to take charity. But what can be done?

Number 2 consists of an elderly man and his wife and an only son, a freshman at Ames [where Iowa State University is located].

The old lady does baking, which the old man peddles around. He also carries the paper route that his boy used to carry. They manage to get by somehow that way, but the relief chairman says she expects to see the old man drop in the street some day.

However, he's chiefly worried about the boy. He's a really fine youngster, the relief chairman said, and the hopes of his parents are all wrapped up in him. The youngster—a rather frail chap—and his parents, too, have always had one consuming ambition. *That he should* go to college.

"Nobody knows how hard that kid has worked," the relief chairman said. "In Iowa these last few years there's been darned little chance for a boy, no matter how ambitious he was, to earn money doing odd jobs here and there.

"But somehow that kid managed to earn a little—and he's saved every cent.

"And now he's down there at Ames, and I hear he's got himself a room and does all his own cooking and lives on a dollar a week. Now what's going to happen to that boy? He'll break himself down!"

Oh, Lord! Well, it's the first old couple that worries *me* more. I'm going out to see them tomorrow, and the relief chairman and I are going to try to figure out something. But it doesn't look very promising.

Tomorrow night—Minneapolis. And letters from you. Oh, my dear, I *do* get so hungry for letters! Some days—it seems that I can hardly bear it, I want some direct word from you so much. It's particularly bad in the morning, to wake up—with the realization that there'll be no letter today.

I must get ready for dinner. And after dinner—expense accounts and bed early. I had breakfast at 6:30 this morning and left Iowa city at 7! And tomorrow will be another long day.

I suppose you arrived in Warm Springs today. Well—I'd probably not be very happy there, anyway. Oh, I guess I'm probably a little jealous.

Forgive me. I know I shouldn't be—and it's only because it's been so long since I've seen you. I'll be good—

Dear one—you are ever in my heart—

H

Eleanor became a close friend to several of the women reporters who attended her weekly press conferences. This letter refers to Ruby Black, a reporter for the United Press news service. Because Black had been feeling ill for several weeks, Eleanor invited her to join the Roosevelts on their annual vacation to Warms Springs for Thanksgiving.

On train getting into Atlanta

November 29th

Dear, We got off last night after a full day & we've had an easy day. Ruby is suffering from what we both fear might be pleurisy but we hope is only muscular.

Well dear all I can think of to-day is that when I get home from here I will soon be expecting you back.[26] I wish you were going to spend Thanksgiving here, it surely would be Thanksgiving, wouldn't it?

I hope you & Tom Dillon[27] don't let that feeling [of] estrangement grow, there are so many other things beside politics you can talk about![28]

[26] Lorena was planning to spend Christmas at the White House.

[27] Lorena was spending Thanksgiving with her former editor and his wife Clarissa in Minneapolis.

[28] Dillon's *Minneapolis Tribune* was one of many papers that had published Republican accusations that Eleanor was selling pieces of Val-Kill furniture to the government to place in the Arthurdale houses to make money for herself. ER had denied the accusations, pointing out that the hand-crafted items from Val-Kill were far too expensive for government housing and, furthermore, that she had never made a cent of profit from the Val-Kill factory. Lorena was angry at Dillon for publishing the accusations, even though Eleanor defended him, pointing out that he also had published her denial.

We are coming in & I must mail this, so goodbye dearest one, all my love to you.

Devotedly,

E.R.

December 1st

Georgia Warm Springs Foundation

Hick dearest, It was so good just to hear your voice yesterday, so good that I didn't much care what you said as long as you were well. At last it is Dec. 1st, fifteen more days & I'll be meeting you!

How would you like to go to Charlottesville & see Monticello[29] & then to Washington & Lee [University] at Lexington & home by way of Luray?[30] We can do it in two days but if you've had too much motoring, we could go to the Farmington Country Club at Charlottesville & stay, those days are yours & if you prefer we can stay in Washington & go out with books, lunch somewhere & walk in the country each day. Darling, I know they [news reporters asking Lorena about the first lady] bother you to death because you are my friend, but we'll forget it & think only that someday I'll be back in obscurity again & no one will care except ourselves!

We all arrived [in Warm Springs] rather weary in time for supper & after it I took Ruby [Black] to the hotel. I was to be so sleepy all day yesterday! I went swimming & lay in the sun & after calling you we came back for lunch & I slept a half hour & then had a walk.

Dear one, I wish you could be here the weather is glorious & you would enjoy it. I had a little longing (secretly) that F.D.R. might think I'd like you to be here & insist on your coming to report to him! You know how one dreams? I knew it wouldn't be true but it was nice to think about!

E.R.

---

[29] Monticello is Thomas Jefferson's home near Charlottesville, Virginia.
[30] Luray, Virginia, is a picturesque town in the Shenandoah Mountains.

In the early 1930s, Nan Cook and Marion Dickerman joined the Roosevelts for their Thanksgiving holiday trip to Warm Springs.

December 3d

Georgia Warm Springs Foundation

Hick dearest, Yesterday was grey but no rain, however we didn't swim—Marion, Ruby, & I took a walk after Marion & I rode & we all listened in on the press conference which was not very exciting yesterday.[31]

We've had a chance to talk these few days & I am relieved to find that F.D.R. is thinking in terms of the next five years.[32]

Last night we waited to hear [William Randolph] Hearst on money at 10[33] & I was entirely asleep long before I went to bed! Ruby looks better too & even these few days seem to have done her good.

Darling, I feel very happy because every day brings you nearer. I love you deeply & tenderly & oh! I want you to have a happy life. To be sure I'm selfish enough to want it to be near me but then we wouldn't either of us be happy otherwise, would we?

Devotedly,
E.R.

December 5th

The White House
Washington

Hick dearest, No letter to-day, but I was spoiled yesterday so I will just read over all those I had yesterday! This has been a busy day. Stuck at my desk till I went to a Thrift Shop doll sale at 12:30. Then lunch, desk

---

[31] FDR's press conference was so lacking in news that the *New York Times* did not even publish a story about it.

[32] Eleanor was concerned that Franklin merely reacted to crises and did not have a long-range strategy for strengthening the American economy to avoid another depression.

[33] In his nationwide NBC broadcast, publishing mogul William Randolph Hearst supported FDR's position of departing from the gold standard and lambasted Al Smith and others opposed to that move, accusing financiers of being driven by the big commissions they would receive on loans to foreign organizations rather than by what was best for the United States.

again till 5, at 6 went up & unpacked X-mas things & distributed them in the various drawers all ready to fill stockings! Fannie Hurst[34] & her husband arrived at 6:15 but I didn't see them till we greeted our dinner party. Forty-four & the Sedalia Choir (colored) sang. It was lovely & I thought of you & wished you were there with me. You would have liked them I know.[35]

I had a funny letter to-day. A woman said she read all I wrote on child labor & she had had 13 [children] & wouldn't I please tell her how to stop it!

One week from to-morrow you will start for home. Oh! dear me that last day will be bad but seeing you & feeling you doesn't seem entirely possible even now!

Ruby [Black] & Bess [Furman of the Associated Press] are both sad that you won't be here for the Gridiron party on Sat. night & so am I.[36]

A world of love & goodnight & sleep sweetly dear one—

E.R.

The first and last paragraphs in this letter contain what may be the most erotic passages in the entire collection of letters. When Lorena wrote them, she had been away from Eleanor for more than two months and was eagerly anticipating their reunion. The fact that Lorena was so intimately familiar with the contours of Eleanor's face that she knew exactly which "soft spot" she wanted to feel against her lips leaves little doubt that their relationship was more than platonic.

[34] Fannie Hurst was a popular novelist in the 1930s.

[35] The Sedalia Choir was composed of African-American students who attended the Alice Freeman Palmer Memorial Institute in North Carolina. The institute received much of its funding by having the choir give musical recitals.

[36] Because women reporters were banned from the Gridiron Club dinners where the president and other male Washington newsmakers socialized with male reporters, Eleanor inaugurated Gridiron Widows parties at the White House for women reporters, women newsmakers, and the wives of the men attending the Gridiron Club dinners.

December 5th

Lyran Hotels
New Hotel Markham and Annex
Bemidji, Minnesota

Dear:

Tonight it's Bemidji, away up in the timber country, not a bad hotel, and one day nearer you. Only eight more days. Twenty-four hours from now it will be only seven more—just a week! I've been trying today to bring back your face—to remember just *how* you look. Funny how even the dearest face will fade away in time. Most clearly I remember your eyes, with a kind of teasing smile in them, and the feeling of that soft spot just northeast of the corner of your mouth against my lips. I wonder what we'll do when we meet—what we'll say. Well—I'm rather proud of us, aren't you? I think we've done rather well.

A beautiful drive today—although slippery. I think the president would have got a kick out of it. We drove for miles and miles, it seemed to me, through second growth pines, a part of the state's reforestation program. Itasca State park, part of it, at the headwaters of the Mississippi. Lord, they were lovely! But the mere still among them when it got dark, and the road—where the sun hadn't had a chance to melt the ice—was terrible. Almost as bad as the time you and I drove down to New York from Hyde Park the Sunday before March 4th. Remember? This is beautiful country, though. I'd forgotten how beautiful it is. We were in one big county today that has within its borders *a thousand lakes!*

I just got a big kick out of something I overheard. I'm writing this down in the lobby—since I want to hear the president's speech and don't want to climb the two flights to my room twice in one evening—and half a dozen men sitting nearby have been talking politics.

One of them said he'd be willing to bet on the president's reelection in 1936.

"Well, I don't know," another said, "a lot of things can happen in three years."

"Oh, Hell," another put in, "he's got more friends now than he had when he went in."

And they all agreed on that.

This has been a funny day. They're so damned slow up here. The cold seems to get into their very muscles and brains and make it impossible for them to do anything rapidly.

(The gang next to me are talking now about recovery.

"I think things will hold just about as they are for awhile," one of them said. "They're just getting organized."

"Yeah—we can't expect things to get going in a big way for a few months," another said.

And they all nodded in agreement and seemed perfectly satisfied!)

I was in one village today where not a single man had been put to work under CWA. They just can't seem to get started. I gravely suspect my old friend [Governor] Floyd Olson[37] of playing politics with relief in Minnesota. I gather that Floyd runs the show himself and is too busy to do a decent job of it. The two states out here where they are doing the best jobs on relief and CWA—South Dakota and Iowa—have the least interference from their governors. North Dakota, Nebraska, and Minnesota—all bad. I tell you—Floyd is for Floyd. And that's that. And if I were Harry Hopkins or Henry Morgenthau or any of the rest of the boys down in Washington, I'd never forget it—not for a moment. Floyd is for Floyd, and, I suspect, a not too scrupulous fighter. He's got brains, too, and that makes him all the more dangerous. There's no point in all this, except that I have a feeling that both Mr. Hopkins and Henry Morgenthau are quite impressed by him. I believe that Floyd would see all the Swedes in Minnesota—except himself—drawn and quartered if it would be to his advantage. He's an ambitious young man, Floyd is.

Darling, I've been thinking about you so much today. What a swell person you are to back me up the way you do on this job! We *do* do things together, don't we? And it's fun, even though the fact that we both have work to do keeps us apart.

[37] Lorena had covered Floyd Olson while she was reporting for the *Minneapolis Tribune*.

Good night, dear one. I want to put my arms around you and kiss you at the corner of your mouth. And in a little more than a week now—I shall!

H

Eleanor's reference in this letter to Lorena's job being "more interesting than mine" speaks both to ER's admiration for Hick and her frustrations with the limits of the role of the president's wife.

On train to Washington

December 7th

Hick darling, I'm writing now because [I had] little time in Washington!

We went to hear F. speak & it really was a good speech.[38] I wonder if by chance you were listening too. Funny everything I do my thoughts fly to you. Never are you out of my heart & just one week from to-morrow I'll be holding you. Of course the long separation has been hardest on you because so much of the time you've been with strangers but on the other hand your job is more interesting than mine. Both jobs are somewhat tiring & we'll both enjoy days to rest, won't we? A world of love.

Just going down to stand up & receive for an hour & a half!

Good night & a kiss to you,

E.R.

Just before the train starts

[December 8]

Hick darling, Two grand letters of the 5th & 6th this morning & your reports. The last one most chilling!

---

[38] FDR told the Federal Council of the Churches of Christ that the church and state should not necessarily be separated in all endeavors but sometimes should work together for mutual goals—such as outlawing lynching.

Dear, nothing is important except that my last trip will be over to-morrow morning before you come & then I hope the next will be with you. Less than a week now. Take care of yourself. I know I won't be able to talk when we first meet but though I can remember just how you look I shall want to look long & very lovingly at you.

A world of love & good night dear one—

E.R.

This letter gives a sense of the roller coaster of mood shifts—from anger to excitement to frustration to pleasure to anxiety—that Lorena often experienced in a short period of time.

December 8th

The Androy
Hibbing, Minnesota

My dear:

I'm feeling confused and indignant. An elevator boy just said to me:

"Are you a Girl Scout leader?"

"Good God, no!" I replied, consternation depriving me of all discretion. "Whatever put any such idea in your head?"

"Your uniform," he replied.

I'm wearing that old dark grey skirt—the one you never liked—with a grey sweater. And to soften the neckline a little, I wear that dark red liberty scarf of mine knotted about the throat. That costume, topped off by a brimmed black felt slouch hat and supported by low-heeled golf shoes—Oh, lord, I wonder how many people in the farm belt these last few weeks have thought I was a Girl Scout leader! My very soul writhes in anguish.

Well, here we are at the end of another day, and *only six more to go.* Darling, I am getting so excited! You're going to be shocked when you see me. I *should* be returning to you wan and thin from having lived on a diabetic diet, but I'm afraid I've gained, instead of losing, weight. Just you or Doctor [Ross] McIntire[39] try to live on green vegetables and fruit, without starch or sugar, in country hotels, where they have nothing but meat, bread, potatoes, pie and cake, and see how far you'd go without breaking over. Besides, I feel so perfectly well, and I'm living such an active life, and yet so hungry. Up here in this clear, cold, Northern Minnesota air, I have an appetite that would do justice to Paul Bunyan himself. Ever hear of Paul Bunyan? He's the legendary hero of the lumberjacks. He used to bite off the tops of Jack pines with his teeth! Up and out early every morning. Good cold mornings. It was five below in Brainerd this morning, and ten below here. In and out of the car. Tramping around over CWA projects. Long, busy days. Lady, I get *hungry!* And I can't think there's anything so *very* much wrong with me when I feel so perfectly healthy—Well, I've been pretty good about sweets. No candy, of course. And very few desserts. (Did you ever eat cracked wheat bread, by the way? Delicious!) And I'm very much afraid I've gained weight. I've just resolved—again—to be good until I get back to Washington. But—I probably shan't.

Oh, by the way, I had a funny experience the other night, in Bemidji. At the table next to me in the dining room were two men, and I overheard one of them say to the other:

"Do you remember that Lorena Hickok who used to be a writer on the Minneapolis Tribune? You know, she used to write all those feature stories. Well, she's in town. Her name's out on the register. She went to New York, and sometimes the Tribune still published her articles. She's registered from Washington, D.C. Wonder what she's doing now."

It made me feel sort of self-conscious and embarrassed, although I *did* get something of a kick out of it.

There is, to be sure, an unemployment problem here that will never be cured probably. In the last three years the open pit mines—the largest open pit mine in the world is at Hibbing—have gone in for modern machinery. They've bought electric shovels, for instance, and one man, with an electric shovel, can do the work of eight men on a steam shovel. Well—among other things we really *have* an industrial revolution on our hands, haven't we?

---

[39] Dr. Ross McIntire was the White House physician who had advised Lorena to lose weight.

Oh, my dear—I can hardly wait to see you! Day after tomorrow, Minneapolis and letters from you. A week from now—right this minute—I'll be *with* you!

Good Night, my dear. God keep you!

H

I'm sleepy. There was a mouse in my room last night, and I lay awake half the night worrying about it. I *would*.

H

December 9th

THE WHITE HOUSE
Washington

Hick dearest, I can't help wondering if my pencil note will reach you which I sent off last night! No letter from you to-day but I had two yesterday so I am just expressing a longing not a complaint!

I've really made a start in Xmas things. A huge pile of packages are actually going off all carefully marked "Do not open until Dec. 25th."[40]

We had all the world to tea! Now I must get ready for dinner & I feel rather weary not a good way to begin the evening is it?

Dear, I never thought you were feeling badly from drinking, it never ever crossed my mind! I never think of that unless it is obvious, I suppose because it does not attract me. I never think of other women doing it![41]

---

[40] Eleanor gave dozens of Christmas gifts to a wide variety of friends, relatives, and people she had come into contact with over the years. She began her Christmas shopping each January in order to complete it by the end of the year.

[41] Eleanor's reference to Lorena's drinking suggests that Lorena may have had serious concerns that she had been suffering from alcoholism. During her newspaper days, Hick had been a heavy drinker, but after becoming involved with Eleanor, she had reduced her alcohol intake. Perhaps now, being hundreds of miles away from the first lady and with the increased attention on alcohol because of the end of Prohibition, Lorena was becoming concerned that she was drinking too heavily again.

Dear one it's getting nearer & nearer & I am half afraid to be too happy. It's the way I felt as a child when I dreaded disappointment! A world of love,

E.R.

December 10th

THE WHITE HOUSE
Washington

Hick dearest, I just sneezed all over this paper, forgive me! Well, I took the party [of White House guests] to Mt. Vernon,[42] got home in time to go to church with F.D.R. taking Anna & Sisty & Buzzie & it was a circus! Buzzie wanted to know where the men went to bed, the surplices of course being night clothes to him![43] The two children were one continuous question til Anna took them out before the sermon.

The [Gridiron Widows] party last night went well. Katharine Dayton[44] was excellent & I got several speeches from them which were good. Ruby [Black] & I tried but she was so embarrassed she wasn't good.[45]

I have a rather pathetic letter from Elliott just here. I think the child is sad at being separated at Xmas time from us all & it makes me feel sorry for him but this is the way life teaches us certain necessary lessons & I know we have to learn them & Elliott needs them but—oh! I am unreasonable!

Only 2 more letters Hick & then I'll hold my breath till you arrive! Oh! dearest I can hardly wait, it is lucky I have a busy week or I would die just waiting.

I love you deeply & tenderly,

E.R.

[42] Mt. Vernon is George Washington's home in Alexandria, Virginia, just south of Washington, D.C.

[43] Surplices are the long, loose-fitting white garments that Episcopal priests wear over their robes during church services.

[44] Katharine Dayton wrote for the *Saturday Evening Post* and Consolidated Press news service.

[45] Eleanor and her guests at the party performed skits and lighthearted speeches.

December 12th

THE WHITE HOUSE
Washington

Hick darling, 2 letters, a report & a wire! this is a rich day & this is my last letter! The day after to-morrow you will be starting East, *don't* fly if the weather isn't good![46]

We'll have tea in my room as soon as you get here Friday & then we'll decide about Sat. & Sunday—

Dearest one, it will be good to see you. All my love till Friday & God keep you safe,

E.R.

Despite Eleanor's exuberant statements about how eager she was to see Lorena after months of separation, the first lady became so caught up in Christmas activities that, during Lorena's first week in Washington, Eleanor barely spent any time with her. After ER promised to commit the evening of December 22 exclusively to Lorena but then spent it with Anna (in the throes of separating from her husband), Lorena blew up. She stormed out of the White House, telling Eleanor she had changed her plans and instead of spending her entire three-week holiday with the first lady she was taking the train to New York and would spend the next two weeks with friends there.

[December 23]

THE WHITE HOUSE
Washington

Hick dearest, I went to sleep saying a little prayer, "God give me depth enough not to hurt Hick again." Darling, I know I'm not up to you in many ways but I love you dearly & I do learn sometimes.

I got in on time & such for Tommy [Thompson, ER's secretary] & she

---

[46] Eleanor's comment about Lorena not flying was a joke—she meant that Lorena shouldn't drive so fast that her car flew. Lorena had never considered taking an airplane back to Washington, as it would have been too expensive.

went with the kids & me to the Fox theatre to give out some things to children.[47] "Sisty" objected to the smell! I'm afraid she's going to be as fastidious as I am which is bad luck for her!

Then I saw the usual people! Lunch early as Missy [LeHand, FDR's secretary] & Tommy were to go off. Missy left in tears, her first Xmas without her mother & I think she would rather have been here but she felt she must go [home].[48] Tommy didn't seem keen to go [to New York City to be with her family for the holidays] but she motored up. In fact no one round me is very happy except the kids & Sisty has a cold! I wonder why we bother so much about it [the Christmas holiday] anyway, tradition I suppose!

The Salvation Army party came off at 2:30 & was nice[49] & then Anna began to dress the Xmas tree helped (or hindered) by Sisty & Buzzie. Anna went out at 6 & Mama arrived & F.D.R., Mama & I have just dined & I must go in & fill envelopes with money in the oval room[50] till Mama goes to bed.

Dearest one bless you & forgive me & believe me you've brought me more & meant more to me than you know & I will be thankful Xmas eve & Xmas day & every day for your mere being in the world. I'd like to hug you.

Goodnight, sleep well, a world of love—

                                                                    E.R.

After calling Lorena in New York City and apologizing on Christmas Eve and again on Christmas Day, Eleanor finally persuaded her to re-

---

[47] Each year Eleanor hosted a Christmas party for some 1,000 children from the Central Union Mission.

[48] Eleanor was mistaken. Missy's mother had died in October 1932, before the previous Christmas.

[49] Eleanor served as hostess for the annual Salvation Army Christmas party that included singing hymns and distributing hundreds of food baskets and gifts.

[50] FDR used the oval-shaped room on the second floor of the White House as his study.

turn to the White House the next Friday so they could spend the last week of Lorena's holiday together.

Xmas night

THE WHITE HOUSE
Washington

Hick my darling, I love all the things from you, most of all the notes! The underclothes are just right, the [automobile first aid] kit I hope I shan't need but I should carry one, the little lemon fork will certainly be useful someday when I am in my own home again & the gun was an amusement to us all![51] I read some of the poems last night[52] & I love many things you have marked, we'll read them together sometime.

Franklin said I could ask Harry Hopkins about Puerto Rico.[53] He said nothing about not flying when I said we'd go that way. I only wonder if I'll be a nuisance for you for of course we can't keep it quiet & there will be reporters & fuss. Would you rather I didn't try to go with you? Be honest, I won't be hurt!

I just talked to you!

We drank a toast to absent friends whom we would like to have with us at dinner & I thought of you dear one as I proposed it— We started with stockings, then breakfast, church & Anna the boys & I walked home. After lunch which the kids had with us we opened presents nearly all afternoon. F.D.R. read parts of the Christmas Carol & John B[oettiger] whispered to me it was the nicest day he'd ever had & he would never forget it! The young ones then went dancing including Fjr. who has had & still has a sore throat! John didn't go & he went out with the dogs & with me & at last I got him to bed. I must go too. It was good to hear your voice & you shall dine in bed & sleep all you want if you'll just stay here & be happy. Don't think I don't know what it is like to be

[51] As a joke, Lorena had given Eleanor a plastic gun, a reference to the revolver that the Secret Service had persuaded her to carry in the glove compartment of her car.

[52] Lorena had given Eleanor a book of poetry.

[53] Harry Hopkins had told Lorena that he wanted her to visit Puerto Rico to investigate the relief programs in that island territory. The schedule for the trip would place Lorena in the Caribbean in early March, which would mean that Lorena would spend her birthday away from Eleanor, as she had the previous year. Lorena had suggested that the first lady go with her to Puerto Rico so the trip could double as a vacation.

jealous, or want to be alone, because I know both emotions tho' I succeed as a rule in subduing them with laughter! When I don't, I give you
& myself a pretty bad time, don't I? But I promise I'll be quite reasonable & in hand before you get here Friday!

A world of love & sleep sweetly,

E.R.

[December 26]

THE WHITE HOUSE

Washington

Dearest, Both your letters reached me to-day written on the 23d & 24th
& I was made happy by them as I know you wished. No dear, you
should not make believe to be happy for me nor like things you don't
like on my account but I should have you all alone!

We've just sent 60 odd children home. They were fun to watch & the
entertainment very good! I told Bill [Dana][54] you'd be here Friday a.m.
& were deigning to sleep here but nothing else & he looked understanding![55]

Dr. McIntire will see you Friday a.m. at 9 or 9:30[56] & your report is
good!

Many thanks dear one for everything, a world of love,

E.R.

[54] Bill Dana was a long-time friend of the Roosevelts who had met Lorena.

[55] Lorena's insistence on doing "nothing else" but sleep probably meant that she would not
participate in any public events at the White House.

[56] Eleanor had made an appointment with the White House physician for Lorena to have her
blood sugar tested.

Three

JANUARY–FEBRUARY 1934

"A World of Love"

During the first two months of 1934, Lorena proceeded to travel the American roadways to investigate the nation's relief programs, and Eleanor proceeded to redefine the role of the nation's first lady. Both women committed a great deal of energy to their individual pursuits, often working twelve- and fourteen-hour days, but each still found the time to write the other—not only religiously but also lovingly, providing constant emotional support and encouragement.

The remarkable epistolary conversation also continued to include references to physical contact—Eleanor kissing Lorena's photograph and dreaming of holding the first friend in her arms. The creamy white pages trailing after Lorena often ended with a phrase of endearment that the first lady had coined and that somehow captured the unique personality of this relentlessly generous woman whose humanity had, by this point, become legend; night after night, Eleanor sent her letter on its way with the final, and resolutely heartfelt, phrase, "A world of love."

In this letter, Eleanor refers to the monthly newspaper articles she had begun writing, with Lorena's encouragement, first for the North American Newspaper Alliance and later for the McNaught Syndicate. She dictated the articles to Tommy Thompson, who corrected Eleanor's spelling, punctuation, and syntax. Most of the subjects she wrote about were routine, such as the purposes of various federal agencies, but others were highly controversial—including married women working outside the home. This letter also contains the first reference to Eleanor and Lorena hoping to meet for a long weekend together in Warm Springs, as Lorena's investigative work had taken her to Georgia.

[January 6]

THE WHITE HOUSE
Washington

Hick darling, Your letter hasn't come to-day so I am glad I talked to you last night & shall talk to you again to-night! Gee! but it is good not to have you too far away. This has been a long day but much is done, all my mail signed, all dictation up to date. Our syndicate article done, & now after a large tea party, Tommy, Missy & I are dining with F.D.R. & we then go at nine to the Tiny & Eddie dance.[1] We'll be home early & then I'll call you & to-night I'm going early to bed.

Dearest one, I miss you very much. I took time out trying to arrange my dates so they wouldn't conflict with any possible time when we could be to-gether & I'll write you fully to-morrow.

I'm going to do 2 [syndicate] articles on prison conditions & F. says I can go to the Atlanta penitentiary when I go down to you. Would you be interested? If so we must meet in Atlanta. Some-day we will do lots of work to-gether!

I love you deeply & tenderly & my arms feel very empty, but it won't be so long.

Devotedly,
E.R.

[1] Mayris "Tiny" Chaney and Eddie Fox were professional dancers who had become friends of Eleanor through Eleanor's friend Earl Miller.

Eleanor wanted to hear Lorena's voice so badly late one night that she finally called her, even though she knew that Lorena had been suffering from fatigue and often did not sleep well. In this letter, the first lady apologizes for disrupting Hick's sleep—up to a point.

[January 9]

THE WHITE HOUSE
Washington

Hick darling, It was a crime to wake you last night but I was glad to hear your voice. Oh! dear one it means so much to me to talk to you for a few minutes even at 2 a.m.! We had a very long & satisfactory meeting on Arthurdale last night & this morning at 11 a.m. Mrs. [Elinor] Morgenthau & I went & visited schools.[2] I had my exercises & swim too! We were late for the ladies of the cabinet lunch but there was nothing to talk about & it was brief.[3] Then mail & preparation for Tommy's tea,[4] 4 p.m. a Hawaiian table presented, 5 Tommy's party & I think she enjoyed it. She had to have a car take her & the loot home! Since then I've greeted 5 house guests & now I must dress for one of our intimate little dinners & receptions![5]

I'd like to be travelling with you! You should be reading John Brown.[6] I'll bring it, we might finish it on our week end!

The schools were interesting to-day because the colored one was so much better than the white—remind me to tell you about it! School lunches especially done with imagination in the colored school & without in the white.

I love you beyond words & long for you but I'm so tired now that I'm glad this is written for it might not have been done to-night! Dear one, I wish you were here. A world of love,

E.R.

---

[2] Eleanor wanted Arthurdale's schools to be more progressive than the public schools in other West Virginia communities. So she and her long-time friend Elinor Morgenthau were visiting various private schools to gather ideas.

[3] Eleanor invited the wives of her husband's Cabinet members to the White House on a regular basis.

[4] Eleanor invited several of her loyal secretary's friends to tea to celebrate Tommy's birthday.

[5] Eleanor's use of the adjective "intimate" was sarcastic, as such White House events typically included dozens—or even hundreds—of guests.

[6] Stephen Vincent Benét's *John Brown's Body* was about the controversial abolitionist.

January 10th

49 East 65th Street
New York City

Hick dearest, I have a little while before tea & I want to talk to you on paper. I can hardly wait to get home to-night & really talk to you [by telephone]! I worked on the train & after a short stop to unpack here (my folding frame with you is on my dressing table) I went to Cousin Susie for lunch.[7] She looks badly & I am sorry for her but, well, she must have ten times your income even now & we spent 1½ hrs talking chiefly about what "she couldn't do" because "they were so poor"! Then I walked up here & am waiting for tea to begin at 4.

Dear me, I miss you & I love you but one week from to-morrow night I will be starting on my way to you [in Georgia]! I'm trying to arrange about going through the Atlanta prison. The [Harry and Barbara] Hopkins' & Rita Halle come to lunch on Saturday. I wonder if the latter will like me, too bad if she reverses her opinion again![8] Bless you dear, my love is yours—

Devotedly,
Eleanor

In the early 1930s, most Americans were still leery of air travel. Eleanor, however, became one of flying's most visible advocates and provided a significant boost to the industry. American humorist Will Rogers found her air travel so noteworthy, in fact, that he wrote in the New York Times *about it: "Out at every stop, standing for photographers by the hour, being interviewed, talking over the radio, no sleep. And yet they say she never shows one sign of weariness or annoyance of any kind. No maid, no secretary—just the First Lady of the land on a paid ticket on a*

[7] Eleanor referred to Susie Parish, her godmother and wife of her Uncle Henry Parish, as "Cousin Susie."
[8] In June 1933, *Good Housekeeping* magazine writer Rita Halle criticized Eleanor for traveling more than any other first lady in history, suggesting that the proper place for a president's wife was at home, but in December Halle praised ER's many activities on behalf of American women.

regular passenger flight."[9] *In this letter, Eleanor refers to her eagerness to go to Atlanta by air rather than train so she can spend as much time as possible with Lorena.*

[January 15]

THE WHITE HOUSE
Washington

Hick dear one, I find I can fly from here at night and get to Atlanta early Friday morning & if the flying [weather] is good I will do it. I'll wire you Thursday evening & I'll blow in on you I hope while you are still in bed!

We had a good press conference this a.m. When I had no engagements over the week end & next week's press conference was to be Tuesday,[10] they smelled a rat but were kind & didn't press me! Gee wouldn't I like to get away with it![11]

I could cry that you won't be here to-morrow to hear [Fritz] Kreisler.[12] We have an intimate little dinner of 76 & 250 for music!

Louis seems better to-day.[13]

Darling, what fun we'll have to-gether [in Warm Springs]. I don't care whether it rains or not my sun will be high in the heavens! A world of love to you dear one & take good care of yourself,

E.R.

Eventually both the Atlanta Journal *and* Atlanta Constitution *covered the first lady's weekend at Warm Springs on their front pages—but only as she was returning to Washington. The stories portrayed Eleanor as an intrepid traveler, with neither making any mention whatsoever of Lorena. One stated that the first lady had come to Warm Springs for*

[9] Will Rogers letter, *New York Times*, 7 June 1933, 17.
[10] Eleanor's press conferences were routinely on Monday.
[11] To escape briefly from her public life and spend time alone with Lorena, Eleanor was attempting to keep her planned four-day trip to Warm Springs a secret.
[12] Fritz Kreisler was an Austrian violinist whose interpretive artistry placed him among the world's foremost musicians of the early twentieth century.
[13] Louis Howe, whose White House bedroom was directly across the hall from Eleanor's sitting room, had become seriously ill with consumption. By this point, FDR's long-time political adviser rarely left the second floor or dressed in anything but pajamas.

"rest and quiet"; the other quoted her as saying of the weekend, "It was all one could possibly wish."[14]

January 22nd

Hotel Upson
Thomaston, Georgia

Dear You:

Got out of Atlanta late. Gay Shepperson,[15] whom I found on more extensive acquaintance to be a grand person, kept me talking until 1. Then I had lunch with that nice lad, Wright Bryan, of the Atlanta Journal. I took him to lunch, thereby easing my conscience a little for the way I treated him Friday.[16]

Darling, I'm sending Gay Shepperson to see you. Maybe I'll bring her myself—she doesn't know just how soon she'll go up to Washington. I *know* you'll like her. She's simply swell. She's a most unusual woman, truly. Attractive and feminine, and yet she has the breadth of viewpoint and the impersonal attitude of a man. She's extremely interesting about Georgia. She feels that the money we are pouring into Georgia—in the rural sections—is being wasted really—that this isn't an emergency down here, but chronic, and she's deeply interested in some sort of subsistence farming rehabilitation program, instead of relief.

Oh, Lord, dear—this *is* a fascinating job of mine! I was terribly low and felt lost this morning after I left you. I always feel that way. But Gay Shepperson and Wright Bryan—and now I'm sitting on top of the world again—even though I had a little ache when I unpacked my briefcase and realized that I was in the cottage at Warm Springs, *with you,* when I packed it early this morning.

Dearest, it was a lovely weekend. I shall have it to think about for a long, long time. Each time we have together *that* way—brings us closer, doesn't it? And I believe those days and long pleasant hours together

---

[14] "Wife of President Terminates Week-End of Rest at Warm Springs," *Atlanta Constitution,* 22 January 1934, 1; "Mrs. Roosevelt Tells of Eluding Press on Warm Springs Trip," *Atlanta Journal,* 23 January 1934, 4.

[15] Gay Shepperson was head of the Federal Emergency Relief Administration in Georgia.

[16] When the *Atlanta Journal* initially heard that the first lady might be coming to Georgia and reporter Wright Bryan telephoned Lorena to ask her if the rumor was true, she hung up on him.

each time make it perhaps a little less possible for us to hurt each other. They give us better understanding of each other, give us more faith, draw us closer—

I *am* wound up, "nicht wahr?"[17] Well, I must go to dinner.

Good night, dear, *very* dear! You have my gratitude and all my love—

H

In this letter, written only a few days after the Warm Springs trip, Eleanor refers to an incident that had taken place during a lunch at the Roosevelt townhouse in New York soon after the 1932 election. FDR's haughty Aunt Kassie Collier had criticized Eleanor for having had so many newspaper articles written about her. Lorena, then still an Associated Press reporter, came to Eleanor's defense by responding that it was difficult for someone of ER's public stature to avoid publicity. Aunt Kassie then loudly announced: "Nonsense! I have never talked to a newspaper reporter in my entire life!" After nearly laughing out loud, Lorena remained silent for the rest of the meal, never revealing that she was, in fact, a reporter. The incident became a joke that Eleanor and Lorena shared for years to come.

[January 23]

THE WHITE HOUSE
Washington

Hick dearest, It seems years since we sat & read & read & were alone to-gether. I loved every minute & I am going to live on it during these next few weeks.

Well, we landed peacefully at Greensboro [North Carolina] to be told we could go no further & our pilot transferred to the mail plane & took the mail through. We all lunched to-gether first & saw the little mail plane come in which he was to take on up & I got a feeling of what a lonely epic this flying the mail all alone is! Then I went to a hotel for three hours & was discovered but I wasn't bothered. The train landed

---

[17] *Nicht wahr?* is German for "Don't you agree?" or "Isn't that right?"

me here at 1:40 a.m. but I slept curled up most of the way. I sent you a wire [from] Greensboro & another on arrival here where I found your wire. Also the last letter was here which gave me a thrill!

This day has been busy. Press, subsistence farmstead, lunch Mr. [Harold] Ickes,[18] dedication of new wing in Home for Incurables.[19] Several for tea & now a big family group—Mrs. Collier who never talked to a newspaper woman! & her children. A little dinner of 68 & I must now go & see Louis [Howe] & I hope Anna will come in so I can see her for a minute before dinner.

Dear one, take care of yourself & remember I love you—

Devotedly,

E.R.

January 23rd

Hotel Colquitt

Moultrie, Georgia

Dearest:

I've just come in from a conference with the county relief administration that left me gasping. She told me about a Negro girl that gave birth to a child at 9 o'clock the other morning—and at 4 o'clock that afternoon, when she went there with a doctor in response to a call for help, *the cord had not been severed yet.* Did you ever hear anything much more awful than that? The baby died, but the mother lived.

She's quite a person, the relief administrator here. She got an idea for a project for better educated women that is a honey. It would consist in placing them in grocery stores where food orders are cashed to advise the women what to buy, and I'm not so sure that it wouldn't be the solution for a problem that has been bothering relief people all along. Remember Mary Bittner up in New York and her beloved diets that she couldn't "sell" to the people on relief? Her chief difficulty was a proper—or workable—contact with the women. The case worker

---

[18] Harold Ickes was secretary of the interior.

[19] The Home for Incurables was the predecessor of St. Elizabeth's Hospital, a facility for the mentally ill in Washington, D.C.

couldn't do it. People on relief are apt to be too antagonistic—not *apt* to be, but *are*—toward the case worker, for that. These would really be "shoppers" in the groceries. I wonder if it wouldn't work. Something of the sort is needed very badly in these rural communities, where, as she says, the people are "eating their way into pellagra."[20]

Tomorrow morning she's taking me out into the country to visit the homes of some of the farm tenants and laborers, white and black, to see how they live. Then I'm to see some of the more prominent farmers and business men and leave for Tallahassee about 4 o'clock.

I've been rather lazy today, I'm afraid. Left a call for 5 o'clock, intending to leave Thomaston [Georgia] at 7. It was foggy and rainy at 5, however, and I was terribly tired. So I went back to bed and slept until 6:45. Sent off a lot of money orders and a wire to you and finally got away about 9. Hoofed along the road. It was warm, sunny, lazy weather, and, anyway, I was afraid to drive very fast on account of the damned stock in the roads. Had to come to a dead stop twice—once for a calf and once for two very small piglets. Lunched on doughnuts while driving.

I was distressed this morning when I got your wire and realized what a terribly long day you'd had. I hope it didn't destroy all the good effects of the weekend. Well, even so, you got home sooner than if you'd made the whole trip by rail. But you must have been terribly tired.

Darling, I *do* love you so!

H

January 24th

THE WHITE HOUSE
Washington

Hick dearest, It was good to get your letter to-day & to find you had got over the first wrench [of being apart] well. I always have a lost feeling & then the infinite succession of things takes hold & though I'm not always interested at least I am numb!

---

[20] Pellagra is a chronic disease caused by niacin deficiency and characterized by digestive disturbances and eventual mental deterioration.

I'll look forward to seeing Gay Shepperson & I enclose a note from Alice Davis[21] which may interest you & will show you that you make an unforgettable impression on people! To-day I've worked for my living, mail all a.m., an interesting time on Puerto Rico & several other things with your boss. The final conclusion is that relief should be stopped & public health go in there [Puerto Rico] on TB [tuberculosis] etc. but the problem is economic & he wants me to go & return, then they'll call a meeting of sugar owners etc. & dramatise [sic] the whole situation. Imagine you'll go down to get data for that meeting! Anna said to-day she might want to go with us. I'd rather go alone with you but I can't hurt her feelings & we do have fun to-gether but I may suggest she take Betsey.[22] What would you think of that? Also she said she wanted to take the children to Nevada next summer so I will be free while F.D.R. is away.

Mail till 3:30 & when I had a regular succession of Dorothy Dix interviews.[23] The [Albert] Einsteins arrived & are priceless, so German & so simple with many wise gentle German qualities.[24]

Darling I love you deeply, I never want to hurt you. You are dearer to me than you can guess—I kiss your photograph & wish every blessing for you.

A world of love,
E.R.

In this letter, Eleanor mentions Molly Dewson, the driving force behind the Women's Division of the Democratic National Committee. Eleanor had known Molly and her life partner Polly Porter since the early 1920s, as they lived in the apartment across the hall from Nan Cook and Marion Dickerman in Greenwich Village. Eleanor also had vaca-

[21] Alice Davis was a Quaker woman who was involved in the Arthurdale homestead project.
[22] Betsey Roosevelt was James's wife.
[23] Dorothy Dix popularized the personal advice column in American newspapers.
[24] Albert Einstein, the German-born theoretical physicist who formulated the theory of relativity, and his wife Mileva Maric Einstein were overnight guests at the White House.

tioned with Molly and Polly in their summer cottage in Maine. The final line in this letter provides an example of ER being caustic in her assessment of her godmother's character.

January 25th

THE WHITE HOUSE
Washington

Hick dearest, I've missed you all day probably because I got no letter & you've been so much in my thoughts. I do love you so dearly—

Elliott appeared about 11 a.m. He looks well & happy but I've not seen him alone & don't expect we'll get down to anything beyond being glad to see each other. Funny world! He & two friends are all having dinner upstairs, no proper clothes & want to sleep! A bit like you![25]

I had Molly Dewson to lunch, then work till tea & more people to tea & the Pattersons came.[26] I have them & Laura Delano[27] over the week end & it weighs a bit heavy on me as I have a fairly heavy schedule!

Now I must dress, dear one I long for you but wherever you are my love is reaching out to you.

Sleep sweetly & goodnight, a world of love,

E.R.

My poor old colored laundress of years ago came to see me to-day. She's been on relief & the rate is pathetic. I've got to try & help her but she is old & it will be hard. Cousin Susie is worried about finances. I wonder how they'd like to change places.

---

[25] When staying at the White House, Lorena liked to dine privately on the second floor with Eleanor—in the West Hall in winter, on the South Veranda in summer—rather than in the more public rooms on the first floor.

[26] Eleanor Medill Patterson was editor and publisher of Washington's *Times-Herald,* and her brother Joseph Medill Patterson founded New York's *Daily News.* They were grandchildren of *Chicago Tribune* founder Joseph Medill.

[27] Laura Delano was Sara Delano Roosevelt's younger sister.

January 26th

THE WHITE HOUSE
Washington

Dearest Hick, Your Tuesday letter & report came to-day & that is the best report yet! How you can write!

That grocery store idea is rather good.

This has been some day! I hurried everyone this morning & left at 10:35 for Warrenton[28] with Elinor Morgenthau, Agnes Leach[29] & Laura Delano. We got there at 11:30. Had all the county workers there & we had an interesting 3/4 of an hour discussion. They are making surveys in all states of the rural life in one or more counties, 1st present conditions, 2d plans for renovation & improvement of existing houses, barns, etc., 3d replacement of houses & complete rehabilitation when necessary. Cost by counties etc. I got a lot of dope & got home & to Mrs. [Ilo] Wallace[30] for lunch at 1:25. A little late but we had driven 80 miles an hour most of the way! 3 o'clock I was in your boss [Harry Hopkins]' office & we settled school lunches [for Arthurdale]. 4 o'clock took all guests to F's press conference, 4:30 received the Soviet ambassador & his wife, they are nice but she only speaks french [sic], 4:40 drove with Elliott & his friends to the airport, 5 had this large household to tea, 6:15-7:15 read mail & wrote. Isabella [Selmes Greenway] brought the Emmets[31] to dine, they sail for Holland the 7th, 9 movies but I had a meeting with Mr. [M.L.] Wilson[32] & Mr. [Clarence] Pickett[33] & 8 colored leaders. It lasted till midnight but it was a good thing I believe. They won me to their point of view in the long run. Remind me to tell you all about it next time that we are to-gether.

Now dearest one I must sign mail & go to bed. I am getting tired again but I still have some sleep to fall back on & so many happy mem-

---

[28] Warrenton, Virginia, is located about fifty miles southwest of Washington, D.C.

[29] Agnes Leach was a women's rights activist who had become a close friend of Eleanor's while both were active in the League of Women Voters.

[30] Ilo Wallace was the wife of Secretary of Agriculture Henry Wallace.

[31] Ellen "Bay" Emmet and her cousin Lydia Field Emmet, both artists, had been friends of Eleanor and Isabella Selmes Greenway since their girlhoods.

[32] M. L. Wilson was director of the Subsistence Homestead Program.

[33] Clarence Pickett, executive director of the American Friends Service Committee, was involved in the Arthurdale project, as the Quakers worked hand in hand with the federal government on subsistence homesteads in West Virginia.

ories! I love you deeply, tenderly darling & I would like to put my arms around you. Goodnight, sleep well, dream sweetly very dear one,

E.R.

The restless tone that dominates this letter gives a sense of Lorena's emotional instability during this period.

January 26th

The Angebilt
Orlando, Florida

Dear:

I wonder what is happening with you tonight. I feel restless, unable to settle down to anything. I must settle down very shortly, though, (in bed!) I'm getting up at 5, to get a good early start out to Lakeland and Avon Park, to get a lineup on the citrus situation. Discovered there was no use trying to get it in Orlando, so I'm leaving early, spending the day down there, and driving on into Tampa in the late afternoon. In the meantime, I've accomplished little today. I have an uneasy feeling that things aren't going well in Florida, but I can't put my finger on the trouble.

I did a crazy thing tonight. I had my dress off and was in my dressing gown when, glancing out the window, I was sure I saw Bluette[34] parked in the street down in front of the hotel. In as much as she was supposed to be safely bedded down in a garage, I didn't care for the idea. So I put on my dress and went down. It wasn't Bluette at all, but a Pontiac—almost the same color, though, and with the same accessories, trunk rack, two tail lights, two spare tires in metal covers, two windshield wipers, and so on. I slunk back upstairs, feeling very foolish.

Oh. I don't like Florida much, even though this part of it *is* beautiful. Too many Middlewestern voices. Too God damned many old people from "Ioway"—sitting in the sun. It's just like Pasadena, and I loathe

---

[34] Bluette was the name Eleanor and Lorena had given to Lorena's dark blue Chevrolet convertible.

Pasadena. And I get bored with talk about the weather—forever comparing this climate with that of California.

Something has bitten me, six times and savagely on my left ankle. I don't know when it happened—discovered it yesterday morning. Don't know whether it was a mosquito, a flea, bed bug, or, maybe, a spider. If it was a flea or a bed bug, there must have been only one. No bites anywhere else, and I haven't seen or felt anything. But there they are—six great big bites, and my ankle is swollen up. They are draining so much that I had to put a dressing on today. If they are any worse tomorrow, I'm going to see a doctor.

A week ago tonight, darling—we were very happy. But thinking of that has nothing to do with my being out of sorts tonight. I don't know *what is* the matter. Heat, perhaps.

Good night, dear you. Sleep well and have sweet dreams!

H

The first lady ends this letter with a litany of the "little things" she misses and yearns for when she and Hick are separated. The items on Eleanor's list—especially the feel of Lorena's hair—suggest a good deal about the physical intimacy that the women shared when they were together.

January 27th

THE WHITE HOUSE
Washington

Hick darling, Your letter of Wednesday is here with the report, which is good but not as interesting as the last one which was one of your very best!

How well I know that Florida landscape. I might like it with you, it may just be that I knew it best in my stormy years & the associations are not so pleasant.[35]

---

[35] Eleanor and Franklin traveled to Florida while he was serving as assistant secretary of the Navy between 1913 and 1920. During that same period, Eleanor discovered her husband was having an affair with Lucy Mercer.

Oh! I'm so glad you think you can make it by the 20th.[36] I'll get home that morning or late the night before & we'll go to that concert together & I'll be all caught up on mail so we can spend the evening catching up & the next night, the 21st[,] there is a symphony concert, too!

I spoke at noon at the Pennsylvania Women's lunch, then at 1:30 with Secretary [Harold] Ickes at the National Housing Conference. Went out to the Colonial Dames at 4 & dropped Laura [Delano] at a friend's home & had Mrs. [Frances Parkinson] Keyes to tea.[37]

Mrs. K came in & said to the doorman "Oh! What do you do without Mr. Hoover?" With a startled look he replied "This president is doing very nicely Ma'am!" He had forgotten "Ike" & she "Herbert"— how short are human memories![38]

Gee! what wouldn't I give to talk to you & hear you now, oh, dear one, it is all the little things, tones in your voice, the feel of your hair, gestures, these are the things I think about & long for. I am trying not to think about your next trip. You will seem so far away.[39]

A world of love,
E.R.

January 29th

THE WHITE HOUSE
Washington

Hick darling, I hope you are safely in Miami resting after your long drive. I notice your unrest & I doubt if it is the heat, politics have always as far back as '28 been rotten in Florida & they may well be [involved] in the relief picture.

Meantime John [Boettiger] objects to Anna going away for as long as the Puerto Rico trip would take & when I told her I was flying she said

---

[36] Lorena had arranged her schedule so she could return to the White House on February 20 and stay with Eleanor until they departed for Puerto Rico in early March.

[37] Frances Parkinson Keyes was a Washington socialite who wrote occasional magazine articles and achieved considerable popularity as a novelist.

[38] Ike Hoover, the long-time usher at the White House, died in 1933 not long after the Roosevelts moved in.

[39] After Eleanor and Lorena's trip to the Caribbean, Lorena was scheduled to travel south to Alabama and Louisiana before heading west to Texas, New Mexico, and Arizona.

she'd hate it so I don't think she'll go! She talked with me till 12:45 last night & she is fine & oh! I hope those children will be happy some day. Seeing Elliott made her restless & moody & want to get things settled [regarding her marriage] & John was sweet to her & very understanding.

Press conference this a.m., lunch, mail, received people 4:30-6 & now I must dress. We leave at 8:10 to go & dine with the Vice President [John Nance Garner] & I understand Will Rogers is to be there!

People are never satisfied Hick dear, unless things are done for them. It is unfortunate that we have to do it, they like doing for themselves. Human beings are poor things, think how much discipline we need ourselves & don't get too discouraged.

A spider undoubtedly bit you they are horrid & I only hope you had no further trouble. Dear, I would like to be with you all the time! I love you deeply & tenderly,

E.R.

In this letter, Eleanor talks about a range of feelings— including wanting to wrap her arms around Lorena and hoping to share a home and a life together at some point in the future, and then expressing jealousy of Lorena's former same-sex relationship. The last sentence in the first paragraph is one of the most memorable that Eleanor would ever write about her relationship with Lorena.

[February 4]

THE WHITE HOUSE
Washington

Hick darling, I just talked to you, darling, it was so good to hear your voice. If I just could take you in my arms. Dear, I often feel rebellious too & yet I know we get more joy when we are to-gether than we would have if we had lived apart in the same city & could only meet for short periods now & then. Someday perhaps fate will be kind & let us arrange a life more to our liking [but] for the time being we are lucky to have what we have. Dearest, we are happy to-gether & strong relationships have to grow deep roots. We're growing them now, partly because we are separated, the foliage & the flowers will come, somehow I'm sure of it. I dread the western trip[40] & yet I'll be glad when Ellie [Morse Dickinson] can be with you, tho' I'll dread that too just a little,[41] but I know I've got to fit in gradually to your past & with your friends so there won't be closed doors between us later on & some of this we'll do this summer perhaps. I shall feel you are terribly far away & that makes me lonely but if you are happy I can bear that & be happy too. Love is a queer thing, it hurts but it gives one so much more in return!

Every day you are one day nearer, the 20th is only 2 weeks & 1 day off now!

A world of love & I do put my arms around you in my dreams dear one,

E.R.

As Eleanor wrote this letter, she was nearing the end of the annual series of special events arranged in observance of FDR's birthday on January 30.

[February 8]

49 East 65th Street
New York City

Hick darling, I was glad the cold was better Wednesday but they do get such a hold on you & make you so miserable. I wish I could be with you.

I went to Arnold Constable[42] & got two spring dresses, cheap but they don't look as smart as Milgrim![43] Emma [Bugbee][44] drove me to the train. She may be sent to Puerto Rico if I go! Well, Ruby [Black] will

[40] Lorena was scheduled to travel to the West Coast in April.

[41] Ellie Morse Dickinson was the woman Lorena had lived with for eight years in Minneapolis and San Francisco.

[42] Arnold Constable was a clothing store in Manhattan.

[43] Milgrim's was one of the most fashionable women's apparel shops in Manhattan.

[44] Emma Bugbee was a reporter for the *New York Herald Tribune* who covered the first lady.

have a companion & in a way it will be easier! Tommy & I worked hard all the way down & both [syndicate] articles are written.

Walter Lippman [sic][45] is just now conversing with F.D.R. I'm wondering whether they will get on better, they have never really liked each other.

This is our last reception & I feel like skipping it. I was busy & tired yesterday but I feel better. My heart is light too because I'm going to talk to you to-night, dearest. I can hardly wait. I love you—

Later. I just talked to you & dear it was a relief to hear your voice. I wish I were with you but someday we will go back to all the places we've enjoyed seeing & enjoy them to-gether. That is a tall order for I have a great many places abroad I want to show you. Bless you dear one. I wish I'd been there when you felt rotten & wanted me! All my love,

E.R.

February 9th

THE WHITE HOUSE
Washington

Hick darling, Your report is grand! I'm still happy because I talked to you last night! I'll call you in Raleigh Monday morning. I expect to get home Sunday but it will be one or two in the morning & I think I'd better wait till 8:30 or 9 to call you.

To-day has been an easy day, work till 11, Elinor Morgenthau met me & we walked to Galt's[46] where I bought a birthday present for Gus [Gennerich].[47] His brother-in-law & nephew are here for his birthday to-morrow & I've asked them all to tea & we'll have a cake! Home &

[45] Eleanor misspelled the last name of the most influential newspaper columnist in the country. Although Lippmann generally voiced social and political views that were far more conservative than Eleanor's, he was an early and enthusiastic supporter of the New Deal.

[46] Galt's is a jewelry store on Fifteenth Street a block from the White House; it was founded and owned by the family of First Lady Edith Bolling Galt Wilson.

[47] Gus Gennerich was a bodyguard FDR brought with him from Albany.

we had a lunch for Molly Dewson,[48] 36 at table & a young colored singer afterwards who sang very well, then a woman from Baltimore & her 16 yr. old daughter, polio case, whom I'm going to try & get to Warm Springs. Tea from 4:40 to 6 & now dress for dinner & the Junior League dance to-night.

Darling, only 10 more days. Dear one I love you & the nicest part about my desk is looking at your picture & kissing it goodnight. Bless you, take care of yourself. You get too tired or you wouldn't have a cold.

Ever devotedly,

E.R.

[February 12]

THE WHITE HOUSE
Washington

Hick darling, A quiet day, which was just as well! Lots of work, & at 10:30 a visit from Gov. [Paul] Pearson of the Virgin Islands. He's doing a swell job & I think we'll fly over for a day with him [during the Puerto Rico trip]!

The Rector [from Harvard] wrote me to-day that John had an attack, very mild appendisitis [sic] so he'll probably have to be operated on in this vacation. I hope he gets no acute attack before that.

I lunched to-day with the "little Cabinet"[49] & returned to work till 4 when I went to lay a wreath with F.D.R. on the Lincoln Memorial then home & a bunch for tea & then the last big dinner & music.

I love you dear one deeply & tenderly & it is going to be a joy to be

---

[48] Molly Dewson was Eleanor's friend from the 1920s.

[49] The "little Cabinet" was an informal name for members of the administration just below Cabinet rank. FDR had been, as assistant secretary of the Navy, a member of Woodrow Wilson's "little Cabinet" from 1913 to 1920.

to-gether again, just a week now. I can't tell you how precious every minute with you seems both in retrospect & in prospect. I look at you long as I write—the photograph has an expression I love, soft & a little whimsical but then I adore every expression. Bless you darling.

A world of love,

E.R.

And will you be my valentine?

A Holiday Gone Bad

As Lorena was driving toward Washington to rendezvous with Eleanor and prepare for their trip to the Caribbean, *Time* magazine dealt her a crushing blow. The story as a whole was positive, complete with a flattering cover photo of Harry Hopkins and an equally flattering one of Lorena on an inside page. The lengthy paragraph about the country's chief investigator of relief programs, however, was not so complimentary: "His [Hopkins's] chief field representative and investigator is Miss Lorena Hickok, who for eight years worked for the Associated Press. She is a rotund lady with a husky voice, a peremptory manner, baggy clothes. In her day one of the country's best female newshawks, she was assigned to Albany to cover the New York Executive Mansion where she became fast friends with Mrs. Roosevelt. Since then she has gone around a lot with the first lady, up to New Brunswick and down to Warm Springs. Last July Mr. Hopkins, who is a great admirer of Mrs. Roosevelt, hired Miss Hickok and now she travels all over the country using her nose-for-news to report on relief conditions. Last week when it was announced that Mrs. Roosevelt planned to visit Puerto Rico in March, it became known that Miss Hickok would also go along to look into relief work there."[1]

Lorena was livid. As an old-style newswoman, she could not understand what her *girth* had to do with the country's relief work—or her *voice*, or her *manner*, or her *wardrobe*. She also was concerned what the Washington harpies might do with the suggestion that she and Eleanor were *fast friends*—whatever that meant. And besides, the magazine couldn't even get its basic facts right—she'd worked for AP for five years, not eight; she'd been assigned to go to Puerto Rico *first*, so

[1] "Relief," *Time*, 19 February 1934, 11.

Eleanor actually "would go along" with *her*. The article unleashed a verbal tirade from Hick. Her first attacks were on the relief administrators she blamed for passing on the details to the magazine. "Believe me," she wrote Hopkins, "the next state administrator who lets out any publicity on me is going to get his head cracked!" She had strong words for journalists as well. "I'm so fed up with publicity I want to kick every reporter I see," she raged to Hopkins's secretary. "I suppose I am 'a rotund lady with a husky voice' and 'baggy clothes,' but I honestly don't believe my manner is 'peremptory.' Why the Hell CAN'T they leave me alone?"[2]

The article put the emotionally volatile Lorena into a decidedly foul mood by the time she and the first lady began their trip—Eleanor going to the Caribbean to show the administration's commitment to Puerto Rico and the Virgin Islands, Lorena going to investigate relief programs. Nor was the first friend's attitude helped by the fact that what she and Eleanor originally had envisioned as a reprise of the idyllic vacation of the previous summer had evaporated; four women reporters would now join Eleanor and Lorena to provide daily news coverage of the first lady's activities. A good sense of how Lorena was feeling about the trip emerged in a letter that Eleanor wrote her daughter on the first day of the trip. The first lady had booked a private drawing room for Hick and herself on the midnight train from Washington to Miami where they would depart for Puerto Rico. The conductor asked if the first lady would autograph a timetable for him, and Eleanor graciously agreed. But according to Eleanor's letter to Anna, as the conductor closed the door to the compartment, Lorena barked—not the least bit graciously— "I hope he chokes."[3]

By the time they reached the Caribbean, however, Lorena had cooled off. Her mood may have changed at least partly because of the view that opened up to the women as they looked out the window of their Pan American bi-plane; the tranquil setting would have soothed any soul. The dazzling blue sky, an azure sandbar protruding gently from the crystal clear water, reefs in shades of lavender, rose, and turquoise just

---

[2] Hickok letter to Harry Hopkins, 7 February 1934, Hickok Papers; Hickok letter to Kathryn Godwin, 18 February 1934, Hickok Papers.

[3] Eleanor letter to Anna Roosevelt Dall, 6 March 1934, Eleanor Roosevelt Papers.

below the surface of the shimmering Caribbean—a seascape straight out of paradise. To make the moment complete, one of the reporters later would recall, as the shadow of the clipper scudded across the water below, a fire-fish leaped from the sea to catch the glint from the early morning sun.[4]

Once on land, the first lady did all she could to see that the official trip doubled as a tropical holiday in celebration of Lorena's forty-first birthday. In San Juan, Eleanor arranged for the two of them to stay in a private bedroom in the magnificent seventeenth century La Fortaleza mansion (complete with marble floors, gold-encrusted ceilings, and mahogany staircases); in St. Thomas, Eleanor arranged that she and Hick slept on the third floor of the nineteenth century Government House palace. In both cities, the four reporters stayed in hotels far away from Eleanor and Lorena. The first lady found other ways to spend time alone with her friend as well—dining privately in their room on several evenings, swimming in the ocean, and skipping rope on the beach in the early morning while the reporters were still sleeping.

Only when Eleanor wanted the reporters for her own purposes (often with Lorena's counsel) were they summoned to appear and document specific activities. On the flight from Miami to San Juan, for example, Lorena suggested that Eleanor add another notch to her ever-lengthening belt of press innovations by conducting what the reporter-cum-publicist dubbed "the first ocean-flying press conference" in the history of American journalism. The reporters obediently accommodated, turning the event into a story that American newspapers trumpeted across page one the next morning.[5]

On another occasion, the reporters dutifully cooperated when the first lady suddenly saw the chance to create an impromptu photo opportunity. She had insisted on seeing the worst slum in all of San Juan, and as she walked through the narrow streets, a crowd of clamoring men, women, and children began to form behind her—calling out "La Presidenta! La Presidenta!"—with a few barking dogs and snorting pigs following on the fringes. Suddenly Eleanor stopped beside a muddy rut

[4] Bess Furman, *Washington By-Line: The Personal History of a Newspaperwoman* (New York: Knopf, 1949), 197.

[5] Emma Bugbee, "Mrs. Roosevelt Off for Survey of Puerto Rico," *New York Herald Tribune*, 6 March 1934, 1.

and puddle of stagnant water in the middle of the street, swarming with flies. She huddled with the reporters for a moment, asking if she could direct their photographer—all four of their news organizations had sent one man, Sam Schulman, to take photos that they all shared—to document the scene. When the reporters agreed, Eleanor called out, "Sammy, I want you to take a photo of this. I want the American people to see what it's really like here!" Later that day, Schulman sent his film on a flight back to Miami, and the next morning newspapers all over the country showed not only the squalor of Puerto Rico but also the first lady, in a crisp white dress, standing smack dab in the middle of the filth, the sludge, and the human suffering.[6]

Those were only two of a continuing stream of events that ultimately turned the first lady's trip into a public relations bonanza. The *New York Herald Tribune,* for one, carried stories about Eleanor fifteen days solid, with most of them on the front page and several accompanied by photos—ER conducting her in-flight press conference, ER visiting a thatch-roofed school, ER addressing the first mass meeting of women in the history of the Virgin Islands. With Lorena on hand to help with the writing, Eleanor also crafted several public statements that portrayed her husband in a glowing light; one front-page story quoted her as saying to the people of San Juan, "As long as my husband is in office, you have a friend in Washington." Also with Lorena's counsel, Eleanor adroitly—though sometimes disingenuously—dodged tough questions; when asked to comment on the dicey issue (then as well as today) of Puerto Rican independence, Eleanor said, "I make no recommendations. I leave politics to my husband."[7]

On a personal level, however, Eleanor and Lorena's trip to the Caribbean ultimately fell far short of a triumph—at least for the more temperamental woman. What propelled Lorena into an emotional whirlwind was, as so often in the past, the press coverage.

For most of the trip, Lorena had successfully avoided being in the public eye. But on the return trip from San Juan to Miami, a tropical storm forced the Pan American airliner to land in Haiti. When reporting

---

[6] Furman, *Washington By-Line,* 197, 200.
[7] Emma Bugbee, "Puerto Ricans Hail Arrival of Mrs. Roosevelt," *New York Herald Tribune,* 9 March 1934, 1.

on the bumpy flight, Emma Bugbee of the *Herald Tribune* wrote—in a page-one story—that Eleanor was unperturbed but that Lorena became so "squeamish" and "nervous" that the first lady had to put down her knitting and "play a guessing game" with her friend—as if Hick were a child. Lorena was not only irritated by that reference but also by the fact that Bugbee repeatedly referred to her as "*Mrs.* Hickok." Seeing the story as another in a long series of instances when the press focused more attention on her than she wanted or deserved, Lorena began to sulk.[8]

Lorena's frustration escalated into rage after the trip ended. Spending the last week of her respite in Washington, Lorena looked through the stack of newspapers at the White House to see exactly how the national press had covered the trip. Lorena soon discovered the single image that the newspapers had found most compelling was the one of Eleanor standing amid the squalor of the San Juan slum. Showcasing the first lady reaching out to the Puerto Rican peasants was important because it focused public attention on the economic deprivation on the island, Lorena knew, but what she also realized when she saw the stack of newspapers was that the photo captured not only the first lady—but also the first friend. That meant that the photo of her spread all over the country would alert thousands of people to her friendship with Eleanor—exactly what Lorena did *not* want! Nor did it help that Hick's image was not exactly flattering. Eleanor stood tall and pristine in her long-sleeved white dress, white hat, white shoes, white stockings, white purse, and white gloves. Slumped to one side, Lorena was not only bare-headed, bare-armed, and bare-legged but also wearing a dress that had a flamboyant tie flowing down the front—the more newspapers Lorena saw it in, the more that tie looked like something a clown would wear to the circus rather than something an official of the United States government should have been wearing on the job. Lorena grew angrier and angrier as she started to count up how many papers had published the photo. There she was standing within arm's length of the first lady (none of the newspaper women was anywhere to be seen) in the *Washington Herald* and *Pittsburgh Post-Gazette* and *Birmingham News* and

[8] Emma Bugbee, "Storm Forces Mrs. Roosevelt Down in Hayti," *New York Herald-Tribune,* 16 March 1934, 1.

Chicago Tribune and *San Francisco Chronicle*. And the proliferation of this particular image could not be attributed to some *Time* magazine reporter or to Emma Bugbee or to any of those other irresponsible reporters who, in Lorena's estimation, were now dominating the American press. This time the blame rested solely on the shoulders of the first lady herself. Eleanor was the one, after all, who had gone out of her way to instruct Sammy Schulman to take the photo, even though she knew full well—indeed, better than anyone else on Earth—how much Lorena absolutely *loathed* being in the public eye.

So as Lorena's mind churned over the consequences of the trip, she saw the Eleanor–Lorena scorecard as far from even. Because Lorena had suggested that the first lady join her on the trip to the Caribbean, Eleanor had received a surfeit of positive press that would further enhance her public image. In return, because Eleanor had suggested that Schulman take the photo in the San Juan slum, Lorena would have to struggle even harder to shed the public mantle of the first lady's "fast friend" from which she, for more than a year now, had been desperately attempting to distance herself.

In short, by the end of the Caribbean trip, Lorena did not see it as anything remotely close to the tropical getaway that she had envisioned in celebration of her birthday. Nor would she soon forget the disappointment. Although the biography that she would write about Eleanor three decades later contained thirteen pages on their 1933 holiday to French Canada, it did not so much as mention the trip to the Caribbean.

Four

MARCH–JULY 1934

"To Put My Arms Around You"

The four months that followed Eleanor and Lorena's ill-fated holiday in the Caribbean were marked by a dizzying mixture of highs and lows. On the one hand, Eleanor repeatedly spoke of longing to kiss and hold Lorena in her arms; the first lady even pressed a rose inside one letter before sending it. This also was the period during which Eleanor spoke wistfully of spending her old age with Lorena and of wanting to buy a special corner cupboard to furnish the home that she dreamed that they would someday share.

On the other hand, the correspondence during these same months was dotted with references to Lorena's struggle with emotional instability—brought on partly by physical exhaustion and a near-fatal automobile accident, but clearly influenced as well by the simmering uncertainty regarding the future of her relationship with Eleanor. In April, Lorena cried, "Oh my dear, love me a lot! I need it!" The next month, Eleanor hinted that she was finding Hick's volatile nature to be discomfiting, saying that she was tiring of the "bad things" that Lorena's temperamental nature did to her. The frequency of such unsettling comments accelerated in the early summer, with Lorena pleading, "I *must* pull myself up. But *how?*" and Eleanor cautioning Hick to be weary of the "mental and emotional depression" that habitually plagued her.

As Lorena and Eleanor prepared to meet for the West Coast holiday that ultimately would prove to be even more disquieting than the one in the Caribbean, Lorena's words suggested that her emotional state had escalated beyond depression and that she was teetering on the edge of suicide. "I wonder if it will be like this when I die—a feeling of remoteness from everything," Lorena wrote. "Oh, my dear, I'm so sick of the whole miserable business!"

As Lorena struggled with the emotional demons raging inside of her, it was left to Eleanor to provide stability to the relationship. In keeping with that role, the first lady ended more than one of her letters by expressing her longing "to put my arms around you."

Lorena's destination after the Caribbean trip was the Deep South, followed by a trip across Texas and into New Mexico and Arizona.

[March 26]

THE WHITE HOUSE
Washington

Hick darling, I believe it gets harder to let you go each time, but that is because you grow closer. It seems as though you belonged near me, but even if we lived to-gether we would have to separate sometimes & just now what you do is of such value to the country that we ought not to complain, only that doesn't make me miss you less or feel less lonely!

After you left I took Tommy to the amaryllis show. Then went to see John,[1] had a peace conference which was dull, lunched & spoke for the National Symphony Orchestra[,] went back to see John & came home with F.D.R. I spoke to him about CWA[2] & he says the delay is mostly in state & locality but he thinks when he gets back another $50,000,000 will have to be allocated to H.H. [Harry Hopkins] to continue CWA thro' May, but this of course you must not mention.

Darling, I ache for you & wish I could be expecting you later. I will call you for I do feel as if those I loved were very far away—& always much love dear one,

E.R.

[March 29]

THE WHITE HOUSE
Washington

Hick darling, I am getting that hunted feeling—so much to do & no time in which to do it.

Well, the opera was like a musical comedy last night & we all enjoyed it. Your boss was very fit & more cheerful. Didn't F. get walloped in

---

[1] John Roosevelt had just had an appendectomy at a Washington hospital.

[2] In response to Lorena's reports that many government workers who were supposed to be being paid by the Civil Works Administration were not receiving their checks, Eleanor had raised the issue with the president.

both the House & Senate?[3] Anna says F. was wild over the House vote. Louis just says "a defeat will be good for the young man" & "he must see more of the heads of committees"!

My desk is piled high & I have to do articles to-morrow & speeches!

Darling, I'd be a horrid companion if you were here but I wish you were. I miss you very much & love you very much, more & more deeply as the weeks roll on.

Good night sweet, a world of love—

                                E.R.

                                       [March 30]

THE WHITE HOUSE
Washington

Hick darling, Having just taken an aspirin to beat a headache which has hung over me all day, I'll busy myself thinking about pleasant things till it works so I'll write to you! Sorry you had such a hard day.

The day has been busy but not quite so bad! Spent 3/4 of an hour with a lady about the [cherry] blossom festival, then a photograph with Easter lilies, then mail till lunch. At 2:30 was presented with an invitation to attend the opening of some park & visit a girls' camp & they gave me a lovely piece of homespun [handwoven] material! Isabella [Selmes Greenway] came at 2:15 & we talked over a difficult situation. [Speaker of the House of Representatives Henry] Rainey had been in & told Louis [Howe] she was the greatest influence *against* the administration & Louis stormed in to me & said if she wanted to defeat F. she could & would be responsible for his downfall.[4] I laughed & said it was

---

[3] On March 27 and 28, the House and Senate overrode the president's veto of legislation to provide financial bonuses for veterans of World War I and the Spanish-American War. The override was a major political defeat for FDR, with many members of his own party defecting from his camp.

[4] Greenway had joined the majority of House members voting to override the president's veto on the bonuses for war veterans, the political debacle that had begun to make the Democratic leadership worry that the New Deal initiatives might be sputtering to an end. Greenway then had voted against certain provisions of the National Recovery Administration, which was aimed at stimulating industrial production. In May 1935, the Supreme Court ruled that the NRA was unconstitutional.

flattering that they felt a woman had gained that much influence in so short a time. *She* came in to tell me Rainey had said this to her plus the statement that F. was the greatest man who had ever lived & everyone must do just as he said on every subject! Doesn't it seem unbelievable? Well I took her in & let her talk to Louis & then at 3:15 I took them for a drive & let him tell me all his worries. Since 4 I've worked, had tea & now I need to dress.

Darling, I love you & I have just marked five days off on the calendar. May seems so far away[5] & yet I know I'm going to be busy & so are you & it will pass but dear one when I sit here just before dinner I wish the door might open & let you in. I wonder if always I'm not going to feel that a day is incomplete which we don't start & end it to-gether? Well, I don't on paper anyway. So much, much love & bless you dearest one.

Devotedly,

E.R.

The second paragraph of this letter refers to an incident that occurred in Alabama a few days earlier. Thad Holt, the director of the state's relief programs, had read the Time *magazine article about Lorena. So when she walked into his office, Holt shook her hand enthusiastically and gushed that it was a real honor to meet Mrs. Roosevelt's "fast friend." Lorena exploded. She said it was foolish for a person to believe everything he read, and then she turned and stalked out of the office. Holt ran after her, but Lorena kept walking.*

Easter Sunday
[April 1]

THE WHITE HOUSE
Washington

Dearest, A telegram & two letters from you to-day. They came just after I had sent my wire to you, you see it has been a very blessed Easter & I

---

[5] Lorena was not scheduled to return to Washington until May 11.

have hoped all day you were happy too. Tommy came over early & we went to the 7:30 service in Arlington[6]—it didn't rain but oh! it was cold. We came back & sat in front of the fire on footstools in my room till our feet warmed up & by that time breakfast was ready. Afterwards Tommy & I worked till John & I went to church. It was a long service & I couldn't hear the sermon so I sat & thought about you & prayed I might make you happy & care in the way which would make me plan & foresee enough so as to never make the one I love unhappy. I think my real trouble is not that I don't care enough, but that for so many years I've let my work engulf me so as to have no time to think & now when I should know how to shake it, it has become my master! Darling, do try not to get so tired. This is a long trip with no breaks & if you go on as you have begun you will be worn out. I'm being good, please be good too!

I can just see how annoyed you were with that Thad Holt for emphasizing your friendship with me, but it was natural. They probably think if they didn't know, you'd mind, if they only knew! Well, I'm glad you don't mind being Mrs. Doak's friend anyway but she must remain obscure!

I took Louis for a two hour drive with the top of my car down. It was sunny & so different from the early morning. I was hot & we drove to Great Falls on the Virginia side.[7] We'll take a picnic there sometime it has real possibilities if you could walk a little. Louis wanted to get out but 10 yards was about all his legs would stand. At 6 Isabella & Jackie [Greenway],[8] Anna, John [Boettiger], Sisty, Buzzie & I are having supper & then when the kids go to bed Anna who went off at 9 to ride with John & has been gone all day I think will go back & dine with him. Her Father's being away she feels free![9]

---

[6] An Easter sunrise service is traditionally conducted at Arlington National Cemetery in Virginia.

[7] Great Falls is a section of rapids on the Potomac River in northern Virginia just outside of Washington.

[8] Jackie Greenway was Isabella Selmes Greenway's son.

[9] FDR did not approve of Anna being seen publicly with John Boettiger while she was still legally married to Curtis Dall.

I've wanted you badly all day but dear one I hope for May 11th & I'm going to do the best I can till then & try to be free for you & for my own joy!

A world of love,
E.R.

[April 4]

THE WHITE HOUSE
Washington

Dearest Hick, This has been a busy day & no letter from you but I'm just hoping to find several in Columbus.[10] I do feel lost with no news! Worked & took Louis driving & had a talk with your boss [Harry Hopkins] this a.m. He's worried about white collar people & his own staff the country over for he feels they are discouraged & that bothers him. He's got a new plan brought about by you in part to open separate offices for the proffessional [sic] group & loan them money on a relief basis, it is still nebulous but his mind is working.

Elliott wants you to call his house in Fort Worth when you arrive & he is most anxious to see you.

He brought the news that F.D.R. had been in bed with a cold ever since he got on the boat except for getting up to greet the Governor General in Nassau.[11] He had quite a fever & ached & they were all worried stiff but Elliott said he was better yesterday & a wire came from James to-night saying "all better everyone happy."

Dearest, I miss you & wish you were here I want to put my arms around you & feel yours around me. More love than I can express in a letter is flying on waves of thought to you—

Devotedly,
E.R.

---

[10] Eleanor was traveling to Columbus, Ohio, to give a speech.
[11] Franklin, James, and several other men were on a sailing trip to the Bahamas.

[April 6]

THE WHITE HOUSE
Washington

Hick darling, I think this may catch you in New Orleans so I am sending it off just to say "I love you." I've been very much 'Mrs. R.' all day![12] I loved your wire this a.m. & it brought you nearer. To-morrow I shall wire you.

This day began with Girl Scouts at 8:30 & then a few words to a State Grange meeting, then conferences til 12. [Royal] Copeland so dull![13] Tommy & I had lunch to-gether in our living room, 1:15 radio, then conference with a speech from [Postmaster General Jim] Farley & E.R. who suddenly felt like being herself & not like the first lady said several things the first lady shouldn't have said. So goodnight & bless you dear one.

A world of love,
E.R.

April 9th

Hotel Monteleone
New Orleans

Dearest:
This will be just a note to tell you I love you. I've had a long and busy day, it's after 10, and I'm getting up at 5 to start for Texas. I think I'll make Houston by tomorrow night alright.

I ended a long day of conferences—pretty gloomy conferences, for New Orleans is apparently, from the commercial standpoint, just a charming corpse—with dinner at Arnaud's,[14] and, it being my last real meal in New Orleans, I made it a memorable one: two gin fizzes, some kind of a marvelous shrimp concoction known as shrimps Arnaud, pompano baked in a paper bag, potatoes soufflé, a pint of sauterne,

---

[12] Eleanor referred to spending time in the traditional role of the president's wife—such as hosting tea parties and shaking hands in receiving lines—as "being Mrs. Roosevelt."
[13] Royal Copeland was a Republican senator from New York state.
[14] Arnaud's is a famous News Orleans restaurant.

crepes Suzette (I think I'll never order them anywhere else!) and black coffee. You never tasted such food! What a town for a glutton!

Dined with Maude Barret, state social work director, and she told me some marvelous stories. The best was about one of her parish directors, out in the state, when they were recruiting boys for the CCC camps a year ago.[15] The director had been told, among other things, that no boys with flat feet would be accepted. There was no doctor to examine her boys' feet. So she lined them up in a vacant store, bare footed, and had them step into a pan of water and out onto the dry floor, so she could herself eliminate those who were flat-footed and spare them the disappointment of going to camp and then being sent home. Isn't that a peach?

I must go to bed. Darling, I love you, devotedly. And I'll wire you from Houston tomorrow night.

H

April 11th

Sam Houston Hotel
Houston, Texas

Dear You:

This is a pretty gloomy report [enclosed with this letter]. Well, it *has* been a day. It wound up with dinner with some social workers who are handling unattached people, including single women on a basis which you will see from the report is terribly low. Most of the young ones, she said, supplement their relief by having lovers or practicing prostitution. Those who have lovers, she said, probably would anyway. But about those who have become prostitutes we both wonder.

One of the male social workers put on old clothes one night and went down & had himself put through the transient set-up, to see how tran-

---

[15] The Civilian Conservation Corps was a government program that hired unemployed workers for conservation projects such as preventing soil erosion.

sients were treated. Several girls solicited him as he walked along the streets.

"'I can't. I have no money.'

"'Oh, that's all right,' she said wearily. '*It only costs a dime.*'"

Well, it's 1:30 a.m., and I have some packing to do before I go to bed. Got your wire tonight and sent you another one.

Oh, my dear, love me a lot! I need it!

H

[April 15]

The White House
Washington

Hick darling, I've had such a house full to-day that even the fact that they were growing less didn't seem to alleviate my sense of crowding! It was good to get in & find your two letters & one report even tho' it was so gloomy. I shan't show it to Franklin! What a mess Texas always is politically. I hope somewhere you can find things more cheerful!

Jimmy & Betsey left to-night, Marion [Dickerman] & the [Joseph P.] Kennedys.[16] I'm just oppressed by my calendar the next two weeks & fussing about things I can't help & I shouldn't be writing you for I'm in the mood when I should be alone, also it is 2 a.m. So dear one goodnight, forgive me I'm an ungrateful wretch, instead of being glad you are somewhere on this continent I feel rebellious because you are not here! Anyway, I love you dearly & I'll be very happy to see you on [the] 11th of May! A kiss to you,

E.R.

---

[16] Joseph P. Kennedy, a wealthy businessman and supporter of the Democratic Party, and his wife Rose had been guests at the White House the previous several nights. The Kennedys were the parents of President John F. Kennedy.

This letter contains the first mention of Eleanor and Lorena's plans to reprise their summer vacation of the previous July, though they had not yet decided on a destination.

[April 16]

THE WHITE HOUSE
Washington

Hick dear one, Two letters & the New Orleans report to-day & dearest I am glad you haven't had any more publicity. It would hurt terribly & make work very hard, we must be careful this summer & keep it out of the papers when we are off to-gether. No, I am *always* glad you were assigned to me in 1932 & I am glad if you feel the same way for I sometimes think Europe & Prinz would be easier & pleasanter [sic] but you are seeing your own country in a unique way & Europe & Asia & the rest of the world will perhaps come later![17]

To-day has been a better day, more interesting I guess for it has been just as busy & yet I am less weary in mind & body. We are funny, I think I was worried because they told me how annoyed Fjr. was with me because he never comes home & yet I know one can never do anything for one's children & decided years ago not to try!

Press conference this morning, then 2 women from the South to lunch who have been active in the anti-lynching society & have a new angle with their problem. They fear no harm [to] themselves but harm to the negro if there is much agitation & say the poor whites are so badly off that they are jealous of the negro & of their supremacy.

Then Mary Anderson[18] & a group working on domestic employment, then I ran over to see Mary Miller[19] in the hospital, drove Louis for 20 minutes, received the Turkish Ambassador, 2 women from Boston & 1 from Louisiana & one from Missouri at tea & Rose Schneiderman[20]

---

[17] At various times during 1933 and 1934, Lorena expressed interest in returning to news reporting as a war correspondent in Europe, perhaps even taking her German shepherd along. Eleanor discouraged the idea, however, saying she would hate for Lorena to be so far away from her.

[18] Mary Anderson was a union activist who worked with Eleanor in the Women's Trade Union League.

[19] Mary Miller was a long-time friend of Eleanor's whose husband Adolph Miller was a member of the Federal Reserve Board.

[20] Rose Schneiderman was a working-class labor activist who worked with Eleanor in the Women's Trade Union League.

who wants the working women to present my portrait to the White House! I put off the decision for a year! It may not have to be done!

Now I have ten minutes to dress for dinner!

A world of love dear one,

E.R.

This brief letter contains one of Eleanor's strongest statements regarding her dream of someday sharing a home with Lorena.

[April 18]

49 East 65th Street

New York

My dearest one, I got in early & then came at 8:30 to breakfast & I looked at all the new models.[21] One corner cupboard I long to have for our camp or cottage or house, which is it to be? I've always thought of it as in the country but I don't think we ever decided on the variety of abode nor the furniture. We probably won't argue!

Now I am off to the train. Dear one, do you realize *if* you get home the 11th it is only 3 weeks from Friday? I can hardly wait.

A world of love & bless you,

E.R.

[April 19]

THE WHITE HOUSE

Washington

Hick darling, I found your two letters from Austin [Texas] of the 14th & 15th when I got in this morning, read them & ached at your writing

---

[21] At various times, Eleanor joined Nan Cook and Marion Dickerman for showings of pieces of furniture being crafted at the Val-Kill factory.

when you were so tired on Saturday night & rejoiced at the restful Sunday.

I'm so glad, dear, the separations get easier. I don't think I've been very good this time but that is purely myself, & you know me well enough to know I will have moods, don't you? Remember you must never worry about my being depressed or cross for it is just a passing mood with me & it never tears me the way it does you!

Well, this a.m. I again dressed for riding, got delayed & up at Ft. Myers[22] 1 hour later just as it began to pour! However, I drove up & back & haven't had a bad day. Ruby [Black] brought her Father from Texas & sister & brother-in-law. I liked the old man. He's 87 & after lunch I took him in to shake hands with F.D.R. Then mail & at four I went down to see Buzzie's [birthday] party begin & the marionette's [sic] did Peter Rabbit in an enchanting way! I forgot to say that I had an interesting talk with Walter White[23] from 12:30 to 1 on the anti-lynching bill. At five I took old Harriet May Mills[24] who's staying here & went to the West Va. congressional reception & a New Hampshire one at Mrs. [Frances Parkinson] Keyes getting home at 7. Mrs. K. has some nice collections of maps, crucifixes[,] fans & dolls in foreign costume & for her lecture she has the real costumes to display on mannikens [sic], rather clever, it makes your trips pay. We must [use] our brains to do what we want & make it pay for itself!

I am sorely tempted to take a radio contract, $3,000 a week & picked up wherever I am![25] Tommy & I have worked all evening & F.D.R. has 80 publishers still downstairs firing questions at him! Dear one, a heart full of me would like to fly to you to-night.

Devotedly,
E.R.

---

[22] Eleanor often went to the Ft. Myers army base in Virginia to ride her horse, Dot.

[23] Walter White was the head of the National Association for the Advancement of Colored People.

[24] Harriet May Mills had been the first director, in the early 1920s, of the Women's Division of the New York State Democratic Committee.

[25] Eleanor did, in fact, sign a contract with the Simmons Mattress Company to provide five radio commentaries on highlights of the week's news. She used the money to support various charities and social causes.

When Lorena's travel schedule took her to Fort Worth, Texas, she stopped to see Elliott Roosevelt and his wife Ruth. Eleanor was eager to receive Lorena's report, as the first lady had met her new daughter-in-law only briefly and had not been supportive of Elliott remarrying so soon after he had divorced his first wife, Betty. The exuberant tone of this letter also demonstrates how Lorena's attitude toward life, although generally melancholy during this period, could sometimes soar to the point of ecstasy.

April 19th

The Texas
Fort Worth, Texas

Dear You:

Well, I had lunch with the kids today. And, as I wired you tonight, a nice time.

I was very much impressed with Elliott. He's changed a good deal, I think, since I saw him last, which was back before the inauguration. Quieter, not so restless, *much* more mature.

As for Ruth—she really is a *vast* improvement over Betty, I should say. She's the *neatest* sort of person and darned attractive—even when pregnant. There certainly is nothing sloppy about her, mentally or physically.

Elliott was called to the telephone before lunch, and she and I were left alone. The situation might have been darned awkward—I certainly felt flushed—but she turned to me with a smile and said, "Tell me, are they *all* as vigorous as Elliott?" Or something to that effect. Then she said very simply—I like the way she said it:

"They must be grand people. I hope I'll get to know them sometime later."

At lunch, which was a very excellent lunch, by the way, we discussed aviation, politics, and various phases of the recovery program. She certainly held up her end. I doubt if Betty could have. I think she really is quite a person, darling. I honestly liked her.

I liked the home, too. It's just comfortable upper middle class. As a matter of fact, you get the feeling that Ruth and her mother actually keep house. They only have one maid, whom Elliott told me they pay $6 a week—good wages here—and a yard boy, who also waits on table. There was a kind of daintiness about the place that appealed to me.

She and Elliott are sweet together. Apparently very much in love. He's sweet to her. So nice and solicitous. This girl is interesting. You don't have to "talk down to her." You get the impression of capability and steadiness. And I *do* have a lot of respect for a woman who keeps herself up when she's going to have a baby. Ruth is just about as big as a house, but she looked attractive. She hadn't let herself go.

They were amusing about the baby. Elliott said they had an unlisted phone because apparently a lot of people thought it was a "shotgun wedding." There'd been a good deal of gossip in Fort Worth, and several times cranks called up the house. He said something about it's being pretty close at that. Ruth added with a chuckle:

"Don't forget, dear—we have three days of grace!"

Oh, yes, when we were alone, I said something about you. She said she thought you were a wonder and added:

"Elliott adores her."[26]

And I think he really does, dear. He seemed honestly concerned about your getting so tired and hating Washington, but said he thought the Puerto Rico trip had done you a lot of good, and I think he and Ruth are counting a good deal on your visiting them this summer.

I told Elliott I was really worried about the state of mind of people these days. He said he was, too.

"The trouble with Father," he said (Please don't repeat this to the president!) "is that he has too much of a tendency to compromise."

I remarked that I thought he'd got by best right after he took office, when he was really *tough*. He said he thought so, too.

Darling, your Sunday night letter *did* sound low, although you seemed to be feeling better Monday night. I asked Elliott why F., Jr., was so annoyed with you. He said he wasn't really, that it was mostly kidding.

---

[26] ER adored Elliott as well. She felt closer to Elliott than to any of her other sons because he was the most like the father whom, during her childhood, she had idolized. Eleanor also feared that Elliott, like her father, was prone to alcoholism and instability. After he failed the entrance exam to Harvard, he continued to have trouble getting his feet on the ground, moving from one career and one woman to another.

Darling, I must go to bed. It's 12:30, and I've got to get up at 6:30. Don't work too hard, dear. Try to get some sleep. Oh, damn it, I wish I could be there when you feel as you did Sunday night and take you in my arms and hold you close. Well, I'll try to make you happy every minute while I'm there in May—

Good night, sweet.

H

April 20th

The Texas
Fort Worth, Texas

Dearest:

The end of a busy day. I drove over to Dallas this morning, spent the day in conference with relief people and business men—finding the picture still pretty gloomy, I'm sorry to say—and drove back, arriving here about 7:30. Since then I've done a bit of reading, dined, done all my packing except the things I need tonight, and have gone through a big batch of stuff that arrived from the office. It's now 10 o'clock, and as soon as I finish this I'm going to bed. I'm leaving at 6 tomorrow morning. Drive 273 miles to Big Spring.

Darling, I hate to sound so gloomy all the time, but *I* can't see much chance for reducing our relief rolls in the next 90 days. Not even here in Texas, and Texas, I believe, is much better off than many other states. There *is* reemployment going on, but industry is not hiring people off the relief rolls. They are taking back their own people, most of whom—the best of them—managed to stay off the relief rolls, possibly because they were the last to lose their jobs. They were the last ones let out—and the first taken back.

I was somewhat shocked tonight to read in the paper that [Postmaster General Jim] Farley is going to issue a Mother's Day stamp *in your honor* May 3rd. God knows you are a mother alright, but not old enough to be honored in connection with Mother's Day! I always think of the Mother's Day mother as an old lady with a wistful expression and a cap and shawl.

And now I'm going to bed—to try to dream about you. I never do, but I always have hopes. The nearest I ever came was one night this week—I think it was the night I ate the Mexican dinner. My dream that night was that I was going to marry Earl [Miller], and your mother-in-law was simply furious! Isn't that a honey? The truth is, I almost never dream.

I've been thinking a lot tonight about Prinz and wondering if he misses me as much as I miss him, the dear pup.

Well, good night, dear. Sweet dreams!

H

[April 25]

THE WHITE HOUSE
Washington

Darling one, I got no letter to-day so it will be Friday before I hear again, which seems a long time!

This has been a nice day—lovely weather & I got out at 10:45 & rode with Anna & John [Boettiger] & enjoyed it. We got in at 12:45 I had some National Theatre people to lunch. Afterwards I went to a Thrift Shop entertainment, a Kentucky mountaineer work sale & called on poor old Nora [Duse].[27] It is sad to be helpless & poor & old, isn't it? I hope you & I to-gether have enough to make it gracious & attractive!

You will be amused to hear that a Denver hotel man wired me to-day ordering a "suite" of furniture! Wouldn't it be a joke if old [Senator Thomas] Schall, meaning to do me harm[,] had brought me a new source for revenue?[28]

Fifteen more days! Dear one, I would give a great deal to put my arms about you to-night!

A world of love,
E.R.

---

[27] Eleanora Duse was an Italian actress Eleanor had known since her childhood.

[28] Senator Thomas Schall of Minnesota had led the attack on Eleanor and the subsistence homestead project, accusing the first lady of selling Val-Kill pieces to the government to furnish the homes at Arthurdale. Eleanor responded that she had founded the factory to provide employment for rural laborers and that she had never made a cent of profit from it.

On April 29 as Lorena was driving on a country road near Tucson, Arizona, she hit a patch of loose gravel and Bluette went hurtling down an embankment. Even though the convertible rolled over several times as it tumbled down the hill, Lorena walked away unscathed. "I had apparently carried most of the weight of the car on the back of my neck while it was rolling over," Lorena later wrote. "You have to have a darned good neck to get away with anything like that. I think mine had no doubt got toughened up these last five or six weeks from carrying the weight of the world on it."[29] Lorena sent a wire to the White House immediately after the accident, prompting a frantic telephone call, telegram, and letter from Eleanor, who offered—apparently in earnest—to abandon her official duties and become Lorena's driver. The resilient chief investigator spent only one day resting before she resumed her work, but the bottom of that Arizona hill was the end of the road for Bluette.

[April 29, 1934]

WESTERN UNION

[from] THE WHITE HOUSE WASHINGTON DC
[to]   MISS L A HICKOK
        PIONEER HOTEL TUCSON ARIZ
TOO SORRY WILL TELEPHONE YOU TONIGHT OR TOMORROW ABOUT
PLANS LOVE AND THANKFUL YOU ARE NOT BADLY HURT ANYTHING ELSE
CAN BE QUICKLY REMEDIED

ELEANOR

[April 29]

THE WHITE HOUSE
Washington

Hick darling, I've just talked to you & hearing your voice has scared me. Your wire did worry me for fear you were worse hurt than you realized & the "what might have happened aspect" I can't face even now.

---

[29] Hickok report to Harry Hopkins, 4 May 1934.

Darling, I ought to drive you! I'm glad though you aren't off [afraid of] driving & gee! you are swell about it. Of course you must have a car & I'll send whatever you need.

A world of love & I will say a prayer of thanksgiving to-night. Bless you!

E.R.

[April 30]

THE WHITE HOUSE
Washington

Hick dearest, I would telephone again to-night just to be satisfied about you but decided I wasn't justified [in spending the money] unless you weren't well! I have a feeling you will be more upset to-day than yester-day but perhaps I'm wrong & I certainly hope so. I still tremble when I think about it but I haven't told anyone outside the house because I thought you'd rather tell those you wanted to have know.

To-day has been a busy day. People to see from 9:30 on, 2 guests to breakfast, press conference 11-12:45, the press girls to lunch, 2 Girl Scouts from Maine to greet, hair & nails, then people to see till 6:30[,] now I must dress for dinner!

I'm nearly over my cold but going slow for a day or two when I can but haven't been able to this day!

Oh! dear one I love you & long to be with you when things go wrong. Bless you & a warm kiss to you.

Devotedly,
E.R.

[May 3]

THE WHITE HOUSE
Washington

Hick darling, To-day has been an easier day. I drove Louis one hour & a quarter this a.m., had people to lunch, several appointments—then with

F. & the Daniels[30] to the unveiling of [William Jennings] Bryan's statue down by the [Potomac] river in the rain but a fine figure & as I listened to Mr. Daniels I decided he [Bryan] accomplished a great deal but I did not like him.[31]

We returned to Anna's party & the kids enjoyed seeing "Papa" [FDR] spank her. She is 28 & how much further ahead than I was at her age.

We are having a dinner to-night for [Puerto Rican] Gov. [Blanton] Winship who arrived here a few days ago. I haven't found out what is happening but will know more when you arrive.[32]

A world of love to you dear one. I will be happy to hold you in my arms on the 11th.

> Devotedly,
> E.R.

Eleanor and Lorena were at the White House together from May 11 to 23, but the visit ended on a sour note when Hick wasn't able to spend the final morning alone with the first lady, whose letter written immedi-

---

[30] Josephus Daniels, as secretary of the Navy, had been Franklin's boss from 1913 to 1920, and his wife Addie Bagley Daniels, a socially concerned aristocrat, had worked with Eleanor in creating the Navy Red Cross.

[31] The Bryan statue that the president dedicated was located near the Theodore Roosevelt Bridge entrance to West Potomac Park; in 1961 it was moved to Bryan's birthplace in Salem, Illinois. Bryan, who served as secretary of state during the Wilson administration, ran for president in 1896, 1900, and 1908. Eleanor disagreed with many of the stands that Bryan supported. Among many other causes, Bryan was a leader of the Fundamentalist Movement, the Prohibition effort, and the campaign to prevent Darwinian evolution from being taught in American schools.

[32] Eleanor soon learned that quite a lot was happening. After returning from their Caribbean trip, Eleanor and Hick had made a number of recommendations to FDR (during a White House dinner for three), and during the next few months, several of their suggestions were transformed into reality. The responsibility for administering the island was transferred from the War Department to the Interior Department (Eleanor and Lorena's recommendation), where a separate division of territories was established (also Eleanor and Lorena's recommendation). In addition, the Puerto Rican Reconstruction Administration was created to expand and stabilize the economy (another Eleanor and Lorena recommendation). Other changes that soon occurred on the island also had their roots in Eleanor and Lorena's trip—a minimum wage scale was established for women who stitched garments in their homes, federal money was used to replace rickety schools and prisons made of bamboo with new buildings of brick and stone, and codes were established to ensure that products made in Puerto Rico were sold for decent prices.

ately after they parted included one of her increasingly frequent apologies.

[May 23]

THE WHITE HOUSE
Washington

Hick dearest, I know how you felt to-day, you couldn't let go for fear of losing control & being with me was hard & I imagine I made it worse by sending you to say goodbye to Tommy but she spoke of it at breakfast & I was so afraid she'd come & stay & spoil our little time together. Darling I love you dearly & I am sorry for letting my foolish temparament [sic] make you unhappy & sorry that your temparament [sic] does bad things to you too but we'll have years of happy times so bad times will be forgotten. July is a long way off but when it comes we'll be to-gether.[33]

Perhaps this will reach you to-morrow night so sleep sweetly & a world of love dear one,

E.R.

This letter provides another example of Lorena's dramatic mood swings. Despite her near-fatal accident, her general fatigue, and the gloomy tone of most of her letters before and after this one, the tone of this particular letter was euphoric.

May 24th

Dayton Biltmore
Dayton, Ohio

Dear You:

I saw my first subsistence homestead today, and, lady, did I get a kick! The contrast between those homesteaders, busy, planning, working, *really happy and hopeful,* and people on relief—gosh! You just must have seen some of the things I've been seeing these last few weeks to appreciate it, that's all.

---

[33] Eleanor and Lorena were hoping to vacation together in July.

I found one family actually living in their house! A neat, attractive, *clean* house, with rugs and couch covers, colorful things, that the woman had woven herself, on a hand loom. Outside was their garden, well underway, with strawberries almost ripe, and a sow with four little pigs, a big flock of chickens, and some rabbits, for eating, all in excellent condition. And, darling, *you should have seen the expression of contentment on that woman's face* as she showed me around.

Furthermore, those people are going into debt only a little over $500 for their house! The people who are going to live there are building the houses themselves, helping each other, under good supervision. So they go into debt only for the cost of the material. The land was bought by the community, and each homesteader will pay rent on his share to the community—between $3 and $6 a month—covering taxes, amortization of the debt for the land, and so on. One of the homesteaders and I figured out this afternoon that a man with a family of five could get by there on $40 a month cash income.

Oh, my dear, you'd get a kick out of this place! I'm so thrilled about it.

I could go on and on, but I'll have to do it in a report, I guess. Elizabeth Nutting, who runs the cooperative here, just called to say she'll be stopping by for me in ten minutes to go out to dinner! More later—

Later: It's now nearly 11. Elizabeth is a wonderful person. She is practical and a good business woman. She is a very attractive woman and yet has the mind of a man. I must take my bath and go to bed. I'm getting up early tomorrow morning to write a report.

Good night, dear. I hope your day has been happy and not too crowded.

H

[May 30]

49 East 65th Street
New York

Hick darling, It was good to find your Saturday & Sunday letters here & I hope for word to-morrow. Dear I'll try to do my share towards living up to our resolutions. I will try to keep on an even keel from now on.

The one thing I wanted to take you to task for is that phrase "she has the mind of a man." Why can't a woman think, be practical & [be] a good business woman & still have a mind of her own?

We went to "Tobacco Road." Never have I seen on a stage a more revolting 1st act, then 2nd & 3rd were horrible but interesting but I don't really think that type of play helps even the poor whites.[34]

Well, dear one, I love you tenderly & I wish you were here with me to-night, but you are happier & interested & I'm feeling well & rested so we are going to look forward to a grand two weeks to-gether in July. Where shall it be? Goodnight, sleep well & my thoughts are with you.

Devotedly,

E.R.

Eleanor sending Lorena a pressed rose from the garden at Val-Kill was a romantic gesture that the first lady hoped would soothe Hick during her difficult times.

[June 3]

Val-Kill Cottage

Hick darling, I wonder if any of the sweetness of this little favorite rose of mine will linger by the time it reaches you? My garden at the cottage was a lovely sight in full bloom & unconsciously I wanted you to see it with me.

We got here [Hyde Park] at 9:15 & at 10:30 I went out with F. in his car & drove over all the little roads on this side of the place & some on the other. I hope Franklin has a few years here. He would really enjoy it & I believe he would enjoy it even with Mama here. I kept thinking of the mess we had made of our young lives here & how strange it was that

[34] *Tobacco Road*, originally a novel published by Erskine Caldwell in 1932, is the story of a degenerate family of poor whites living in Georgia. In many ways, the family represented the dregs of society with few redeeming human qualities, which may have been the reason Eleanor found the play distasteful.

after all these years I return here as indifferent & uninterested as a stranger & I doubt if any child has any feeling about it because nothing has ever been his or her own here. It is a pity one cannot live one's life once again but at least we can try to keep one's children from making the same mistakes.

We got in at 12:30 & I had a swim & talked with Mama for an hour. She is unhappy & I see why & yet I feel so strongly she brought it all on herself but she can't help it for she just doesn't understand.[35] She'll be 80 in Sept. & I must make an effort to make it a happy day for her. I've been such an unsatisfactory daughter-in-law.

God bless you dear & good night. I would like to really kiss you tonight but I do in spirit,

E.R.

June 6th

Hotel Negley
Florence, Alabama

Dear You:

Today has been strenuous. I took a quick look at the transient setup—thousands come here looking for work, you see, and present quite a problem—and spent the afternoon looking over Muscle Shoals—Wilson dam and power house, Wheeler dam, the houses they are building there for the engineers and their families, the construction camp and so on.[36] It's all on such a huge scale! But darned interesting. Always in the background, though, is this dreadful relief business—dull, hopeless, deadening. God—*when* are we going to get out of it? As nearly as I can figure it out, most of the relief families in Tennessee are rural, living on sub-

---

[35] Sara Delano Roosevelt was a controlling person who ruled the Springwood mansion at Hyde Park as if she were a queen. After dinner when the family retired to the living room, for example, Sara sat in one of the tooled leather wingback chairs by the fireplace and her son Franklin sat in the other, leaving Eleanor to sit on the floor.

[36] Muscle Shoals was a series of rapids in the Tennessee River that was the site of a massive hydroelectric power project the federal government began in 1918. After spending $15 million on the project, Congress halted it in 1921. After the Roosevelt administration came to power, the Tennessee Valley Authority was established and took over the properties and used them as an example of regional planning.

marginal or marginal land. *What* are we going to do with them? And, so low are their standards of living, that, once on relief, low as it is, they want to stay there the rest of their lives. Gosh! TVA is now employing some 9,500 people.[37] But it doesn't even make a dent!

Well, I must stop and order my dinner. I'm pretty tired. I've simply *got* to get a report off tonight, and it's very hot. So I'm having dinner in my room, in my nightgown, and will start the report as soon as I've eaten—

Good night, dear. I hope the train isn't too hot tonight. And that the roadbed won't be too rough!

H

P.S. With the possible exception of the one on Puerto Rico, this is probably the poorest report I've ever written. I *must* pull myself up. But *how?* I *am* so tired.

H

[June 8]

The White House
Washington

Hick darling, Your letter of Wednesday night troubled me. You cannot get so tired it always results in mental and emotional depression & that feeling of the "utter futility" of all things is a result of weariness. Darling, do take care of yourself.

The decision [on our vacation] is up to you. Either I meet you in Banff[38] or in San Francisco. If it is the latter I can probably make it the night of the 10th if it is the other by the 12th anyway.

Your report is *very* good, you are too tired to judge.

---

[37] The Tennessee Valley Authority was a corporation designed to plan for the proper use, conservation, and development of the natural resources of the Tennessee Valley drainage basin.
[38] Banff is a resort city in the province of Alberta and surrounded by the Canadian Rockies.

I've worked all a.m. & am now off to lunch with Frances [Perkins] & Isabella [Selmes Greenway]. A world of love & I wish I could put my arms about you,

E.R.

In mid-June, Anna filed for divorce from Curtis Dall in Reno, Nevada. To fulfill the Nevada residency requirement for a divorce, the first daughter would stay with Bill and Ella Dana, long-time Roosevelt family friends, on their ranch near Reno for the next several months.

June 15th

Burlington Hotel
Akron, Colorado

Dearest:

The Denver papers just arrived with pictures of Anna and the story plastered all over the front page. Poor child—she barely got out of Washington before it broke. I'm afraid this will make it a pretty hard trip for her. Too bad she couldn't have got out there and settled before the whole thing got out. Well, it had to get out *some*time of course.

Well, I entered the Colorado drought area today—in hail and a cloudburst! It was very funny really. As I drove out of Fort Morgan, about 35 miles west of here, young Terry Owens, one of the field engineers who is driving me about, announced with a flourish, "You are now in the drought area." He had hardly got the words out when simultaneously we got a flat tire and it started to pour! Hail, too! And there has been a severe electric and hail storm here tonight, with a regular cloudburst. They had one last night, too, and they now consider the drought broken in this part of the state. Too late to save the small grains, but they think there will be plenty of good grazing and possibly some corn. The rain, after its long delay, brought tragedy to some. One farmer, living on lowland, lost all his stock in last night's rain. Forty-two head of cattle, all drowned. Isn't it ironic? Yesterday he was worrying about his cattle starving to death because the drought had burned up all their food. Today his stock was all dead any way, drowned, and everything else swept away—his house and his barns under water.

I spent most of today tramping around in the beet fields. I had my first look at child labor—children 8 & 10 years old working in the beet fields. It was not a nice picture. I ought to write a report tonight, but I've gritted my teeth so much these last two days that the roof of my mouth is all raw. So I think I'd better go to bed.

Darling, I hope Anna won't have too bad a time, and that you and she both will be bothered as little as possible.

Good night, dear person. Akron, Colorado, is many, many miles from Washington, D.C., but I'll be thinking about you tonight, as I drift off to sleep.

H

Eleanor wrote this letter while visiting her godmother Susie Parish, whose husband Henry Parish was ill.

[June 17]

Undercliff

Orange, New Jersey

Hick darling, I am feeling better to-night than I was last night which means I suppose that I feel more charitable! I breakfasted in bed, talked to Cousin Susie & spent an hour & a half this morning in the hospital with Cousin Henry. He is an angel & how he stands his life I don't know. He only worries about her! She & I had lunch on the porch, then she rested & I wrote letters & at five we had a tea party, about 30 people. Now she is resting again. Will you tell me how anyone could sleep at night for she spent the whole morning in bed! I'd love to make her live your life for a week. I do hope you are not completely exhausted & I can hardly wait to hear your decision on a car.[39] I rather like the idea of us both having Buicks!

If you can't take more than two weeks holiday, I'll go along on your schedule the last four days & you can work while I look on & then I can

---

[39] Lorena was trying to decide what kind of car to buy to replace Bluette. Eleanor was providing the money.

take a night train from wherever we are into Seattle.[40] Only don't be too far away from a train!

Dearest one, I love you dearly & I think of you so much, take care of yourself.

Devotedly,

E.R.

Eleanor and Lorena's travel plans were falling into place, propelled by the various people they hoped to visit during the trip. Eleanor would spend several days in Chicago with her brother, Hall Roosevelt, before flying on to Sacramento to connect with Lorena. Then the two women would drive to Colfax, California, to visit Roy and Ellie Dickinson, the woman Lorena had lived with in Minneapolis. From there they would drive to the Dana ranch near Reno, Nevada, to see Anna for several days before completing their holiday alone in Yosemite National Park and San Francisco.

[June 18]

THE WHITE HOUSE

Washington

Hick dear, I came in & found your letters & wire. I hope we hear soon about the car but if you don't have it in time I'll try to arrange to rent a Buick in Sacramento. Let's do this, I'll fly from Chicago early on the 10th & get in late at night. We'll go to Colfax & spend 5 or 6 quiet days. Then we'll get the car, motor to Anna & back over a lovely route—thro' the Yosemite & in to San Francisco. Two days there & 3 or 4 days up to Seattle. This leaves us leeway to move slowly from Anna to San Francisco & stay over a day or so if we like. I have maps & directions & will arrange a way by which I can get a ranger as guide if you wire me to Washington that this plan suits you!

I really think the papers have been fairly decent about Anna but she

---

[40] Eleanor was planning to meet Franklin on the West Coast after he returned from a trip to Hawaii. The meeting point initially was Seattle but later was changed to Portland.

did get caught in one interview & she was very tired & writes Sisty & Buzzie kept her awake most of the night. I hope she is getting rested.

Also floods in the drouht [sic] area are ironic but so like us as a nation, we always deal in extremes. Poor man, who lost his cattle, that was [a] tragedy! I hope you will think as little as I do of the sugar beet industry.[41] I forgot you'd never seen those conditions. I saw them years ago in the 1920 campaign trip.

I'm so sorry about the teeth & hope your mouth got well. It is a bad sign to grind your teeth like that, you must be less intense!

Mama when in London is going to stay with the King & Queen of England, Lord, how I would hate it & how she will love it![42]

Now dear one good night. Bless you, I love you always & I wish my arms were around you.

Devotedly,

E.R.

July 3rd

HOTEL BARBARA WORTH

El Centro, California

Dear You:

Phooie, but it's hot here! Someone said it was *128* yesterday, and I believe it.

This valley[43] is the damnedest place I ever saw—except Southern West Virginia and Eastern Kentucky. There is the same suspicion and bitterness all through the place. An unreasoning, blind fear of "Communist agitators." If you don't agree with them, you are a Communist, of course.

They have no use for the Administration. One of the leading citizens told the state field man for the relief administration that he'd like to lead the pack & give [Assistant Secretary of Agriculture] Rex Tugwell a beat-

---

[41] Eleanor was critical of the sugar beet industry because of its dependence on child labor.

[42] Sara Delano Roosevelt was planning a holiday in London, staying at Buckingham Palace. Sara relished ceremony and luxury as much as Eleanor abhorred them.

[43] Lorena was in the Imperial Valley on the southern tip of California.

ing if he "ever showed his face around here." He was here last summer, as a matter of fact, but they were never aware of it. And they call Harry Hopkins a Communist.

You, Washington, the apartment in New York, Prinz—they all seem very far away this morning. I wonder if it will be like this when I die—a feeling of remoteness from everything. Oh, my dear, I'm so sick of the whole miserable business!

Goodbye for now—

H

Eleanor wrote this letter while visiting her brother Hall in Chicago. It suggests that Eleanor sensed that her upcoming vacation with Lorena might be less than idyllic.

July 10th

The Blackstone

Chicago

Hick dearest, This probably won't reach you before you leave for Sacramento—but it will be there for the record! I went to the [Chicago] Art Institute, & walked home followed by camera men & then stayed in all day. Had some friends of Hall's to lunch, worked, had more friends to tea & went to dine. I was followed, they [the photographers] waited for me & saw me home. I just pray I may get out to-morrow but!

I can't quite understand why you are so worried dear, why can't you just be natural? Of course we are going to have a good time to-gether & neither of us is going to be upset.

Good night dear one & bless you,

E.R.

Another Holiday Disrupted

As Eleanor and Lorena moved along their individual routes toward the Sacramento hotel room where they would meet, their respective paths were separated not only by hundreds of miles but also by two very different sets of needs and commitments. Since she had reluctantly accepted the mantle of first lady sixteen months earlier, Eleanor had rewritten the job description. Initially with Lorena's counsel and assistance but increasingly on her own, the first lady had found ways to use her position to advance her own social and political agenda—her own vision, her own destiny. After a lifetime of starts and stops caused by the decisions and the needs of other people, Eleanor was finally establishing a life that reflected her own values and priorities—and on her own terms. She had the potential, in other words, of doing precisely what she had been endeavoring to do for forty years: She could make a difference in the world.

Lorena was in a very different place. Her accomplishments had come early, though certainly not easily, when she had proven during her teenage years that she was perfectly capable of taking care of herself. During her twenties, her combination of raw talent and even rawer grit had helped to change the world of journalism, transforming an all-male profession into one in which a woman, at least a few of them, could carve out a niche. During her thirties, she had grown still more, emerging as one of the most admired journalists—male or female—in the country, becoming a top political reporter assigned to the most sought-after of news beats. Her path had changed abruptly when she had fallen in love with Eleanor, but once again she had proven herself by adapting to the situation and becoming the best relief investigator anyone could ask for, while at the same time serving as the behind-the-scenes adviser who helped reinvent the position of first lady. Now in her early forties and with so many achievements to her credit, Lorena had set her sights on a very different goal. She had found the love of her life, and she was ready to settle down into a quiet and peaceful existence with her.

Eleanor was poised to change the world; Lorena was ready to retreat from it. Eleanor was eager to commit her energies to humanity; Lorena was eager to focus her energies on a single person. Was it possible for two such dichotomous sets of priorities to survive in a single relationship? When Lorena wrote the chapter in her book that described the West Coast trip, she rephrased that very question with her choice of a title—"Last Attempt."

By early August of 1934 when the two women would again part, the question would be answered. But first, Eleanor and Lorena would complete the twenty-two-day Western trip that would be the same length, to the day, as their French Canadian adventure of the previous summer. This time, though, their travels would bear scant resemblance to a blissful holiday but would provide an experience more like an emotional roller-coaster ride neither woman would soon forget—nor wish to remember.

From the outset, the getaway was troubled by press coverage, as on this trip the first lady was not inside the protective bubble provided by her press "girls." Eleanor and Hick tried to keep their rendezvous point—the Hotel Senator in Sacramento, an out-of-the-way hotel chosen in hopes of avoiding attention—a secret, but when Lorena arrived to spend the night before Eleanor arrived the following morning, she found a gaggle of reporters waiting in the lobby. Lorena later wrote, "Somebody—I suspected the airline press agent—had broken the secret and released the name of the hotel to the press. I then proceeded to do the silliest thing I ever did in my life. As the reporters undoubtedly put it, I tried to 'out-smart' them." By the time Lorena wrote those words in 1962, she had calmed down. But in 1934 when it seemed like her private holiday with Eleanor was about to be transformed into a media event, Lorena was furious.[1]

Newspaper coverage of the activities that followed eventually captured a sense of that fury. But first they described Lorena's effort to evade the reporters; the scheme read like the script of a spy movie. En-

[1] Hickok, *Reluctant First Lady*, 157–58.

listing the help of the state troopers assigned to travel with the president's wife, Lorena had the District of Columbia license plates on her new Plymouth convertible removed and replaced with California plates. (She ultimately had decided on a Plymouth rather than the Buick that Eleanor had wanted her to buy.) Then she parked the car outside the back door of the hotel. On the morning that Eleanor arrived in Sacramento, Hick took a cab to the airport—with a crowd of reporters on her heels. As soon as Eleanor disembarked from the United Airlines plane, Lorena hustled her into the cab, and when they arrived back at the hotel, Lorena got out of the car to run interference. "I used to be a newspaperman myself," she told the reporters. "I know you want to interview Mrs. Roosevelt, but she's just finished a long, overnight flight and she's feeling grimy. Would you please let her wash her face first before you talk to her and take her picture?" The reporters agreed. The first friend then led the first lady into the lobby and onto the elevator. Instead of going *up* to their room, however, the two women headed *down* to Lorena's car where a trooper was waiting to whisk them away. They threw their bags into the rumble seat and took off.[2]

"It was a swell scheme," the *Sacramento Union* wrote in a page-one story the next day, "except that one pair of reporters had thought she would do just what was done to elude them." The two reporters hopped in their car and raced after Lorena's, while the trooper tried his best to outrun the reporters by putting, as Lorena later wrote, "a heavy foot on the accelerator, and with dismay I watched the speedometer go up and up and up—50, 55, 60, 75, 77 miles an hour." But Lorena's car wasn't built for racing. So after fifteen miles, the trooper finally had to pull off to the side of the road.[3]

On the details that followed, Lorena's and the *Union's* accounts differed significantly. She wrote in her book that Eleanor graciously invited the reporters to interview her over breakfast at a restaurant in the tiny town of Roseville—"Jim's Coffee Shop, Booths for Ladies," the sign read. The news stories, on the other hand, described an agitated Lorena shaking her fist at the reporters and shouting "You're a pair of bum sports!" (Those were about the saltiest words that newspapers were al-

[2] Hickok, *Reluctant First Lady,* 159.

[3] John L. Sullivan, "President's Wife Tells Union She Plans 'Secret' Auto Tour of California," *Sacramento Union,* 13 July 1934, 1; Hickok, *Reluctant First Lady,* 159.

lowed to publish in 1934.) Lorena remained angry throughout the meal—at least according to the paper. ER initially ordered orange juice with her coffee and toast, but then, when reminded that peaches were in season in California, changed her order to peaches and cream. Lorena was not so conciliatory. "Miss Hickok was too mad at the interview to change over to peaches," the *Union* reported. "She lit a cigarette. Mrs. Roosevelt did not smoke."[4]

The newspaper stories that appeared for the next two days—the Associated Press picked up the novel story of the first lady trying to elude the press and distributed it nationwide—were decidedly complimentary to Eleanor. One began "Merry Mrs. Roosevelt," others described her as "smiling" and "laughing," and still others talked about her "being gracious toward" and "playing hide and seek with" the reporters. Nevertheless, the first lady's press adviser was anything but pleased. Maybe the president's wife flying to California was newsworthy, Lorena acknowledged, but did the whole country really need to know—on page one, no less—that the investigator of the nation's relief programs had shouted at a pack of reporters and had opted not to eat California peaches? Adding to Lorena's frustration was the fact that one story incorrectly stated that she wrote her reports *for* the first lady. As with Lorena's earlier portrayals in newsprint, there was also a characterization that she simply didn't understand; in this case, the paper said she had "a police-woman complex." Maybe that was supposed to be something like her being *peremptory,* Lorena wasn't sure. One thing she was sure of, though: It wasn't a compliment. And finally, Lorena shrieked, was it really anyone's business that she smoked cigarettes or that she and the first lady were, as the *San Francisco Examiner*—William Randolph Hearst's notorious voice of sensationalism—characterized them, "intimate friends"?[5]

The next few days of the trip were more successful, as the pair of reporters—after getting their exclusive interview—agreed to let the

[4] Hickok, *Reluctant First Lady,* 161; Sullivan, "President's Wife Tells Union," 13 July 1934, 1.

[5] "Mrs. Roosevelt Visits in Marysville, Colfax," *Sacramento Union,* 14 July 1934, 1; John Lee, "First Lady Loses Race to Reporters," *San Francisco Examiner,* 13 July 1934, 3; Sullivan, "President's Wife Tells Union," 13 July 1934, 1; "First Lady in Mount Cabin," *San Francisco Examiner,* 14 July 1934, 7; "First Lady's Auto Heads for Sierras," *San Francisco Chronicle,* 13 July 1934, 1.

women be on their way. Eleanor and Lorena visited Ellie and Roy Dickinson in Colfax, just north of Sacramento. Then they traversed Donner Pass in the High Sierras and continued north and west into Nevada to visit Anna and her hosts, Bill and Ella Dana, on their huge and wonderfully isolated ranch. Next, Eleanor and Lorena drove into Yosemite National Park just across the California state line and spent their first night at the Ahwanee Hotel, the mountain lodge built from stone and sugarpine logs against the backdrop of the Sierra Nevada mountain range. Lorena gasped in awe when she entered the grand lounge and solarium with its thirty-foot-high, trestle-beamed ceiling and its twinkling chandeliers; it would be the last time she would use the adjective "beautiful" to describe any aspect of Yosemite.[6]

Eleanor had been in charge of planning their three days in the park, but as the details of the outdoor adventure came to light, Lorena began to realize that what she had envisioned as three sublime days and nights of quiet walks in the woods and long evenings holed up in a rustic cabin *for two* was going to be three exhausting days of hiking and riding horses over hazardous trails followed by cold nights of sleeping in crude campsites set up *for seven!* For when the first lady had written in advance asking the park's chief forest ranger, Billy Nelson, to plan a visit for her and a friend, she didn't realize that Nelson and four other rangers would be *joining* the women—the chief ranger wasn't about to take a chance of the president's wife getting injured in *his* park. Though Eleanor hadn't specifically asked Nelson and the other rangers to come along and she, too, was surprised that they kept so close, she was too gracious to tell them to go away.

Hick became even more irritated when the high altitude made it difficult for her to breathe—and angrier still when the first lady, accustomed to exercise because when in Washington she rode her horse almost daily, bluntly pointed out "If you didn't insist on smoking so much, you wouldn't be so short of breath." Another detail that added to Lorena's growing anger was the fact that Eleanor and the rangers found it exhilarating to dash down to a nearby lake every morning to bathe in the ice cold water, while Lorena tried that experience only on the first day and then spent the other mornings grinding her teeth as she lay in her sleep-

[6] Hickok, *Reluctant First Lady,* 168.

ing bag furious that she would have to endure yet another day without a bath and wearing the one set of jeans and shirt that she'd brought along.[7]

The worst moment of all came not at the highest elevation (they eventually climbed to 8,000 feet) but at the lowest. Eleanor, Lorena, and their male escorts had ridden their horses down into a valley when they came upon a river they had to cross. When Eleanor had written Nelson, she had specified that "Miss Hickok will require a quiet, gentle horse, since she has not ridden for some time"—phrasing that, when Nelson read it to Lorena, she found so patronizing that she became even angrier with the first lady. Still, Lorena's little mare had her frisky moments. When Lorena attempted to cross the river, she somehow lost her balance and slipped off her horse and fell backward. The next thing she knew, she was sitting in water up to her chin while Eleanor and the rangers stared from atop their horses—one of the men reflexively chuckling at the sight of the woman plopped down in the middle of the river. Lorena was not hurt physically, but she was humiliated—and irate. She tried so hard to wipe the incident from her memory, in fact, that she did not mention it in her book. The only account of the accident that was preserved is one Nelson later wrote in a note to Eleanor expressing his hope that she would visit Yosemite again. As part of that note—one that Lorena undoubtedly wished had joined the other letters she burned—Nelson wrote, "Tell Miss Hickok that I am wondering if she still dives backwards from her horse into rivers."[8]

Eleanor experienced her own embarrassing moment toward the end of the Yosemite visit. The incident was not the doing of a frisky horse and chuckling forest ranger, however, but of a reluctant outdoorswoman who finally found a release for her pent-up anger. Throughout the three days of camping, the first lady and first friend had been accompanied not only by rangers but also by vacationers. "We couldn't get away from the tourists," Lorena wrote irritably in her book. "They followed us everywhere, in *droves*." After having thirty years to reflect on her own behavior during that long-ago trip, Lorena also admitted

[7] Hickok, *Reluctant First Lady*, 166.

[8] Hickok, *Reluctant First Lady*, 167; Billy Nelson letter to Eleanor, 14 September 1935, Eleanor Roosevelt Papers.

"And there were times when I behaved badly and embarrassed Mrs. Roosevelt."[9]

The particular incident Lorena was recalling began when she and Eleanor spotted a little village of chipmunks so tame that they ate out of a person's hand. "They were charming little creatures, and it was a delightful experience to have one of them perch on your wrist, daintily picking crumbs out of your hand." What Lorena did not find delightful, though, was looking up from the chipmunks to find a crowd of tourists, many of them with cameras in hand, surrounding her and Eleanor—and *not* taking pictures of the chipmunks. Lorena's mood was made no more pleasant by the fact that she wasn't exactly looking at her peak. After three days without washing her hair or changing her clothes, she was in no condition to have her picture taken. Even worse, most of the tourists had decided they could get their best photos of the first lady by stationing themselves to the rear of Lorena, thereby filling their frames with that quite broad behind of hers that was still splattered with mud from her river bed mishap of the previous day.[10]

Lorena lost it. Lashing out not only at the rudeness of the tourists but also letting loose much of the repressed resentment after the nights sleeping on the cold ground . . . and the sweltering hot days of hiking . . . and Eleanor's patronizing comments about her smoking and horse-riding ability . . . and always being surrounded by that entourage of forest rangers, Lorena turned downright surly and started stalking around like a wild animal as she screamed at the tourists to stop snapping pictures and start minding their own God-damned business! The expletives that came streaming out of Lorena's mouth were so colorful—all those years in the newsroom had taught her more than just how to write a news story—that Eleanor finally had to "shush" her and physically pull her away from the stunned assembly of slack-jawed sightseers who stared dumfounded. Eleanor was of a social class that had been trained never to lose one's poise in public, and never in half a century had she succumbed to an emotional outburst; now for her friend to go quite utterly mad in the presence of a whole gallery of the

---

[9] Hickok, *Reluctant First Lady,* 170.
[10] Hickok, *Reluctant First Lady,* 170.

American middle class—the very voters who would decide the fate of her husband's revolutionary New Deal initiatives—was simply beyond what the first lady could possibly find acceptable. Eleanor was not merely embarrassed; she was ashamed.[11]

After Lorena's explosion in front of the tourists, the summer holiday was in shambles. Eleanor herself could endure the wrath of Lorena's temper, but she absolutely *could not* stand by and allow it to be inflicted on innocent people. The price for maintaining her intense relationship with Lorena was simply too high.

The women continued their trip by spending two days in San Francisco, where they were again assaulted by a mob of reporters. The *Examiner* and *Chronicle* both inaccurately identified Lorena as the first lady's "secretary," and the *Chronicle* described her as "plump, ruddy, and hatless" and characterized her as having "played the role of guardian in chief to the First Lady for several years." In addition, the women fell victim to a gang of hooligan souvenir-seekers who broke into Lorena's car and stole, Lorena later wrote, "maps, sun glasses, suntan lotion, chocolate bars, my cigarette lighter, even a little St. Christopher medal which Mrs. Roosevelt had given me, and which I kept in the glove compartment." It was a dismal ending to a dismal trip. When they reached Portland, Eleanor joined Franklin and Lorena resumed her investigation of the nation's relief programs. The women then continued their correspondence, but never again would their letters rise to the level of passion or emotional pitch that they had once reached.[12]

[11] Hickok, *Reluctant First Lady,* 170.
[12] "Mrs. Roosevelt Visits S.F. in Tourist Role," *San Francisco Examiner,* 30 July 1934, 1; "'First Lady' Paying Short Visit to S.F.," *San Francisco Chronicle,* 30 July 1934, 1; Carolyn Anspacher, "First Lady Tries in Vain for Privacy," *San Francisco Chronicle,* 31 July 1934, 1; Hickok, *Reluctant First Lady,* 174.

Five

Letting Go but Holding On

Although the Yosemite trip marked a significant turning point in Eleanor and Lorena's relationship, not every letter they wrote in the wake of that debacle reflected the change. Their letters continued to include words of endearment, as well as a constant flow of support and encouragement.

Still, extremely rare now were the references to the women kissing or lying down together; those sentiments were replaced by a series of apologies for hurt feelings, rearranged schedules, and missed meetings— along with an instance of Lorena verbally reprimanding the first lady for wearing an expensive evening gown. In addition, the letters that Eleanor wrote during the last five months of 1934 were much more likely to contain the familiar words "a world of love" than the more intimate "I love you deeply & tenderly."

Indeed, Eleanor now seemed to save her most romantic words almost solely for the occasions when she wanted to prevent the first friend from going into an emotional tailspin. One such occasion came after Eleanor had set aside an evening early in the Christmas season exclusively for

Lorena but then had altered her plans to accommodate the ailing Louis Howe. "I think I'll have to devote my evening to him," Eleanor wrote, then quickly adding, "You know I'd rather be with you & carefree & dear I love you deeply & tenderly!"

On Lorena's part, her letters from this period were dotted with phrases communicating a variety of negative emotions—agitation and frustration, regret and remorse, pain and torment. "Good night," she wrote Eleanor two weeks after their calamitous western vacation, "I hope you are having a happy, restful time at camp—a happier, more peaceful time than you had with me. Oh, I'm bad, my dear, but I love you so. At times life becomes just one long, dreary ache for you."

After leaving Eleanor, Lorena returned to San Francisco to investigate the relief programs there, and Ellie Morse Dickinson came down from Colfax to spend several days with her.

August 8th

Hotel Worth

San Francisco

Dear One:

Although I shall miss Ellie greatly when I no longer have her with me, it seems good to be here alone, in my dressing gown, for a quiet talk with you. I hate being hurried or interrupted when I'm writing to you, just as I hate it when we are together.

Yes, as you suggest, Ellie and San Francisco have made it easier for me, although there have been times when I've missed you so that it has been like a physical pain, and at those times I've hated San Francisco because you were not here. Not so many times, however, and I've tried very hard not to let Ellie see.

Well, I spent the morning with Mayor [Angelo] Rossi—for three hours. I like Mayor Rossi, a lot. He's temperate, sane, a man of good judgement. Quite different from the fiery type you'd expect an Italian to be. Single-handed, his staff tells me, he fought against setting up martial law in San Francisco during the strike[1] although the pressure brought to bear by the moneyed interests and business men and the newspapers was terrific. It must have taken a good deal of courage, but he won out. I liked him this morning. Several of his "cabinet" were there—the comptroller, the city engineer, the San Francisco county relief directors, and so on. They were pretty sore—there has been a good deal of friction between the city and the state and federal relief administrations—and they lost their tempers and made some pretty wild statements. But he remained calm, corrected some of their more extravagant assertions, and was sweet and courteous to the end.

Good night, sweetheart. I love you tenderly.

H

---

[1] Longshoremen had walked off their jobs in May. After two picketers were killed in a violent protest that became known as Bloody Thursday, the action spread to a general strike in July.

The following three letters show the degree to which the terms of Eleanor and Lorena's relationship had changed after the West Coast trip, with a subtle restraint permeating Eleanor's words.

August 10th

Campobello Island
New Brunswick, Canada

Hick dearest, Two letters from you & I was amused by your conversation with Katherine Beebe.[2] Dear, I hope she gets you in the right frame of mind to enjoy life.[3] I surmise you would be happier if my own attitude were different.

Well, it's lovely here. The drive up was as nice as ever & the two girls[4] are riding in the morning & I'm going to loaf a day or two.

I telephoned F.D.R. & he sounds happy over yesterday & everyone seems to like his speech.[5]

Dear one, take care of yourself,

E.R.

August 11th

Campobello Island
New Brunswick, Canada

Hick darling, Your letter to-day was a joy & I am glad it was easier on the whole but I'm afraid you & I are always going to have times when we ache for each other & yet we are not always going to be happy when we are to-gether. Somehow we must find the things which we can do &

---

[2] Kay Beebe was the Associated Press reporter who originally had been assigned to cover Eleanor during the 1932 campaign but who had transferred to the San Francisco office when she married.

[3] Although Kay Beebe excelled as a pioneering woman journalist for some thirty-five years, she balanced her personal life with her work life and was not as driven by her work as Lorena was.

[4] Nan Cook and Marion Dickerman were vacationing with Eleanor.

[5] In the speech, FDR asserted that the New Deal had brought a rebirth of confidence to the nation and that he was prepared—if he deemed it necessary for the common good—to go to indefinite lengths to extend government control over business.

do them so that what time we have to-gether is as happy as it can be in an imperfect world!

I'm writing you out on the balcony looking over the lake at the sunset & it is absolutely quiet & peaceful & lovely. Major[6] was driven up to-day & he's beside me, at first he didn't seem to know me but he's slipped quickly back to familiarity & follows me around as usual & no doubt will sleep with me or with Earl [Miller].[7] It is nice to have him [Major] though I rather dreaded it & know I shall be an idiot when I say good-bye! I do know how you feel about Prinz & sometimes it makes me ache.[8] I've had a walk & a swim & sun after lunch & then read out under a tree for a couple of hours & now will soon have dinner.

Your work sounds strenuous but are you resting? A world of love dear one, be good!

E.R.

August 13th

Campobello Island
New Brunswick, Canada

Dearest one, Two letters to-day because there was no mail yesterday & I had a grand time all by myself reading them.

Nan & I were left alone for a time this morning, & she was making drawings[9] so I sat on the porch & read in the sun & thought a great deal about you. I am so glad you are feeling better & cutting down on ciga-rettes & above all I'm glad you've been to the ear doctor & it was not so painful. The one ear must have been pretty bad though for probing & scraping is never comfortable! Poor dear, how *idiotic* to think you could do anything political particularly in that California mess.

Yes, I am happy here & one reason, of course[,] is the place but there are other reasons & I was analyzing them to-day, perhaps the main one

[6] Major was Eleanor's German shepherd who had been left at Hyde Park when the Roo-sevelts moved to Washington.

[7] Earl Miller, the former FDR bodyguard who had become a close friend of Eleanor, was va-cationing with her.

[8] Lorena was feeling increasingly concerned about her dog Prinz, who had been confined to a kennel in New York City since she had begun her government job in August 1933.

[9] Nan Cook designed the furniture that was then crafted at the Val-Kill factory.

is that I think I am needed & wanted—I suppose that is why I enjoy being with Anna & John [Boettiger]. So often with the boys I feel tolerated! What curious creatures we are!

Well, dear one, be careful & take good care of yourself, precious person.

Lovingly,
E.R.

My pen just gave out & I am too far from the house to get the ink just now!

In the final paragraph of this letter, Lorena obliquely apologizes for losing her temper in Yosemite and then expresses her hope that Eleanor's life has been more peaceful since that trip. At the very end of the letter, the first friend describes the pain she feels when she is separated from the first lady, followed by a pledge to try to remain emotionally stable.

August 15th

Hotel El Tejon
Bakersfield, California

Dear You:

Well—another day gone. A long day of driving about seeing things, with the chairman of the county board of supervisors and several relief people. The most interesting thing I saw was the little village of adobe houses built by Allan Hoover[10] on his ranch for his migratory workers.

A syndicate in which the former president is said to be a dominant figure owns a ranch, four square miles, near here. They raise mostly cotton and alfalfa. Young Allan Hoover is managing the place.

One of the principal causes of the labor trouble in the Imperial and San Joaquin valleys last winter lay, as you may know, in the unspeakably bad housing provided for the seasonal migratory workers, who come in to pick cotton and harvest the fruit and vegetable crops.

---

[10] Allan Hoover was the son of former President Herbert Hoover.

Tall and thin, with her lumi-nous golden hair piled on top of her head, fifteen-year-old Anna Eleanor Roosevelt was the epitome of the era's fash-ionable "Gibson girl" style.

In her high school graduation picture, eighteen-year-old Lorena Hickok appeared far more shy and sedate than the hard-driving newspaper reporter she soon would become.

Eleanor gave Lorena this photo, ta
as she exited the White House afte
meeting with First Lady Lou Henr
Hoover in early 1933 in preparatic
the Roosevelts' moving into the m.
sion. ER wrote on the photo: "We
only separated by a few yards dea
& I wonder which of us felt most
Eleanor Roosevelt."

Eleanor placed Lorena's photogra
above and slightly to the right of t
center of the mantel in her bedroo
that she could kiss it as soon as sh
each morning and just before she
to bed each night.

...or took this unflattering photo of Lorena ...remote Canadian beach during their road ...The poor technical quality of this photo ...be the reason it has never previously been ...shed.

Lorena took this photo of Eleanor leaning against the porch of one of the log cabins the women stayed in during their "incognito" holiday in French Canada.

...uring Eleanor and Lorena's 1933 holiday, many French Canadians paid more ...ttention to the luxurious Buick convertible than to the woman who drove it, ...ailing to recognize the wife of America's new president.

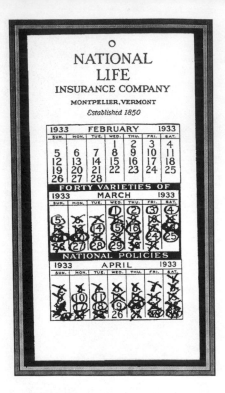

(Left) After Eleanor became first lady, Hick use[d] pocket calendar to record the days the two wo[men] spent together. Lorena circled the days they we[re] together and slashed Xs through the days they [had] to spend apart.

(Right) Eleanor was comfortable wearing fur pieces, gloves, and dresses made of velvet and other rich fabrics, but Lorena generally preferred less feminine attire.

Lorena stood next to Eleanor as the first lady greeted well-wishers who h[ad] gathered in Miami to see her depart for the women's trip to the Caribbean [in] March 1934.

In the spring of 1933, Eleanor posed in front of her brand new 1933 light blue Buick roadster. Lorena can be seen in the background on the far left, with her hands on her hips. The woman talking to Lorena and with her back to the camera is secretary Tommy Thompson.

During a stop on Eleanor and Lorena's July 1933 road trip, in which the two women drove alone to French Canada, the first lady was photographed with two unidentified admirers. Lorena, in the V-neck sweater, put her hands behind her back and chose not to look toward the camera.

This previously unpublished photo, taken by the St. Lawrence River during ER and Hick's July 1933 road trip, illustrates some of the differences between the two women. ER stands tall and slender in a double-breasted pastel suit; she wears a hat and white gloves. Hick is slumped forward and wears a dark sweater woven in a bold plaid pattern, no hat and no gloves.

(Left) This photo, taken as Eleanor and Lorena arrived in Puerto Rico, shows the women walking forward side by side. The first lady still wore her hat and remained poised after the flight from Miami; Hick, however, had discarded her hat and jacket, and her linen dress was looking decidedly rumpled.

(Right) This photo was taken on [Lor]ena's forty-first birthday (March [7], 1934) and shows Hick and ER standing on either side of Virgin Islands Governor Paul Pearson.

[Lo]rena became angry when dozens of American newspapers chose to publish [th]is photograph that showed the first lady—but also her first friend—visiting a [Sa]n Juan slum.

During her years of working for the New York World's Fair and the Democratic National Committee, Hick wore tailored business suits and no jewelry.

On the twentieth anniversary of ER's first White House press conference, Eleanor hosted a reunion at the Algonquin Hotel in New York. Lorena is on the far left wearing eyeglasses and a shawl.

Though the growers are supposed to provide decent housing and sanitary conditions for these people, they don't. Most of the workers live in tent colonies, with no water and no sanitation. Many of them live on the banks of the irrigation ditches and drink the ditch water.

Some of the more liberal growers have started a movement to provide better housing, but, so far, young Hoover is the only one who has actually done anything. I visited his ranch today. Fortunately he was away. I think we both might have been somewhat embarrassed had he been at home.[11]

It's funny, but ten miles away from the Hoover ranch, on the outskirts of Bakersfield, is a place called "Hoover City"—a jungle of tents, cardboard houses, built out of cartons, no sanitation whatever. In "Hoover City" live 100 families, wretchedly—itinerant farm workers, oil workers out of jobs, unemployed of all sorts. It's a terrible place, like thousands of other terrible places growing up on the outskirts of our towns. The tent colony in West Virginia really wasn't any worse, except that the winters are colder in West Virginia. What *are* we going to do with these people?

Last night I was looking at maps. Many, many miles lie between us, dear one.

Good night, I hope you are having a happy, restful time at camp—a happier, more peaceful time than you had with me. Oh, I'm bad, my dear, but I love you so. At times life becomes just one long, dreary ache for you. But I'm trying to be happy and contented.

H

August 18th

Campobello Island
New Brunswick, Canada

Hick darling, Yesterday p.m. yours of the 13th came & this morning the one sent on the 14th. So as I had missed for a day[,] I feel very rich. They

[11] Lorena was part of the Roosevelt administration that had defeated Allan Hoover's father.

are amusing too & your efforts to be polite[12] are most praiseworthy but I know how you have hated it. Poor dear, what I have put you through! We won't do public things any more & you'll be spared all this.[13] I can just see you writhe!

At least you sound as though work were of interest again & I am awaiting the reports with anticipation!

I went off for three hours yesterday to see Elinor Morgenthau. Her mother is at Loon [Lake] & I do think she is far from well so for once I could be really sympathetic.

One week is over & a week from to-day, the 25th, I will be home & for the rest of the year, with only a week end or a few days now & then, I will be "Mrs. Roosevelt"—we'll try to have our times to-gether in N.Y. quiet & unobserved however!

The sun is out & we are off to float around in the motor boat.

I miss you dear & think of you so much & love you dearly,

E.R.

The third paragraph of this letter is one of many apologies that ER offered during this period.

August 21st

Campobello Island
New Brunswick, Canada

Darling, I hope stepchild[14] gets you back safely but I don't like the way she is behaving & if it continues we'll turn it in for a new one!

Thanks for the "Post" [article] but I had seen it.[15]

Yes, dear, you are right I give everyone the feeling that you have that I've "taken them on" & don't need anything from them & then when

---

[12] Lorena had to struggle not to become angry when people recognized her as the first lady's friend.

[13] Lorena detested spending time with Nan Cook and Marion Dickerman; Hick considered the same-sex couple snobs. She also was jealous of the time Nan and Marion spent with ER.

[14] "Stepchild" was the Plymouth that had replaced Bluette after Lorena's accident in Arizona.

they naturally resent it & don't like to accept from me, I wonder why! It's funny I know & I can't help it, something locked me up & I can't un-lock!

A world of love dear, I'll be in Hyde Park on Sat.

Devotedly,

E.R.

In late August, Lorena had written from Salt Lake City that she had be-come ill with severe intestinal pains. Eleanor offered to cut short her va-cation and fly across the country to be with her ailing friend. But in keeping with Eleanor's new restraint, she did not speak of wanting to cradle Lorena in her arms or lie down beside her. Also, Eleanor's state-ments in the letter clearly suggest that she felt sorry for Lorena in the same way that she did for the recently divorced Earl Miller—both were people to be pitied.

[August 31]

Val-Kill Cottage

Hick darling, I was so distressed by your letter to-day. Did you ever have typhoid inoculations? I sent you a wire to-night for I felt I wanted to know how you really were. If you are really ill I will fly out of course.

Well, as far as I'm concerned, a ride this a.m. & work at the cottage with Tommy til noon, a talk with a Miss Roberts, who has been after the stock exchange for 14 years & is about to publish her case, lunch,

---

[15] In its August 4 edition, the *Saturday Evening Post* had published a devastating exposé of the subsistence homestead project in West Virginia. The article reported that Louis Howe, eager to respond to the high priority the first lady had placed on the project, had ordered fifty Cape Cod prefabricated houses to be shipped to Arthurdale. The houses were fine for a young couple on summer vacation at a beach resort, but they were totally inadequate for large Ap-palachian families enduring harsh winters. Also, the former coal miners who were in charge of erecting their own houses had mis-measured the dimensions. Only after the houses had been shipped and assembled did the homesteaders realize that the houses didn't fit the cinder block foundations they had built. This combination of errors meant that the inexpensive houses had been constructed and painted, then torn down, then rebuilt and repainted, and then modified and repainted once again. The estimated $2,000 that each was supposed to cost had soared to a staggering $10,000.

the [Henry and Elinor] Morgenthaus with three men from the Treasury,
2 women to see me about a radio idea, then work again till 6. The [Rex
and Florence] Tugwells[16] & [Harry and Barbara] Hopkinses arrived &
Mr. Hopkins seemed to know you were ill. Both were much concerned.
Tommy & I worked & we are up on back mail & have part of my radio
address done.

Oh! dear one, what wouldn't I give to have you here with me to-night
& know just how you are & be able to take care of you. I always feel
that you & Earl [Miller] need me more than anyone when things go
wrong for neither of you have anyone much nearer to turn to whom I
must remember not to offend!

A world of love & I hope I hear you are better to-morrow—

Devotedly,
E.R.

*Lorena ultimately realized, after medicating herself around the clock for
three days, that her intestinal pains had been brought on by water she
drank from a desert spring intended only for cattle.*

September 1st

Val-Kill Cottage

Hick darling, Your letter to-day was a relief in one way as I was afraid
of typhoid tho' I hoped you had been inoculated. However, I am worried now because I wired you last night & got no answer to-day. I'll
send another wire to-morrow if I don't hear for I must go to you if you
are really ill & yet I hope you are up & about again. Mr. Hopkins said
to-day that your reports would be the best history of the depression in
future years. He says he had sent you word to drive all the way home as
he wants you to stay in the East for a time. I fear this means you won't
get back quite as soon. Well, let me know when you can & I'll meet you
in Washington & we'll manage some quiet days to ourselves whatever

---

[16] Rex Tugwell was assistant secretary of agriculture.

happens. I'm glad you'll be in the East for I like to have you a little more accessible!

It has been a hectic day the men have been conferring & [Assistant Secretary of the Interior] Oscar Chapman has joined us for the week end. We all went to the Morgenthaus' for a clambake this evening. It was a grand party & Franklin was in grand form. He is very angry with [Budget Director] Lewis Douglas for choosing this moment to resign tho' he's glad to have him out[17] & somehow he worked his rage out by having a grand time!

Bless you dear one,

E.R.

Perhaps as the first lady's way of showing that she still needed Lorena, Eleanor had begun sending the former reporter drafts of articles that she was planning to submit to magazines before she sent them to the editors. The article that Eleanor mentions in this letter was about the Great Depression's impact on the American people. The revised article appeared in Cosmopolitan *three months later.*

October 3d
[Fort Worth]

Darling, It was good to find your two letters to-day & I am terribly grateful for all the work you did on that article.

We had a smooth & quick flight here & Elliott & Ruth have such a nice place. The house is charming & the baby [Ruth Chandler Roosevelt] so like Elliott at her age!

I'll leave early Sunday & it will be good to see you dear & we will have a peaceful time!

A world of love,

E.R.

[17] Lewis Douglas had vehemently opposed FDR's departure from the gold standard, predicting that it would result in "the death of Western civilization."

*The peaceful time that Eleanor had been hoping for was not to be. Al-
though the details of the incident are not clear, this note shows that she
and Lorena had a conversation that Lorena had found quite distressing.
Eleanor apparently was agitated as well, as she wrote this note so hur-
riedly that she neglected to date it. A White House servant hand delivered the note to Lorena.*

Hick my darling, That cry of "I want something all my own" is the cry
of the heart & I was near to tears last night. You told me once it was
hard to let go but I found it was harder to let go & yet hold on. Love as
much & yet share. Gosh! I sound horrible but I mean that you taught
me more than you know & it brought me happiness & I wish I could
bring it to you. I bring you *un*happiness & if I didn't think in the end it
would make you happier I'd be desperately unhappy for I love you &
you've made of me so much more of a person just to be worthy of you—
Je t'aime et je t'adore,

                                                            E.R.

I hope you overslept but I fear you had a bad night.

*The tone of this letter demonstrates how Lorena's moods could over-
whelm her and affect everything she did—including reading newspaper
stories. Her criticizing Eleanor for wearing an expensive dress is the first
example in the correspondence of Lorena confronting the first lady so
boldly.*

                                                    November 2nd
                            Lord Baltimore Hotel
                            Baltimore, Maryland

Dear You:
Damn the newspapers! Here I am, keen to know what you said last
night and how it went.[18] And what do the papers carry? One of them

---

[18] Eleanor had given a speech in New York City.

described you in a blue velvet dinner gown, described all the prominent people present and "Mrs. Roosevelt" leaving after her speech but not a word on the content—I hated it.

I'm feeling pretty "red" tonight. Contact with relief clients makes me that way. And I've had a lot of it these last two days. God damn it, none of us ought to be wearing velvet dinner gowns these days. Not when, as the chief attendance officer in the Baltimore public schools said today, 4,000 Baltimore children couldn't go to school in September because they didn't have clothes. As she was saying that, the thought of you in a blue velvet dinner gown—even though you are my friend and I love you—irritated me profoundly. Sometimes I get so sick of this whole damned mess!

I must go to work on my notes. Darling—in a blue velvet dinner gown or out of it—I love you.

H

Eleanor and Lorena had planned to celebrate the beginning of the Christmas season with an evening in New York City—dinner, then the symphony. But as this letter shows, when the ailing Louis Howe asked the first lady to spend that same evening with him, she could not refuse.

[November 3, a.m.]

THE WHITE HOUSE
Washington

Darling, Of course I want you Dec. 13th but Louis wants to be there if he feels well enough & if so I think I'll have to devote my evening to him. You & I can have an hour alone & then we can all dine to-gether but if Louis is here he will want to come back [to the Roosevelt townhouse] & talk [after the concert] & I think you'd better stay the night at the apartment.[19] Can you go down to Washington with me on the Wed. midnight or must you go back & work before you come in Thursday? The concert is at 8:45 & we'll dine at 7:30.

---

[19] Now that Lorena was working on the East Coast, she was spending part of her time in her New York apartment.

My dear, I know you will be disappointed & I am distressed but Louis seems so miserable I would feel horrible to tell him I couldn't look after him that evening. You know I'd rather be with you & carefree & dear I love you deeply & tenderly!

A world of love,

E.R.

[November 3, p.m.]

Val-Kill Cottage

Hick dearest, Here we are & the country looks nice! The morning was spent at the dentist, then a Women's Trade Union League meeting at the house with photographs & the reporters to play up their concert & then Nan & Tommy & I had crackers & milk. I came over to the cottage & have cleaned up lots of odds & ends.

I must go back to dress for dinner in a few minutes—but wanted to get this off to tell you I think I'll get in about 4:30[20] & we could have tea at five if you'd pick me up at the house & then walk to the apartment & I can stay till 6 or we can stay in my room [at the Roosevelt townhouse] & shut & lock the door for a quiet hour.

Your letter has just come. Darling, if we all stopped wearing velvet dresses there would be worse times than there are, if you have money you must spend it now, so I don't feel as guilty as you do, of course if you could give it all where it would do the most good that would be grand but we can't always do that!

A world of love dear,

E.R.

The first paragraph of this letter, which Eleanor wrote during the Thanksgiving holiday, indicates that Lorena was still agitated—this

---

[20] Eleanor was planning a trip to New York City where Lorena also was staying.

time feeling inadequate professionally. Eleanor's comments suggest that she was becoming frustrated with Hick's recurring emotional up-heavals.

November 22d

Georgia Warm Springs Foundation

Hick darling, If only it could be proved to you that as a reporter & holding successfully the job you do you had earned recognition & that knowing me had nothing to do with it, you would get some satisfaction out of your well deserved recognition but as it is you can't. I doubt if anyone can ever make up to you for having saddled you with such a burden, oh! well, there is nothing I can do about it!

It is gray—rained hard all night so I didn't ride but we swam & then Nan & Tommy & I lunched with F.D.R. & have now left him to talk & come down to work ourselves. At three I am going to have a hair wash & manicure & if it clears I may ride at 4:30 but it still looks gray so I probably won't!

The mail must go. A world of love,

E.R.

After the disaster that resulted from Lorena trying to stay at the White House for Christmas a year earlier, Eleanor had suggested that it might be best if Lorena spent Christmas Day in New York City and then came to Washington the next day, after most of the public activities had ended.

Xmas Eve

THE WHITE HOUSE
Washington

Hick darling, This may greet you to-morrow evening when you return a bit weary from a long day so I want it to tell you that I love you dearly & am deeply grateful every day for your love & friendship. I get more than I give on every side I know.

This has been a busy day. 9:45 Fox Theatre, returned saw everyone, dressed Xmas tree, 12 Executive Office Building, 2:30 Salvation Army, 3:30 house staff & all the others, 5 municipal tree lighting ceremonies, then did up things for Xmas dinner & now I am dressing with interruptions to hang up the chicks['] stockings & write this! After dinner carols then fill stockings & Tommy's going with me at 11:30 to St. Thomas'[21] for the service & then I'm going in with her for a minute—to take her her presents!

I'll be talking to you in the morning, till then Bless you & all my love,

E.R.

Xmas night

THE WHITE HOUSE
Washington

Hick darling, Even tho' I know you may come home to-morrow[22] I want to tell you how I loved your presents all by myself after I got home from midnight service & a visit with Tommy last night! It was X-mas so I opened them when I could do it leisurely & enjoy them & above all I loved the notes. Your telegram to-day was grand too & dear one I do hope the worst is over for you & many happy days are in store this coming year for us to-gether.

My travelling cases & hankies are going to be in constant use & the wool undies are so soft I think I will like them for riding. You knew I had a weakness for little brown pots & for honey! I can hardly wait to get the dress to suit the buckle or to share the poems with Sisty—& the dog with a sponge & my beast of burden for the menagerie are going to delight me, also the head band when I get to know how to put it on! You were fearfully extravagant but I enjoyed your extravagance too much to scold you! A thousand, thousand thanks.

---

[21] St. Thomas' Episcopal Church is located at the corner of Eighteenth and Church streets in Washington.
[22] Lorena was coming down from New York to spend a few days between Christmas and New Year's at the White House.

It has been a happy day for everyone I think & I think it worked out well for Anna & John too. Dinner went well for them & everyone seemed to enjoy it.

A world of love & gratitude for you & your love,

E.R.

I'm calling in the a.m. to find out when you leave.

Six

1935

"Life's Rough Seas"

Although Eleanor and Lorena continued to write lovingly and support-
ively to each other during the new year, on more than one occasion their
letters revealed that the first friend was not happy with the first lady's
decision to reduce the intensity of their relationship. Numerous times
during this year of transition, letters from Lorena included either verbal
attacks on Eleanor or references to instances when Hick had behaved
rudely. Sometimes the first lady allowed the comments or actions to
pass; other times she fired back—saying she wanted to *shake* Lorena,
chastising Lorena for overreacting, refusing to accept anything short of
a full apology for a hurtful comment. As the fireworks in the letters at-
test, this was a year during which, as Eleanor wrote in her valentine,
they were definitely navigating over "life's rough seas."

ER's letters also revealed that the first lady and the president were
traveling over waters that were sometimes other than tranquil—even to
the point that Eleanor considered leaving him.

As 1935 began, Lorena was living in Washington while Harry Hopkins decided where he wanted her to travel next. After ten days, Lorena became so restless and irritable staying at the White House with nothing to do—the first lady was busier than ever with her various duties and commitments—that she went to New York City.

[January 20]

THE WHITE HOUSE
Washington

Hick dearest, I am so sorry you had such a bad time, things always are serious with you & I ought to know it. Well, I hope you are better today.

I walked around the Tidal Basin[1] this a.m., had several people to lunch & then the colored group from Charleston sang spirituals. I wish you could have heard them, it was lovely & they looked charming.

Hick darling, I want you too but you would be more unhappy, as you were, hanging round here while I went thro' this deadly round. At least in N.Y. you've got people you like & a city you enjoy.

I love you dear one[,] late this evening I will telephone,

E.R.

After a month of waiting idly to return to work, Lorena became depressed; she had too much time to lament the course that her life had taken. Her complaints to Eleanor prompted the intriguing—and perplexing—statement in the first paragraph of this letter.

[February 1]

THE WHITE HOUSE
Washington

Hick dearest, Of course you should have had a husband & children & it would have made you happy if you loved him & in any case it would

---

[1] The Tidal Basin is the lagoon in front of the Jefferson Memorial a few blocks from the White House.

have satisfied certain cravings & given you someone on whom to lavish the love & devotion you have to keep down all the time. Yours is a rich nature with so much to give that the outlets always seem meager. Dear one, I do love you & appreciate the fight you make not to make me unhappy, but there is no use trying to hide things from me because I know just how you feel!

Took Louis Howe [for a drive],[2] worked a bit till had Mrs. Woodrow Wilson[3] to tea with the family. Swam with F.D.R., rested an hour & [had] just the household for dinner.

Haven't had a minute to read as I must get these [syndicate] articles & sample broadcasts done.[4] When I get them in shape I'll send them to you. I really am trying to do better work but it is hard to find the time.[5]

Earl [Miller] has a new girl he thinks he is or may be in love with, but he is a skeptic on anything lasting & his state of mind & his letters are reminiscent of others I have known![6] What a nuisance hearts are & yet without them life would hardly be worthwhile!

Well, I've talked & knitted all evening so now I must get to work on the mail. A world of love & I wish I could put my arms around you,

E.R.

The valentine that Eleanor sent Lorena showed a black and white puppy holding a small heart that read "To My Valentine." The following verse that the first lady hand wrote on the back of the card ended

[2] FDR's political mentor, now a near invalid, continued to live on the second floor of the White House. Eleanor often took him for drives to get him out of the mansion.

[3] Eleanor had become friends with Edith Bolling Gault Wilson when FDR was serving in President Wilson's administration.

[4] Eleanor was continuing to write monthly newspaper articles for the McNaught Syndicate and now was also attempting to persuade Selby Shoe Company to sponsor a series of radio programs.

[5] ER earned $70,000 for her radio broadcasts during 1934 and 1935. In one memorable program, she enlisted the help of her press "girls" to stage a White House press conference broadcast live on the air.

[6] Eleanor's comment about Earl's discontent with life may have been an allusion to Lorena's similar feelings.

with a phrase reflecting the troubled nature of their relationship at the time.

[February 12]

May the world be full of sunshine,
And our meetings frequent be
Hours of joy & quiet time,
Take us over life's rough seas.

Lorena had announced that she was coming to Washington without first consulting with Eleanor. Because of her busy schedule, Eleanor couldn't spend as much time alone with the first friend as Hick wanted. Lorena exploded—expressing her anger through what the first lady considered rude behavior.

[February 20]

THE WHITE HOUSE
Washington

Dearest, I think you can scarcely realize how you made me feel to-night. I did not ask you to dine to be rude & yet you made me feel that I had been. You went right by me at the studio [where Eleanor was doing a radio broadcast] without speaking. You told me you would entertain yourself in Washington before I had time to tell you whether I was busy or not, you barely spoke to Earl [Miller] & Jane [Earl's companion] at the play who were my guests & certainly did nothing rude to you & when I asked you to go in so you could sit by me[,] you deliberately changed & sat as far away as possible. I am sorry if I've done something to offend [you] but I'm so deeply hurt to-night that I almost wish I had no friends. Acquaintances at least preserve the social amenities & make life pleasant on the surface. I was happy to be seeing you but evidently you were not. For Sat. & Sun.[7] at least let's try to be cheerful & polite & not make everyone around us uncomfortable!

E.R.

---

[7] Eleanor had asked Lorena to join her in the various activities she had planned for the weekend.

In April, Harry Hopkins sent Lorena to Michigan to assess the relief programs and the political climate in that pivotal state with its combination of industrial and agricultural bases. Meanwhile, Eleanor's frustrations with her friend were temporarily superseded by her outright rage with members of the first family.

[April 27]

THE WHITE HOUSE
Washington

Hick darling, I've had a most disturbing day, my day began badly last night when James told me that after I'd told Mama it would not break my heart if Franklin were not reelected & I left [the room], she turned to him & said "Do you think Mother will do anything to defeat Father? Is that why she stays in politics, just to hurt his chances of reelection?" Now I ask you, after all these years?

Then he told me that Fjr. said if we didn't make any more effort to understand him he thought he would just leave college & so would I make a little effort! This a.m. comes a letter from Fjr., he will row at Annapolis the 25th & come home afterwards. This last is the most disconcerting for that is our week end on Long Island,[8] could you delay a week & go the next week end? I hate it because I miss you & want to see you but I ought to be here the 25th & see Fjr. row. Let me know what you can manage & please don't be upset.

I love you dearly & very tenderly,

E.R.

By the following letter, the first lady had become furious with her husband's insensitivity toward their oldest son. James, eager to please and be close to his father, had arranged to sell his insurance business in New York and move to Washington to work as his father's personal aide. Franklin originally had approved the plan. But when newspapers accused him of nepotism, the president changed his mind. Eleanor

---

[8] Eleanor had promised Lorena they could spend a weekend alone at the Long Island cottage of friends.

agreed that James should not be given the job, but when her husband lied to both her and their son about the real reason behind his change of heart, her anger rose dangerously close to the breaking point.

[April 28]

THE WHITE HOUSE
Washington

Dear one, I'm ready to chew everyone's head off! Franklin calmly tells me that the doctors think the heat will be bad here [this summer] for James[9] so he is only having him down for visits till autumn. James[,] looking upset & bewildered[,] meets me outside & says his health has nothing to do with it[,] but he thinks F.D.R. is afraid if he gives up his work it will bring more newspaper stories so [James] having [already] spent $1000 on legally getting out of [his] business has been told by Pa to buy his business back. He's going back to N.Y. to-morrow etc. He's hurt & I am so mad with F.D.R.!

　　I'm so on edge it is all I can do to hold myself to-gether just now,

E.R.

Eleanor was so angry at the president that Lorena feared that the first lady was on the verge of divorcing him. In the beginning of this letter, Eleanor confides that she had, in fact, considered making an "open break" from her husband.

[May 2]

THE WHITE HOUSE
Washington

Hick darling, I'm sorry I worried you so much. I know I've got to stick. I know I'll never make an open break & I never tell F.D.R. how I feel. He still thinks I accepted & believed his story [that the doctors advised against James moving to Washington for health reasons] & he has probably persuaded himself by now that that was his real reason. I blow off

---

[9] James had sometimes suffered from various health problems.

to you but never to F.! Of course it is better for James not to be here &
I knew that from the start[,] but it was done in a way which hurt him
because he wanted to come & I hate to see so sweet a person hurt. However dear one, I am quite in hand again so don't worry & I love you very
much.[10]

Darling I do take happiness in many ways & I'm never likely to fight
with F. I always "shut up."

The many teas are making my feet ache so I'll be glad of a letup on
Sat. & Sunday!

Dearest I'm only unhappy [in] spots & heaven knows, most people
are! I'm not a bit sorry for myself there are plenty of people [who]
would enjoy what I dislike & discipline is good for us all so while I like
you to be sympathetic & grieve over me, don't let it really worry you for
I get over it quickly & I don't suffer the way you would.

You do a lot always for me dearest one, & your understanding &
sweetness is a help even tho' I may not deserve it. Ever so much love,

E.R.

*By the following letter, Eleanor's focus had shifted back to her troubled
relationship with Hick. In this letter, she asserts that she would never
allow another scene of public humiliation like the one that had erupted
at Yosemite the previous summer. The first lady felt so strongly about
the importance of maintaining her poise, in fact, that recalling the incident led to one of her rare instances of using profanity.*

[May 7]

THE WHITE HOUSE
Washington

Dearest, One thing I differ with you on, the thing which counts in the
long run is never any *one* person's happiness, it is that of the *greatest*

---

[10] James returned to New York. It was not until several years later that he finally moved to
Washington to serve as FDR's secretary. Curiously, the concerns that his father had raised in
1935 eventually proved valid, as a combination of the stress of the White House job and press
charges that he was using the position for personal gain forced James to resign and seek treatment for an ulcer—two-thirds of his stomach ultimately had to be removed.

number of people. Remember always that you are damned *un*important! No, dear, we won't have scenes. I made up my mind to that last time.

Things are going smoothly dear & I am happy but I wish with all my heart that you were also.

I love you & would like to hug you to-night. I suppose you are off to Flint [Michigan], so good luck attend you wherever you are & bless you,

　　　　　　　　　　　　　　　　　　　　　　　E.R.

In this letter, the first lady describes her philosophy regarding love, while simultaneously trying to explain to Lorena why she had to reduce the intensity of their relationship.

　　　　　　　　　　　　　　　　　　　　　　　[May 13]

THE WHITE HOUSE
Washington

Dear one, Your wire came this morning to my joy & I found 3 letters here which was also a joy, Wed. Thurs. & Friday & the last has made me think & try to formulate what I believe about happiness. I think it is this way, to most of us happiness comes thro' the love we give & the return love we feel comes to us from those we love. There does not have to be a balance however, we may love more or less some since there is no measure of love. Over the years the type of love felt on either side may change but if the fundamental love is there, I believe in the end the relationship adjusts to something deep & satisfying to both people. For instance, I know you often have a feeling for me which for one reason or another I may not return in kind but I feel I love you just the same & so often we entirely satisfy each other that I feel there is a fundamental basis on which our relationship stands. I love other people in the same way or differently but each one has their place & one cannot compare them. I do know for myself that if I know someone I love is unhappy I can't be happy & I would be happier to see or to know they were happy even if it meant giving up my own relationship to them in whole or in part. I'd probably hope to get it back enriched someday but if not, well, I know no one I love I wouldn't rather see happy & I hope they wouldn't worry about my hurt because it would be so much less than watching them hurt. I don't think I'd run away either, unless they wanted me to! I'm always worried tho' for this means that I am a person of little depth & really don't know what suffering such as you go thro' is really like.

Well, I must go to bed. I love you dearly & miss you much dear person. Sleep sweetly,

E.R.

After spending the first weekend in June with Eleanor in New York, Lorena left for Missouri to assess the president's popularity in that largely agricultural state. Lorena planned to finish her trip by the end of the month. Meanwhile, ER was pursuing, in earnest, her magazine writing.

June 6th

49 East 65th Street

New York

Hick dearest, I've looked up in my book & I think you & I had better try to spend the 28th & 29th to-gether in Washington getting back for dinner the 29th.

Young [George] Lorrimer[11] sounded interested & Mr. [George] Bye[12] very nice but Lord knows if I will succeed, however let us hope for the best!

Darling, last week end seems a beautiful dream but it gave me so much that is a joy to think about.

---

[11] George Lorrimer was editor of the *Saturday Evening Post*.

[12] George Bye was a well-regarded figure in New York literary circles who had agreed to become Eleanor's literary agent and help her to publish articles in major magazines.

You will never learn what a strong personality you have & how much people admire you but then I like that about you!

Devoted ever,
E.R.

The topic that Eleanor chose to launch her new effort to earn money as a magazine writer was the modern American woman's role vis-à-vis her husband and children. Because Eleanor saw this article as a major state-ment to American women, she hoped to publish it in the Saturday Evening Post, *one of the most widely read—and highest paying—maga-zines in the country. The first lady sent a first draft of her manuscript to Lorena for editing and would spend the next several months polishing that draft into final form.*

[June 24]

49 East 65th Street
New York

My own dear one, I know you are a perfectionist & just how hard all my writing problems are for you. I think you hold yourself pretty strictly to your standards both in your work & in your life & that is why you are disappointed in others when they fall down.

I've been working on the article to-day & thinking of you & trying to make myself really work on it! I had my hair & nails done too & worked at books, etc. Tommy & I lunched at a soda fountain.

I am sorry you are so tired & hope you won't get home exhausted for it will be hot I fear in Washington.

I'm awfully sleepy to-night & so good night dearest, sleep well & I will be so happy to see you on Friday. Ever so much love,

E.R.

Eleanor spent July and early August at the Roosevelt summer house on Campobello Island. Her secretary Tommy Thompson and her friends

and business associates Nan Cook and Marion Dickerman accompanied the first lady, but her thoughts were often on the time that she and Lorena had spent on the island at the end of their road trip to the Gaspé Peninsula two years earlier.

July 30th

Campobello Island
New Brunswick, Canada

Darling, I've been thinking so much to-day of our last visit here & I am cherishing the memories for it was such a happy time, wasn't it?

The enclosed wasn't ready last night. I hope it will interest you. I put a lot of work on it but I know it is controversial & will cause violent differences of opinion. Marion for instance disagrees with a lot of it! Tommy didn't think I'd handle it this way & is interested but I don't think entirely in agreement either!

You can be as tough as you like in your criticism. I know my tendency to make speeches. I want to do good work & I want the help which you can give me, no one else is half as good as a critic & I'm very grateful to you & don't mind at all!

A world of love to you dearest,

E.R.

Please return air mail.[13]

In late July, Harry Hopkins sent Lorena to New York to gauge the political climate in that populous state with its large number of electoral

---

[13] The article, published by *Cosmopolitan* in October, was, indeed, controversial. It began with a concise summary of the first lady's thesis: "Can a woman be elected President? Certainly, a woman *can* be elected President, in all probability some time a woman *will* be, but she *may* not, in my opinion, be elected at the present time, or in the near future." Eleanor said society's perceptions of women and women's own behavior were both impediments to a woman being elected president. She concluded with practical—but some would also say radical—advice on how American women could move toward having one of their own sex as chief executive: "They must learn to take other women with them. They must learn that only in proportion as women as a whole are educated in public affairs will individual women succeed in positions of importance."

votes. In this letter sent to Eleanor at the Roosevelt summer home, Lorena laments her reduced stature among the many people in the first lady's life.

July 31st

DeWitt Clinton Hotel
Albany, New York

My very dear one:

The sunset at Campobello Sunday night must have been very lovely, and it was nice to think that you wished I were there. You're probably right, though, when you say I'd not be very happy. I'd probably feel like a fifth wheel. Well—never mind, darling! The time will come when it won't matter to me that there are so many others who have priority rights to your interest and affection. Then I daresay we'll all be one nice big happy family. You must admit, though, it's sometimes rather tough to be the most recent of the people who have any claim on you! I have no seniority rating at all. I'm so very much an "outsider." But when the time comes when I don't care so much—or at least not in the *way* I care now—it will be easier. Anyway, I'm glad you're up there and enjoying it. And we'll have our time together later on.

Saw the Works Progress Administration[14] man [for New York state] this afternoon. He's certainly hard boiled enough. Maybe he's right. I don't know. But it *does* strike me that we're slightly inconsistent in our attitudes toward—and treatment of—the unemployed.

We start out, in 1933, by working ourselves up into a sort of frenzy of sympathy for them. We do everything we can to make the acceptance of relief "respectable." We put in a Civil Works Administration program with wages way above those paid in private industry.

And now, in the state of New York in 1935, we turn 'em over to a man who seems to think, rightly or wrongly, that they *are* bums and chiselers, goes at his job with this attitude.

"By God, we'll quit coddling these babies and get 'em off relief!"

I don't know quite *what* to make of it. I know one thing I'm going to

---

[14] The Works Progress Administration replaced the Federal Emergency Relief Administration as the branch of the federal government putting the unemployed back to work.

do, Madame. I'm going to start seeing relief clients again [not just relief administrators], in Syracuse, Rochester, and Buffalo.

In some ways, probably, the WPA man is right. He's making the cities come through with more money, he says. And the state. He said the Governor wanted him to do all the state projects entirely with federal money.

But, my gosh, he seems to think most of the women he's going to have to put to work ought to be working as domestics. God damn it—I just wish some of these people who think all unemployed women ought to be delighted to hire themselves out as maids or scrubwomen had to take a whack at it themselves. Believe, me, Madame, I've *been* a servant—a maid—in a boarding house! I know what it's *like*. People make me sick.

And so it goes!

Good night, dearest. Oh, you *are* a grand person! And I love you.

H

August 2d

Campobello Island
New Brunswick, Canada

Dearest one, Your letter of the 31st came to-day & I had to laugh! No dear, we won't ever be a happy family party here! We might spend a night or even a week end in close proximity now & then but never more, somebody's feelings would be hurt & I'm too old to handle the strain. You & I will always want to have some time alone to-gether where we spend any length of time in a place where life is not in a routine like Washington.

I am much disturbed at some of the things [Assistant Secretary of Agriculture] Rex [Tugwell] is doing in the [subsistence] Homesteads without preparation I fear. You know I think they are all a bit too efficient & not quite human enough. I'm afraid I'm too personal though!

Marion & Tommy & I walked some 3 miles, perhaps four, but Nan has given out & Tommy is pretty stiff! Marion & I also played a set of very bad tennis. This evening I read aloud "Goodbye Mr. Chips"[15] now all have gone to bed except Tommy who is reading.

I'll wire you to-morrow to Syracuse.

I guess you will get more & more grief wherever you go! You should see relief clients, I think it may be valuable in many ways.

I'd like to be able to give you a kiss & hold you very close darling, but I send you many warm & loving & very tender thoughts instead,

E.R.

By the time Eleanor wrote this letter, she had left Campobello and was in Hyde Park.

August 3d

Val-Kill Cottage

Hick darling, Your Tuesday night letter is here & I do hope you get back in the newspaper business soon! Can't you forget you ever knew us, tell them you never see me & can't find out anything!

I am so glad you found that your A.P. work was really what you could stand on & now if you could just stop talking about your friendship for me & ignore it I think you would find it is practically forgotten & no one would think of it now. I don't think you have to go to Europe in order to do newspaper work tho' I can see why it would be interesting & why you want to go but if you get a job in N.Y. I don't think you need fear their [the editors'] demands for I think they don't need you now to get any story they want [from the White House].

John was here when I came back & I read him my article [about women's role] for criticism & have revised it more since. It goes to you air mail & I'll hold it & mail Monday night in the hope that you can wire any corrections you think vital. It interests me but I think the Saturday Evening Post may not like it & I am frankly a bit nervous about it.

---

[15] James Hilton's novel, published in 1935, told the story of a dedicated teacher who guided several generations of boys attending a British boys school.

Dearest, I do miss you tho' I can't say I would want you here for you would not be happy. The quiet is about over![16]
A world of love & take care of yourself,

E.R.

August 7th

Sagamore Hotel
Rochester, New York

My dearest:

Two sweet letters from you on my arrival here tonight, and it was very nice to get them. I hadn't had any since Friday night, when I found three in Syracuse. But your wire came on Sunday, and that helped.

I think one thing that has "got me down," so to speak, is the decided change in attitude toward the president. Two years ago when I was through here, they were mostly *for* him. At least they weren't panning him. Now, almost to a man, they're "agin him"—and it doesn't seem to matter whether they're Republicans or Democrats, although, of course, most of them are Republicans. I really do believe they think he's a bit "cracked"!

Of course one way of looking at it—and it's probably the sanest way—is this:

Most of these people didn't vote for him in 1932. In 1933 they were for him—for a few months, until business began to get a little better. Then they found he meant what he said about social reforms. Now, naturally, they're against him again. But they *do not* represent a loss of strength at the polls, necessarily.

Well—it's all interesting. But damned depressing, when you get it fired at you all day and on into the evening. The most depressing thing

---

[16] Various house guests were scheduled to arrive at Hyde Park within the next several days.

about it is that these business men don't seem to have learned anything at all in the last five or six years. Not one damned thing! I think the president needs to get out around the country. Only even then—everybody will "yes" him.

In my own small way, I'm as bad as any of the others. He'll turn to me and say, "Am I right, Hick?" I don't always think he is, but I haven't the nerve to say so. Even if he weren't president, intellectually he'd always have the advantage in any argument with me.

Well—*you* don't mind my raving on, anyway. Or *do* you?

If you got a laugh out of my idea of the possibility of a "happy family" at Campobello—I was equally amused at your idea that I could get a newspaper job, telling them I never saw you and didn't know what was going on. They'd NEVER believe it, dear—unless I actually did quit seeing you. And that would be expecting a good deal of me. Gosh I'm not prepared to give you up *entirely!* (And I don't believe you would want that, either.)

I must go to bed. Sleep sweetly, my dear, with all my heart I love you.

H

In late August, Eleanor and Lorena spent several days together at the Val-Kill cottage while the other Roosevelts and their guests stayed at the Springwood mansion. Their time together was less than blissful.

August 26th

Val-Kill Cottage

Darling, I hated to leave you this morning, how I wish we could get back to being happy to-gether.

It is lonely here & I went over [to the mansion] at once & saw James before he left for N.Y. The p.m. has been spent on mail & to-morrow Tommy & I will begin on articles.

Darling, I love you & do try to remember that always,

E.R.

August 28th

Val-Kill Cottage

Dearest, It was nice to get your Monday night letter.

Thank you for the article.[17] I've not read it yet because Nan & I left at nine & went across the river to those fruit stands you & I passed last Sunday & bought apples & plums to can, then we picked up Tommy & we have just returned at 5:30 having spent the whole day at the [Dutchess County] fair! I am weary! John won a fourth but at least he wasn't hurt in the jumping. I'm not going to have to ride to-morrow at the show & I am most grateful!

I'm staying at the cottage you know not the big house till F.D.R. comes.[18]

Tommy's working hard at the second draft of the teacher article & I'll send you a carbon as soon as it is done.[19]

I think the war idea is a good one & a woman writing will be a new thing in war journalism.[20] I'll be tempted to join you if war comes in some capacity if by chance F.D.R. doesn't get in but I think he will by a small margin.

You don't know it dear but you did a grand thing for me on Sunday night by showing me that I should never be sorry for myself. I have so much more in life than most people & I am really never unhappy except when I begin to whine & feel sorry for myself & God knows I've no right to do it. You are putting up such a grand fight & have so little to make you happy that you made me feel ashamed.

Ever so much love,

E.R.

---

[17] Lorena had edited a manuscript Eleanor had written about the subsistence homestead program.

[18] Whenever Franklin came to Hyde Park, he insisted that Eleanor move into the mansion with him.

[19] After Tommy corrected Eleanor's grammar and Lorena worked on the content and organization, it was published in the November issue of *Current Controversy*. In the piece, Eleanor argued that the New Deal increasing the government's involvement in citizens' lives did not mean that people should stop supporting private charities.

[20] Lorena had again mentioned the possibility of going to Europe as a war correspondent. Now realizing how badly Lorena wanted to return to newspaper work, Eleanor supported the idea this time.

Having completed her investigation of the relief and political situation in New York state, Lorena was living at the White House. Eleanor was still in Hyde Park.

[September 5]

Val-Kill Cottage

Dearest one, I read your letter through last night after I went to bed![21] It is a grand criticism & has given me a way to analyze what I am thinking which is most helpful. You need not have been afraid that your criticism would discourage me, you see I haven't the feeling that the things are good in themselves. I've always felt it was largely name & I'm glad to have it back because it shows they are wanting something besides name.[22] If I can't do this after giving it a good try then I must do something else that is all & one can only find out by trying.

I think I know what you mean about structure, it comes from not thinking through from the start & building up step by step & I think I can do that better. It is muddy thinking. I am glad to have your analysis but I hate you to do it when you are so tired.[23]

Your trip sounded nice but rather tiring.[24] Gettysburg must have been really interesting & I'd like to see it. Will I ever have any leisure I wonder? I haven't since I was married!

This morning I took the ferry to New Rochelle where Tommy met me by train & we went in the rain to lunch with Esther [Lape] & Elizabeth

[21] The letter was the one containing Lorena's lengthy comments on the manuscript about subsistence homesteads.

[22] Eleanor had been concerned that magazine editors published her work only because of the prominence of the Roosevelt name. She was pleased, therefore, that the public affairs magazine *Liberty* had rejected her first draft, insisting that it was not yet of a publishable quality.

[23] In the first lady's first draft of the article about subsistence homesteads, she had described the program in glowing terms. Lorena's editing comments urged Eleanor to acknowledge at the beginning of the article that the program had been criticized and then to respond to those criticisms one by one. Eleanor revised the article along the line that Lorena had suggested, and *Liberty* published the revision in its November issue.

[24] Lorena and her friend Howard Haycraft, a fellow Minnesotan who was living in New York and often attended boxing matches with her, had spent the weekend in Pennsylvania's Cotoctin Mountains. As part of their trip, they visited the Gettysburg historical site that memorializes one of the major battles of the Civil War.

[Read] & got home at 7:30 p.m.[25] Darling, I must go to bed. A world of love & be careful!

E.R.

Lorena had left the White House and was now investigating conditions in the Midwest. In this letter, she discusses the assassination of Huey Long, a demagogue who used one of the most elaborate patronage networks in the history of American politics to rise to governor of Louisiana in 1928 and then to United States senator in 1932. Long criticized FDR for not having gone far enough in attacking the Depression. Long advocated a radical redistribution of wealth that would guarantee every American an annual income of $2,500. Long had announced in the summer that he might run against FDR in the next election, but he was shot on September 8.

September 9th

Hotel McCurdy
Evansville, Indiana

Dearest:

Well, Madame, what do you make of the Long business? I've been thinking today about all the people who must be secretly hoping he'll die, but who would hate to admit it even to themselves! Boy, it creates an interesting situation! One Indiana farmer today was quite frank. "He ought to have killed him instead of just sending him to the hospital," he said. I take it that with *that* gentleman, at any rate, Doctor [Carl] Weiss[26] is a hero. And I'd hate to bet that, secretly, he isn't a hero to *plenty* of people. But, if Huey dies, he'll be a martyr.[27]

Well—I'm too sleepy to think much more about it tonight. I've a mountain of work to do—stuff to read—but I simply cannot keep my

[25] Esther and Elizabeth owned a country estate near Westport, Connecticut.
[26] Dr. Carl Weiss was the Baton Rouge physician who shot Long and then was immediately killed by Long's bodyguards.
[27] Long died the day after Lorena wrote this letter.

eyes open. So I'm going to bed right after I finish this and [will] get up early tomorrow morning.

It's been a busy and interesting day. Farmers. Prosperous as Hell. And, on the whole, strong for the president. Sentiment out here much, much better than in the East. In one small town today I counted *eleven* new cars—Fords, Chevrolets, one Pontiac—parked at the curb in one short block on Main Street!

Newsboys yelling the Long extras kept me awake until after midnight and started me on one of my terribly dreaded "white nights."[28] But I'll sleep tonight.

I'm more than half asleep now. Good night, my dearest. I hope you are safe and happy.

H

Although the letter that prompted this angry retort from Eleanor has not been preserved, Lorena clearly had become irritated when the first lady's commitments conflicted with what Hick wanted to do during a trip to Washington.

September 21st

Val-Kill Cottage

Hick darling, I could *shake* you for your letter of the 19th. I've never even *thought* of not being in Washington with you. I do have to go to N.Y. on the 8th because I take the apartment that day[29] & want to get all I can out of storage & be settled. I am not going till the morning of the 8th however & I shall be very sorry if you are not in Washington. I probably won't be able to get to Washington till the 6th & of course flying might be impossible but that is not likely at this time of year, if it should happen you might go up to N.Y. with me for a couple of days.

---

[28] *White nights* was the term Lorena used for the nights when she couldn't sleep because her emotions were spinning out of control.

[29] Eleanor had rented a pied-à-terre in Greenwich Village.

I know you felt badly & are tired, but I'd give an awful lot if you weren't so sensitive!

E.R.

September 23rd

Hotel Statler
Cleveland, Ohio

My dear:

The picture I get of the political situation in Ohio is certainly anything but reassuring. God, but that sap Governor [Martin] Davey[30] has made a mess of things! Buzzie[31] could run for Governor of this state and give him the trimming of his life.

It's common knowledge around the state, apparently—I hear it from all sources, political and otherwise—that he is shaking down the liquor wholesalers to the tune of One Dollar for every case they sell in Ohio. And you have to plunk down to Mister Davey's organization *One Thousand Dollars* to get a liquor license. He is also all messed up in the slot machines racket. In Cleveland, where the slot machine racket is said to be very bad indeed, Davey's state chairman recently got into an automobile accident—with *Four Thousand Dollars* on his person!

A newspaper man, who used to be with the AP when I was and who now writes politics for a Republican paper in Columbus, told me that, if things go on the way they are—with the damage Davey is doing the party—and with the president lacking any sort of organization or spokesman in the state—your esteemed husband couldn't be elected dog catcher in Ohio. And the friendly Scripps-Howard [newspaper chain] people—they have six papers in Ohio, you know—say the same thing. Just seeing Davey in Washington a few weeks ago apparently did the president a lot of harm.

[30] Ohio Governor Martin Davey was a Democrat.
[31] Buzzie Dall was Eleanor's five-year-old grandson.

I could go on at length. And undoubtedly shall in my next report!

Dear, I don't think I *quite* deserve that shaking you say you'd like to give me. I was only trying not to be selfish—to treat you as I would Jean [Dixon],[32] Howard [Haycraft],[33] or any of my other friends!

Good night, and please don't be cross with me.

H

September 25th

THE WHITE HOUSE
Washington

Dearest, Your Monday & Tuesday letters both arrived this morning & I liked your explosive one & in spots you are entirely right as to a federal bureaucracy etc. [Governor] Davey I am not surprised to hear about!

I'm glad to know you were trying to treat me like Jean or Howard, but I shouldn't think they'd like it much! Your letters made me feel that in some way I'd given you the impression I really don't care to see you in early Oct. That I thought more of something or someone in N.Y. than I did of you & that you would go about your business & not burden me. No one likes to be burdened by one's friends, sometimes one can't do things, but one wants to do them & I wouldn't give up seeing you after all these weeks for anything except an illness or crisis of some sort & you ought to know it by this time! Darling, I sound like an old scold, forgive me, I treat you badly lots of times I know when I don't realize it!

---

[32] Jean Dixon was Lorena's friend who worked as an actress.
[33] Howard Haycraft was Lorena's friend who worked in a publishing house.

I'll wire you on Sunday to Cincinatti [sic]. A world of love dear one &
bless you,

E.R.

*This letter reveals that Hick had become so depressed that she wished—
as the last line implies—she had never been born.*

September 26th

New Hotel Secor
Toledo, Ohio

Dearest:

It *is* so hard even for me not to feel a little bitter at the "big shots" these
days. The president, [Harold] Ickes,[34] Harry Hopkins,[35] all well fed,
well clothed, warm, and comfortable, complacently starting off on a vacation while out here in places like Cleveland and Toledo thousands of
people *aren't* getting enough to eat, are facing eviction, begging for little
jobs at a wage that none of us could live on.

Of course a lot of my bitterness is directed at your husband, Ickes,
and, yes, to a certain extent, at Harry. Months and months of rowing
about who is going to run the show. And hence—no show running.[36]
Oh, I know it's just human nature, and that it happens all the time in
private industry. God knows I've seen plenty of it there! But, dear lady,
we are dealing with the welfare of millions of helpless people—the food
they eat, their shelter. The federal government "cracking down" on
Governor Davey, who ought to be led out and shot, while thousands of
innocent people——

---

[34] Harold Ickes was head of the Public Works Administration, which constructed federal
buildings, dams, bridges, highways, and other public facilities.
[35] Harry Hopkins was now the head of the Works Progress Administration, which coordi-
nated all relief efforts and federal construction projects.
[36] Under Hopkins, two million people a month were being paid by the federal government.
Some were building facilities such as schools, libraries, parks, and hospitals, while others were
creating artistic works such as plays and murals. Ickes argued that the jobs were only temporary and the only way to relieve unemployment in the long run was by subsidizing private enterprise.

Well, there isn't any use in my raving on any more.

Good night, dear, wherever you are. I feel a good deal as though I were shouting into space!

Tonight's paper says the president is going to speak Saturday in Fremont, Nebraska. My mother lived there for a year once, when she was a girl—probably the happiest year of her life. She was engaged at the time to a man she didn't marry after all. I met him years later, when I was at school in Michigan. A very fine man. Too bad she didn't marry him.

H

Eleanor had now joined Franklin on his campaign train.

September 29th

New Hotel Secor
Toledo, Ohio

Dearest:

I'll be brief tonight, for I must get to bed. Fairly hellish day ahead of me tomorrow. I'm leaving Toledo at 7 a.m. and don't expect to be in Cincinnati before 8:30 or 9 p.m. I have only about 250 miles of driving, but I'm making a lot of stops.

Spent this morning inspecting projects—or prospective projects, since most of them are at a standstill—in a cold, drizzling rain.

It's things like this that are so maddening dear. Seventy-two relief clients had the job of guarding children as they cross the streets—at the schools in winter, at the playgrounds in summer. When the FERA [Federal Emergency Relief Administration] work program stopped in July, these men volunteered to continue without pay—i.e. only for grocery orders—until the project went through under WPA. The project has gone to Washington. Nothing has been heard from it since. The seventy-two men are still guiding the children across the streets. The project and the men are popular. People keep asking them, "Got your pay yet?" "No." And every time it happens, the president loses another friend. Even the Scripps-Howard paper is boiling about it. They carried an editorial tonight.

There's a meat strike on in Cleveland, and one starting here. The Scripps-Howard people investigated and say they found it was being quietly instigated by the Republican women's organization. Pretty clever of the Republican ladies—provided they manage to keep it dark. It certainly wouldn't help their party any with the corn-hog farmers.

Must go to bed. Can't imagine where you are tonight. The papers carry practically nothing—and that under the vague dateline "Aboard the President's Special Train." Just the same, that dateline makes me damned homesick for the business. Three years ago now I was writing copy under a similar one. "Aboard the Roosevelt Campaign Train." Oh, well—

Goodnight, dear. Sleep well.

H

Eleanor had now left the presidential train and was at Hyde Park.

October 7th

Val-Kill Cottage

Hick darling, Two letters from you this morning, one of them the detailed criticism [of the role of women article] which is going to be the greatest help. I've only had time to read the begining [sic] but so far you are entirely right & I will change it for Mr. [George] Lorrimer doesn't like it [the first version]. Mr. [George] Bye was here for lunch & will write me in detail on Monday. I told him I'd consider their suggestions & rewrite or take another subject for them & rewrite this for someone else. Mr. B. tells me they say that Republican audience has pounded a lot for the first article.[37]

---

[37] In the article that *Cosmopolitan* had published in January, the first lady had argued that unless the New Deal included programs for young people, the deprivation of the Great Depression would handicap the entire next generation of Americans for the rest of their lives.

Anna & John [Anna had married John Boettiger in January] are here & we are now going to Elinor Morgenthau's clambake. I exercised all a.m. & have done no work!

I was a pig to give you the impression it was hard here, it is just a life I don't enjoy & I feel rushed & distant & like [I do in] Washington—but I don't really mind! Your life would seem to me much worse!

A world of love,

E.R.

Although Eleanor was very generous herself, it was difficult for her to accept gifts from other people. This cryptic letter suggests that the fiercely independent Lorena believed, and Eleanor agreed, that this trait was contributing to the problems in their relationship. Eleanor's use of the phrase "dearest person" at the end of the letter also may be a telling choice of words, as the restrained tone it communicates is dramatically different from the intimate tone that had permeated the first lady's letters a year earlier. The letter was written when Eleanor and Lorena both were living at the White House, as Lorena was preparing to depart for West Virginia.

[October 10]

Hick darling, I've thought of you so much all day & I wish I had not had to leave you last night, tho' of course I wanted to come & see Anna.[38] You are a grand person dear & don't ever think I don't appreciate what you are going thro' for me. I love the bag[39] & it will be in constant use next summer no matter where I am. I do love presents & I love you to give them to me but I can't let go & be natural that's all. I will try dear to do better work as long as it matters to you! You see I care so little at times, other times I realize if one does anything one should do it as well as one can. I might at least do things to the best of my ability which however is far more mediocre I fear than you imagine!

---

[38] Anna had been hospitalized for severe tension and exhaustion.

[39] Lorena had given Eleanor a tote bag for her fifty-first birthday that was the day after this letter was written.

[40] Lorena's next task was to assess the political landscape in West Virginia.

I hope you are enjoying getting your job started[40] & that it will be fun to do, it certainly will be valuable.

Anna is much better still rather weak but I get her home before lunch to-morrow.

A world of love & good night dearest person,

E.R.

This letter begins with Eleanor's reference to what ultimately became the final version of the manuscript that she, Lorena, and Tommy had been working on for five months. The time and effort proved to be well spent, as the central idea that Eleanor expressed was both remarkable and prescient. Indeed, it was virtually identical to the concept that would, thirty years later, ignite the modern Women's Liberation Movement: Many American women are not satisfied with living their lives inside the strict parameters of domesticity. Calling the belief that all women should live in the shadow of their husband and children "a kind of blindness," Eleanor wrote, "When people say woman's place is in the home, I say, with enthusiasm, it certainly is, but if she really cares about her home, that caring will take her far and wide." The Saturday Evening Post *published the article in its August 24, 1936, issue.*

[October 15]
49 East 65th Street
New York

Darling, I've really worked hard on my Sat. Eve. Post article & we finished to-night.

A dreadful story came out about poor John [Boettiger] to-day & going to T.V.A. & I think he almost decided not to go![41] What a price one pays

---

[41] After John Boettiger had been offered a job with the Tennessee Valley Authority, he was accused of getting the job only because he was the president's son-in-law. Boettiger ultimately opted not to take the job.

when a revered parent decides to serve his country! I'm begining [sic] to think obscurity the greatest boon that we can ask for in this world!

E.R.

The beginning of this letter provides stark evidence of Lorena's deepening frustration—with Eleanor as well as her job and the state of the nation.

October 16th

Daniel Boone Hotel
Charleston, West Virginia

My dear:

Well—your day sounded full. Mine hasn't been exactly *loafing*.

It's 10 o'clock, and I've just finished my first day's toil in West Virginia. Shall I tell you about it? Or save it for my report? Which probably will never be read. Oh, I know you all think this is temperamental with me—that it's impossible for me to see anything but the dark side. But, God, I wish some of the rest of you had to listen to this, day in and day out. I bet you'd all feel gloomy, too. Ten hours of it I've had today—politics, bitter factionalism, greed, personal ambition, downright dishonesty. I'm beginning to think—*not* beginning to think, for I've really been aware of it for sometime—that, if the president is defeated next year the Relief and Works Progress Administration will be responsible. Despite all of Harry's fine idealism, loyalty, unselfish devotion. This West Virginia situation—well, I'm going to recommend that we send in a federal examiner to go over the books of the relief administration. It's that bad. I got my first report on Red House[42] tonight. Their principal difficulty is the same as that of all the other homesteaders. No work, except that provided by the Federal Government.[43]

And God help us if Congress ever really *does* start an investigation of relief and WPA. What they'll turn up—or *might* turn up—in some of

---

[42] Red House, West Virginia, is a city located between Charleston and Huntington. It was the site of the state's second subsistence homestead project.

[43] The subsistence homestead project at Red House, like the one at Arthurdale, had failed to attract any private businesses.

these states won't be pretty. The thing's too big. It's got out of hand. And much of it is so ridiculous. Do you know what I was told tonight—and by one of our own federal people? It may take *100* cards, including duplications, to put one individual to work on WPA and keep him working! Imagine the fun the press could have with *that!* Just damned red tape.

Oh, well, week after next I'll be trying to boil it down into a reasonably coherent and objective report—to be tucked away somewhere in the files. Objective? HELL—I can't be objective.

Well—I leave for Washington the 26th.

I'm sorry this letter sounds so gloomy. Well, it's my job to tell you all what I hear. And I'm telling you—part of it. It's just a sample.

I hope you are having a nice time.

H

When Lorena wrote this letter, Eleanor was on a speaking tour in the Midwest.

October 19th

Daniel Boone Hotel
Charleston, West Virginia

Dearest:

I think my most poignant experience today was this:

One of the homesteaders we visited, a friend of Major [Francis] Turner,[44] had a dog with pups. Just a little white mongrel dog, thin as a rail. The little boy of the family, about 11 years old, took me out to the barn to show me the pups. They, too, didn't look as though they were thriving any too well.

"Aw, she don't get enough to eat," he said gruffly, referring to the mother, whose name was "Missy."

"We ain't got nothin' to feed her, and so she ain't got no milk for the pups."

---

[44] Francis Turner was the relief administrator for the state of West Virginia.

The expression on his face and that in the eyes of the dog made me want to weep. I thought of giving him some money. But that didn't seem to be the thing to do, either.

On the way in, I told Major Turner about it. He stopped the car—so suddenly that I almost went through the windshield!

"By God, I'll send that kid a case of dog food," he said, drawing out a notebook. I'm going halves on the case with him.

I'm going to get undressed now, get into bed, and read for a couple of hours. And I've turned down three dinner invitations tomorrow to stay here and write letters, read, do my expense account, and so on.

Good night. I hope you are having a nice weekend, wherever you are.

H

In Lorena's next emotional outburst, she became angry when the first lady agreed to meet her—Lorena, at the time, was working out of a hotel in Baltimore—at the White House for a quiet hour or so together. The time was set for 6:15, but Eleanor was delayed a few minutes. When 6:30 arrived and the first lady hadn't arrived, Lorena bolted out of the mansion and drove back to Baltimore in a huff. The letter contains Eleanor's gentle suggestion that Lorena may have overreacted; the second paragraph contains a second suggestion that Lorena should not be so sensitive about the first lady's every word, although the precise comment that Eleanor made—and that Lorena found so agitating—is unclear.

[October 31]

THE WHITE HOUSE
Washington

Hick dearest, I am sorry you were hurt dear, but weren't you a bit hasty? I was back at 6:45 & lay on the sofa & read from 7:15-7:45 which was the time I had planned for you. I do plan times dear one to be with you but you have been here a good deal & the steady routine gets on your nerves, in the old days when it was only a day now & then we broke routine & you pine for that & we must do it more often!

You must not think so long of things I say which I really do not mean so seriously. I want you to be happy because I love you, & when I've hurt [you] I am sorry & cross with myself for not thinking ahead & preventing it but I wouldn't give up our times to-gether & our happiness for these little troubles. You have been a brick & don't think that I don't know how hard it is.

It has been a busy day, ride, work, saw Mrs. [Lillian] Evanti the colored singer who wishes to broadcast,[45] Mrs. [Helen] Wilmerding[46] to the chrysanthemum show at 11:45 & at 12:15 took Louis for a drive. Had the Harold Butlers, English (International labor bureau of the League of Nations) to lunch & enjoyed them. Worked till I left at 3:20 to plant a tree in a playground. Then a dash to see John in the hospital. He had his tonsils out to-day. Worked all evening & have just sent Tommy home at 11:30.

Darling, I hope these next few weeks won't be bad & I shall always be sorry for your unhappiness.

Well dear one, sleep sweetly,

E.R.

By December, Lorena was back on the road. This time she was in northern Michigan.

December 10th

Douglass House
Houghton, Michigan

Dearest:

This has been *a day!* Tragic as parts of it have been, I grin in spite of myself. It's so absurd.

I landed in Iron Mountain at 6:30 this morning. Clear, cold weather, with a biting wind from the North. Lots of snow. Curse had come in the night. Cramps.

---

[45] In 1940 the State Department, after much coaxing from Eleanor, finally sent the African-American opera singer to Argentina and Brazil as a goodwill ambassador.

[46] Helen Wilmerding had been a childhood friend of Eleanor's and a bridesmaid in her wedding.

The district WPA director met me at the station with his chief engineer, and they took me out to the attractive and cozy little log cabin in the pine woods, where they "bach it." Then they proceeded to cook breakfast, while I sat around, feeling foolish. Very delicious food. Nice experience.

Then we went out to look at projects. We slithered and slid over ice, snow, and ruts around and up to the top of a small mountain over a road that eventually is to be called "Franklin D. Roosevelt Parkway." Up on top of this hill, in the snow, in a wind that cut to the very bone, some 200 men were at work, clearing out underbrush, digging out stumps, working on the roadway and building a ski jump.

But—

These men, most of whom had been working since November 15th, hadn't yet received any pay.

Some of them were threatening—not desperately or violently, but rather hopelessly—to walk off the job this afternoon. But when we were there they were still plodding along, patient, dumb.

These people had been taken off relief the day they went to work for WPA—almost a month ago. Whether we like it or not, that is what has happened all over this state—and, I suspect in many others—as the result of our cutting out of federal relief. The states and counties haven't got the money—whether they *should* be able to raise it or not—and it's the poor devil on relief who catches it in the neck.

They had gone two weeks and ten days—going on four weeks—on *nothing*. No relief. No pay. Some of them, I was told, have been coming to work with *nothing but onions* in their dinner pails.

I simply couldn't get those men off my mind. Out there in that bitter wind, working on the "Franklin D. Roosevelt Parkway." Neither could the WPA director. Finally he said, "Aw, hell, let's send some food out there." "You bet," I said. "I'll pay for it." "No, you won't," he said. So he gave a man a ten-dollar bill and told him to load up a car with sandwiches and hot coffee and get out there to that job, and God help him if he ever told where they came from. We're going fifty-fifty on it, whatever it cost.

And now, believe it or not, I'm writing in front of a beautiful, glowing grate fire! This is an old-fashioned hotel, not *too* long on plumbing, *but with fireplaces in the bedrooms!*

And thus endeth the Tenth Day of December, Anno Domini 1935!

                                                                    H

This letter provides the first reference to one of the most important contributions Hick made to the first lady's evolution as a public figure—even though it came well after the intense phase of their relationship had ended. Lorena had suggested that Eleanor talk directly to hundreds of thousands of Americans each day through a syndicated newspaper column. When the first lady mentioned the possibility to the head of the United Features syndication service, he agreed to distribute it, and by late December when the column began appearing, some fifty newspapers—including such major ones as the Atlanta Constitution, St. Louis Post-Dispatch, *and* Kansas City Star—*had signed up. The enterprise received another big boost when the Scripps-Howard chain bought the column as well. Eleanor was initially concerned that the daily deadline would be a problem, but the $1,000 a month she would earn persuaded her to give it a try. She would continue to produce a column six days a week (all except Sunday) for the next twenty-seven years.*

December 17th

THE WHITE HOUSE

Washington

Dearest one, The writing is easy so far, they just want one incident out of the day & so far I've had no trouble.

I wrapped packages after lunch & one more day will see me pretty well done I think. I also went to see Louis this afternoon.

Helen Hayes[47] came to have lunch as I found she was crazy to come here. Three Governors were here for dinner, Iowa, Nebraska & Colorado & the talk was interesting.

The diplomatic reception was only a bit over 1,000 & the Hungarians were beautiful & wore the most dashing & romantic black uniforms! My feet however are very weary & I must go to bed. I love you dearly & I look forward to Monday next![48]

All my love,

E.R.

---

[47] Helen Hayes was the Academy Award-winning actress known as the "First Lady of the American Theater."

This letter suggests that by the end of 1935 Eleanor still considered Hick such a close friend that she would help make the first lady's funeral arrangements.

[December 19]

THE WHITE HOUSE
Washington

Dearest, The rest of this day will be hectic so this is just a line to tell you that two packages have come from Detroit but I won't open them till I return on Sunday! Anna wants me to go there that afternoon to open their present which is also yours & I am intrigued & curious![49]

I stayed at the apartment & worked all morning.

Evening I went to dress the Xmas tree & then to the memorial service for Mary Rumsey.[50]

Darling, don't let anyone hold memorial meetings for me after I leave you. It is cruel to those who really love you & miss you & means nothing to the others except an obligation fulfilled & certainly it can mean nothing to the spirit in another sphere if it is there at all! I'd like to be remembered happily if that is possible, if that can't be then I'd rather be forgotten.

Cheer up darling, we will have a good week or rather ten days together & you must not get depressed about your work, that is good & you know it.

I love you tenderly,
E.R.

[48] Lorena was coming to the White House for Christmas.

[49] Lorena and Anna had, at Lorena's suggestion, gone together to give Eleanor a set of cocktail and brandy glasses for her new apartment in Greenwich Village.

[50] Mary Rumsey had been the former head of the consumers division of the National Recovery Administration.

Seven

1936–1939

Drifting Apart?

During the late 1930s, Eleanor and Lorena found it difficult to maintain their relationship—even at the reduced pitch that Eleanor had imposed—because they had entered two distinctly different phases of their lives. ER had hit her stride and was succeeding at a daunting array of activities that were providing her with venues she could use to further her social and political agenda—conducting weekly press conferences, giving speeches and radio broadcasts, publishing substantive articles in major magazines, writing a daily newspaper column distributed to dozens of newspapers across the country. Hick, on the other hand, was struggling to find an occupation that would give her the personal satisfaction and sense of self that news reporting once had; she was also facing major health and financial worries.

Eleanor and Lorena's correspondence during this period is peppered not only with apologies for hurt feelings but also with apologies for proposed meetings that had to be postponed or canceled. Despite the challenges that prevented them from spending more than an occasional lunch or dinner together, the women remained steadfastly committed to providing each other with support and encouragement through their epistolary conversation.

As 1936 began, Lorena was investigating the relief conditions in New York and New Jersey while living in her midtown apartment. The day before writing this letter, the first lady had lunched with Hick in New York City.

January 14 [1936]

THE WHITE HOUSE
Washington

Dearest, Darling, you were low & I know that in some way I hurt you & I am sorry & I wish I had not but all I can say is, I really love you.

I breakfast alone to-morrow which I much prefer when you can't be here. To-morrow Anna & John & Sisty & Buzzie leave & I shall feel very sad.[1] The afternoon & evening are so filled that I imagine I won't be able to miss them till the next day, but I know I mustn't grow too dependent on these four for, as you have so often said(!), one must let go!

I'd like to call you up, just a kind of yearning to hear your voice but I mustn't run up too big [of] bills this month or I might not have the money to pay them on Feb. 1st.

E.R.

Two days before writing this letter, Eleanor had sent Lorena a telegram suggesting that they meet at Grand Central Station. The subsequent meeting, however, was a disaster. Reporters and on-lookers crowded around the first lady when she arrived at New York's busiest train station, preventing her from spending even a moment alone with Lorena.

[February 18, 1936]

THE WHITE HOUSE
Washington

Hick darling, I am so very very sorry. I ought to know it must be alone or not at all [that I see you] & you probably felt I brought you down under false pretenses but I didn't mean to even though I did.

---

[1] Anna and her family were moving to Seattle where John Boettiger would become publisher of the *Seattle Post-Intelligencer.*

A world of love dear always & I hope you don't get too tired to enjoy Prinz & your home!

E.R.

For the two months that Eleanor had been writing her "My Day" column, she had merely listed the activities in her day. This letter documents that it was Lorena who first gave Eleanor the "tip" that the column also could provide the first lady with an instrument for moving important issues onto the national agenda.

[March 13, 1936]

20 East Eleventh Street
New York City

Dearest, Back in N.Y. with no fuss & feathers & $3000 to my credit![2] It has to go out at once in income tax however!

Thanks for the tip about my column dear. I just never thought of it!

Franklin has been much interested in your letters, they can't help being interesting with all the background & knowledge you have. F. may say I don't know what I'm talking about but he can't say that of you.

All my love dear,
E.R.

Although there is no evidence that Lorena ever committed her disappointment to paper, she must have been deeply hurt by the first lady's statement in this letter that "no one will ever be more loyal & devoted"

---

[2] Eleanor had just returned from a week-long speaking tour.

than Louis Howe had been—a distinction that Lorena surely felt be-longed to her.

April 19th [1936]

THE WHITE HOUSE
Washington

Darling, I got in from speaking last night & [White House physician] Dr. [Ross] McIntire called me to tell me Louis had died in his sleep. They just noticed his breathing was changing, called the doctor who did what he could but he never responded & was never conscious. A merciful way for him. We got Franklin as soon as the Gridiron dinner was over & I spent hours getting Mrs. [Grace] Howe & Hartley[3] on the telephone, but finally succeeded & they took it calmly, thank Heavens! I've been doing a thousand & one little things, changes in dates etc. but until Grace gets here we won't know what she will want to do.

This afternoon I've read the papers & written letters. In an hour I shall meet Grace & Hartley & go with them to the undertakers. Read F.D.R. your letter & I think he was much pleased.

I think I felt Louis would always be an invalid but still always there & tho' for a long time the real person has been gone [because of Louis's illness] I shall miss some of the things that made one at times almost resentful. He was like a pitiful, querulous child but even when I complained I loved him & no one will ever be more loyal & devoted than he was.

If I should outlive F.D.R.[,] Missy would be the one I should worry about![4] I rather hope however that I will be the one to go, before I go through this again, it would seem more logical & so restful! However, I feel extremely well so don't be alarmed!

I don't know what you mean about [you] being "an utter fool" but I am certainly not a wise person. We'll hope I'm generous which is after all little enough for me to be!

A kiss to you dear one,

E.R.

---

[3] Hartley was Louis and Grace Howe's son.
[4] Missy LeHand, FDR's personal secretary, was so close to him that some scholars have described her as being comparable to a wife, including having a sexual relationship with the president.

When Eleanor read the first paragraph of this letter to Franklin, his ears perked up. The president had been wanting to publicize the fact that technological advances were, ironically, a major impediment to the New Deal putting people back to work, which was exactly what Lorena's letter—in simple, straightforward language—said. FDR immediately ordered his wife to reprint Lorena's statement about the Youngstown steel mills in her "My Day" column.

[May 4, 1936]

Dear:

Youngstown [Ohio] is terribly depressing. The steel mills are running full blast, 80 per cent of capacity—as good as 1929. And yet in the last three years they've spent Ten Million Dollars modernizing those plants, and the result is that in 1936, with the mills operating at 1929 production, they are employing 10,000 *fewer* men than in 1929![5]

These figures are probably very conservative. And this year Two Million Dollars more is to be put into modernization. That means more men laid off.

The whole population is worried. They see their jobs slipping right out from under them—snatched away by the machine that was supposed to make life a more gracious thing, but which is really taking away their bread and butter.

H

May 7th [1936]

THE WHITE HOUSE
Washington

Dearest, From your Youngstown letter I've written my Monday piece at Franklin & Roy Howard's[6] suggestion. If you mind I'm terribly sorry, I

---

[5] On May 11, Eleanor's column said of the steel mills: "This industry is at present producing as much as it did in 1929. Ordinarily this would mean work for everybody, but since the depression $10,000,000 had been spent in modernizing these particular plants with the result that they are now using 10,000 *fewer* men than in 1929."

[6] Roy Howard was head of the Scripps-Howard newspaper chain and an FDR confidant.

wanted to wire for your consent but Franklin wouldn't let me. I think he wants me to be [his] whipping boy & tho' he can't bring the question [of modernization] out, he wants it out.

Another busy day. Army & Navy Rummage Sale, 2 teas, conference on textile bill, & visit from Gov. [Theodore Francis] Green[7] & 1 1/2 hours receiving new citizens![8]

Darling, I've a basketful of mail to do so good night. Bless you & all my love,

E.R.

By the summer of 1936, Eleanor reluctantly agreed to be an active participant in her husband's re-election campaign. She did so partly because her reshaping of the first lady's role had become a campaign issue among proponents of the status quo. A Republican campaign button captured the sentiment: "We don't want Eleanor, either!" When she wrote this letter, she was on her husband's campaign tour through Texas.

On the campaign train
June 11th [1936]

Hick dearest, We got off at 6 & heaven knows when we get back so I decided I'd write now. Our train is cool when we are on the move but when we got off at 9:30 it was hot & yet people lined the streets of Houston & seemed enthusiastic. The trip by canal was pleasant to San Jacinto & F. made a nice speech. We heard [Alfred M.] Landon was nominated.[9]

F. remarked he was really interested in the [Republican] platform, I've just read it & it seems to me the same old bunk. I hope ours is not so long but it is foolish to hope it will be any less "bunk-ish"!

[7] Theodore Francis Green, a Democrat, was the governor of Rhode Island.
[8] To honor immigrants completing the steps necessary to become American citizens, Eleanor routinely hosted group receptions for them at the White House.
[9] The Republican Party had nominated the governor of Kansas for president.

I'm weary of cheering crowds (I'd like them less if they booed but I'd be more interested!) How you continue to travel & bear it I don't know. I want to settle down & stay put two months [in one place] at least! A world of love,

E.R.

As Eleanor was writing this and the next letter, the Democratic National Convention was underway in Philadelphia.

June 25th [1936]

THE WHITE HOUSE
Washington

Dearest, You are right that your bad times when we are to-gether are hard on us both but oh! dear, why do you have to *feel* in a way which makes you have bad times, we ought to have such good & happy times to-gether. Perhaps we will some day when I am no longer driven & we are both calmer!

This evening has been nice because I could talk to Dr. Alice Hamilton[10] & she is such a dear, so gentle & unassuming & yet look what she's done! A lesson to most of us who think we have to assert ourselves to be useful & particularly good for me as I was feeling rather annoyed with F.D.R. Nothing unusual just a little feeling on his part that he was abused because I didn't co-operate with his plans about Hyde Park when I wasn't asked at the time to sit in or express an idea![11] Then my pride was injured at his perfect forgetfulness of a political suggestion I had made on the train & I was annoyed till I realized to-night how small it all was sitting by the sweet faced woman who has probably given the impetus to workmen's compensation & research into industrial diseases & saved countless lives & heartbreaks.

---

[10] Alice Hamilton was the country's leading authority on industrial medicine.
[11] FDR was making structural changes to the Springwood mansion.

Now I hear the platform read over the radio as I write. It seems to be going smoothly, tho' I heard F. say before dinner to [political adviser] Jim Byrnes that one change was "weasly"!

I am sensing you may think I shouldn't go with you on a working trip, how would it be to meet me in Warm Springs? Perhaps we can have at least a week end or two.

All my love,
E.R.

Eleanor's casual reference in this letter—as well as in many others—to hosting a tea party belies the enormous quantity of time and energy she devoted to formal entertaining. In a single year, ER had received 9,211 tea guests, 4,729 dinner guests, and 323 house guests. Serving as hostess for so many White House visitors while balancing her myriad other commitments meant that Eleanor typically began her day at 7 a.m. and did not go to bed until 3 or 4 the next morning.

June 27th [1936]

THE WHITE HOUSE
Washington

Dearest, This is a peaceful day! Only a presentation of Bibles for guest rooms at the White House by the Gideons(!) & a tea party at four! We leave at 5:15 for Philadelphia & I've read F's speech which is good, not specific enough for me but I am doubtless wrong on that.[12]

The magnolias out of my window are in bloom & they look beautiful at night. I listened [to the convention] last night & wondered if in 1783

---

[12] FDR had fashioned his acceptance speech to inspire party regulars rather than to give details of his second term. The crowd of 105,000 offered its loudest cheer—the *Washington Post* dubbed it a "mighty roar"—when the president alluded to his inaugural speech in 1933 and boasted, "We have won against the most dangerous of our foes—we have conquered fear!"

they whooped it up so much. It seems undignified & meaningless but perhaps we need it!

It has always been so saner a business for me (living I mean) & I guess this quality of abandon is a grand thing to have.

Gee! I wish I could be excited about all this, I can't & I hate myself!

Bless you dear one, I'll wire you from Hyde Park to-morrow.

All my love,

E.R.

Did you ever long to be a mouse & burrow in the ground?

Near the end of this letter, Eleanor mentions the session in which she joined Franklin and his most trusted political advisers, on the heels of the Democratic National Convention, to plot the strategy for his re-election campaign.

[July 2, 1936]

THE WHITE HOUSE
Washington

Dearest one, Your Saturday & Sunday night letter reached me here to-day forwarded from Hyde Park & you sounded very happy & made me wish to be with you.

This has been a busy day begun by breakfast with Ruby [Black],[13] Tommy, Bess [Furman],[14] & Martha [Strayer][15] the other guests. Then [visited] 2 WPA projects in Alexandria [Virginia]—a pitiful little day nursery for colored children & a white women's sewing project but the relief rolls are way down which is encouraging. 11 [a.m.] Press Confer-

---

[13] Ruby Black covered the first lady for the United Press.
[14] Bess Furman covered the first lady for the Associated Press.
[15] Martha Strayer covered the first lady for the *Washington Daily News*.

ence. 2:30 [p.m.] I spent 2 hours with F.D.R., Jim Farley, [Charlie] Michelson, Stanley High & Forbes Morgan.

Ever so much love dear one,

E.R.

July 11th [1936]

Stevens Hotel

Chicago

My dear:

The heat sadly reduces my energy! Partly—or largely—because it keeps me from sleeping at night. Last night I had to get up five times and wring a bath towel in cold water and put it over me. I can't really decide whether I'm cooler with or without it, although it does make sleep possible, for a few minutes at least. I'm grateful though, for the fact that in the late afternoon and early evening this room, on the lake front, is fairly comfortable. It's when I have to close the door and go to bed that Hell starts. How the rest of Chicago survives is beyond me. Along the beaches you can hardly see the water for people. And they tell me that, with the wind blowing from the West—blowing the water out instead of in—the water becomes very impure. At a time like this last year, they tested the water at Oak Street, the most populous beach, and found it almost 50 per cent urine! Humanity along the lakefront these days is not a very lovely spectacle. I'd not mind nudism so much if only the human body were beautiful! It certainly is *not,* usually. (No, Madame, *I'm* not doing any boasting, either!)

While I was touring the projects yesterday, six men keeled over on one project, and we had to close part of the office down on Michigan Avenue in the afternoon. So I guess the old lady still has some endurance left in her if she can stand ten hours of it—8 a.m. to 6 p.m.—driving around in the heat, climbing in and out of the car, tramping around over the projects.

Tonight we [Lorena and a local relief administrator] dined at Colisimo's, one of the less lurid night clubs, which is famous chiefly for its Al Capone connections. For the most part, we found it depressing. The inanities of sin! There was one funny thing. They had billed one June St. Clair, "America's most alluring woman." After waiting all evening, we finally saw her. She was fat, forty, very much bleached. Her hair looked like cotton. She bustled about the floor for a few seconds, looking for all the world like a worried, frowsy, housewife. Then she stopped in front of the curtain, dropped her dress, which was all she had on, and stood there for a split second—naked and very UNlovely. We laughed and left. Came back and found several dozen flat-chested gals and anemic young men, delegates to a Baptist young peoples' convention, singing "Old Black Joe" in the lobby!

I've got to try for some sleep now.

Good night. I hope it's cooler there!

H

Lorena's next destination was the Dakotas, taking her back to where she had spent her miserable childhood. Meanwhile, the president and his sons were returning from a sailing trip.

July 27th [1936]

Campobello Island
New Brunswick, Canada

Dearest, Your Friday night letter came to-day & I hate your driving alone thro' that country & it sounded so depressing & you had to spend the week end there poor child!

The "boys" sailed in for an hour to-day just to show off their beards! F. has side burns & looks just like his Father's portrait. Funny how men love to grow hair, I think it makes them feel virile!

I have a feeling the tide is setting pretty hard against F.D.R. just now but there is time to turn it. I feel, as usual, completely objective & oh! Lord so *indifferent*!

Good night dear & bless you. I wish I could send you some of our cool air or better still that you could get on the magic carpet & come & share my room to-night, but you wouldn't enjoy these *days* any more than I do!

Be careful of yourself dear on bad roads. I love you very tenderly always,

E.R.

July 31st [1936]

St. Charles Hotel
Pierre, South Dakota

Dearest:

Your Monday night letter came today, and I'm wondering if you or I—or any other enlightened person—really has any right to be as *indifferent* about the outcome of this election as you are. Oh, I know—you hate it all. The "position." And so do I when I'm with you. I can't even be polite about it. You can. I know that you at least *think* you would be happier if you were not in Washington. Perhaps you would. And you are disillusioned, being too close to the whole thing. I get that way, too, when I'm around there too much. A daily dose of Missy,[16] along with all the fuss and pomp and adulation the man receives, will distort anyone's view. And you, personally, would like to be free. Well—it all boils down to this: All your personal inclinations would be to rejoice in defeat. And, so far as evaluating the president and his administration go—you "can't see the woods for the trees." I think I may have a little better perspective now. I've been out of the mess, more or less, for a couple of months. With all the faults—and the faults of some of the people around him—I still think he is a very great man. His defeat—and I'm awfully afraid he may be defeated—will be a terrible calamity for millions of people in this country. The poor and the lowly. Forgive me if I have offended you.

I wonder if that Spanish business *is* going to lead to an European

---

[16] Lorena found Missy LeHand's constant adoration of FDR to be irritating.

war![17] Boy, if it happens, I'll be tempted to drop everything and go to New York and try to land a job as a war correspondent in Europe!

Good night, darling. I'll wire you tomorrow.

H

August 3d [1936]

Val-Kill Cottage

Dearest one, Your letter sounded like an effort to convert me but really my dear I am doing all I can do without being accused of trying to run F.D.R. One can be personally indifferent & yet do one's duty. As a matter of fact it is only when one is oneself very unhappy that one ever thinks about the individual right to the pursuit of happiness. When you reach my age, it comes less & less often & I judge that for the moment you are not thinking about it much either. Europe is in a bad state but F. hopes it won't blow up & after [the] election perhaps something can be done.

Let me tell you a secret dear. I know I'll not be happy in Washington nor out of it so the surroundings don't matter much. I'll get on alright anyhow & tho' I'm not sure anyone is very important still I agree that we must make all effort for what is apparently best! Incidentally tho' I don't flatter myself that it matters if I care or don't care! Your reports are read carefully I know so don't get to feeling you are off in the wilderness forgotten by all!

Had a good ride this morning, worked & swam before lunch. Sat in on a conference of the bigwigs from 2:30-4:30.[18]

Tommy & I are now off to spend the night with Elizabeth [Read] & Esther [Lape] in Connecticut to-morrow.

---

[17] Spain was in the grips of a violent civil war between democratic forces and fascist rebels led by General Francisco Franco. When the fascists seized several major cities but were defeated in Madrid and Barcelona, Adolf Hitler in Germany and Benito Mussolini in Italy came to their aid.

[18] During this session, Eleanor joined FDR's inner circle of political advisers in deciding how the president—now in the heat of his re-election campaign—should respond to the fear of war that had swept the country because of the Spanish Civil War. ER agreed that, for his political sake, Franklin should reassure the country that he would do everything possible to avoid America being drawn into a foreign war, but she argued that the United States should stop the rise of Spanish fascists as soon as the election was over.

Darling, I feel like a beast to be having such an easy life when you are so uncomfortable,

E.R.

This letter provides an example of Eleanor giving Lorena support even to the point that the first lady was willing to denigrate her own accomplishments.

August 9th [1936]

Val-Kill Cottage

Dearest, I'm afraid my reasons for thinking I will probably never be much happier than I am are different than yours dear. You think some one thing could make you happy I know it never does! We are not happy because we don't know what would make us happy, we may want something & when we have it, it is not what we dreamed it would be, the thing lies in oneself! Of course dear it matters if we care enough about people not to be greedy hogs but my particular variety of imaginative interest is not very useful & I truly don't think that what I do or say makes much difference, someone else *could* do equally well what I do. Now you are different. You have gifts & can really get somewhere & I think you will.

You are a swell person dear & deserve to get that inner satisfaction or peace which we all should acquire.

I made popovers which came out well & so feel very satisfied with myself. Had hair & nails done, went to a meeting of colored preachers & then up to my new exercise lady. Boy, does she work you! I'll have some good ones [exercise tips] to give you & I think I'm going to learn someday to stand on my head!

A world of love,
E.R.

This letter contains references to two major undertakings by Eleanor and Lorena. Eleanor had decided, at her friend's urging, to become the

only first lady ever to write her autobiography while she was still in the White House. Lorena's project was to begin, in earnest, efforts to find a job that was more personally gratifying to her.

[September 10, 1936]

Val-Kill Cottage

Dearest, Mr. [George] Bye has two firms of publishers bidding for *my* autobiography up to 1920! I told them you were writing my biography but the most interesting time for that came after 1920 I think.

Went to lunch with Mama. Told her about the book & she is horrified.[19]

I'd hate to go to Europe & see a war but if you really want it I'll speak to Roy Howard if you think it would help.[20] Tommy thinks [Grover] Whalen would give you the N.Y. Fair publicity job.[21] Well, we can talk things over.

A world of love,
E.R.

Eleanor's activism remained an issue throughout the campaign, with the wife of Republican candidate Alf Landon proudly proclaiming that she was not *joining her husband in campaigning and, if he was elected, would* not *be involved in reform issues but would devote all of her time*

[19] Sara Delano Roosevelt felt it was unseemly for a proper lady to write publicly about herself.

[20] Although the head of the Scripps-Howard newspaper chain was such a close political confidant of the president that he came to dinner at the White House often, there is no indication that Eleanor ever talked to Roy Howard about hiring Lorena.

[21] Grover Whalen was chairman of the 1939 New York World's Fair then in its planning stages.

to caring for her family. ER wrote this letter while the FDR campaign train was headed for Nebraska and Wyoming.

just left St. Louis

[October 14, 1936]

Hick dearest, We are surfeited with candy & flowers & crowds! I never have seen on any trip such crowds or such enthusiasm. If it doesn't mean votes then we are a dissembling people for they answer F.D.R.'s questions with a roar. I begin to feel they are getting on the band wagon & if they really have all this faith I hope he can do a good job for them.

Another stop so good night dear one. Take care of yourself & much love always,

E.R.

How I hate being a show but I'm doing it *so* nicely!

FDR's re-election victory was decisive. He won 62 percent of the popular vote—the most he received in any of his four races for the White House. Immediately after the election, Eleanor contacted Grover Whalen and arranged for Lorena to interview with him for a job on the World's Fair public relations staff. On the morning of the interview, Eleanor sent Lorena a telegram wishing her good luck.

November 11th [1936]

10 Mitchell Place
New York City

Dearest:
You were a dear to send the wire. Oh, you always do the nice things—and I always blunder. How you can even *like* me is beyond me.

I wrote the enclosed for Mr. Whalen today. I hope I haven't puffed myself too much. Darling, I've *got* to land that job if I can. I'm taking it down there tomorrow after I've been to the dentist. I don't think Ishbel [Ross] would mind my using her book to help land a job.[22] Grover impresses me as the sort of person who would probably be impressed by that sort of thing. I hope I'm not wrong!

I'm not very well satisfied with myself, darling. I never am, but these last few days I've been even less so than usual.

I love you a very great deal!

H

Hon. Grover A. Whalen, Chairman
New York World's Fair Inc., 1939
Empire State Building
New York City

My dear Mr. Whalen:
You asked me yesterday to send you a memo about myself and what I had done.

I have been most of my life a newspaper reporter. I was in the business for twenty years. The last five years I was with the Associated Press, in New York. I have covered just about every kind of story that happens—including sports. While I was with the Associated Press I covered, among other things, politics. I covered Democratic National headquarters in 1928 and again in 1932 and in 1932 made the big campaign swing around the country with President Roosevelt.

If you wish for more details, you will find them in the accompanying volume, Miss Ishbel Ross' "Ladies of the Press." I have clipped together the pages dealing with my biography.

---

[22] In 1936, Ishbel Ross, a former *New York Herald Tribune* reporter, wrote the first history of American women journalists, titled *Ladies of the Press.* Ross devoted eight pages to Lorena, labeling her a "star" reporter and writing, "She did it on sheer capability. She covered straight politics, which is considered the most difficult and unsuitable work for newspaper women."

In the Summer of 1933 I went to work for Mr. Harry Hopkins, Federal Emergency Relief administrator. My job has been to travel about the country, watching the relief load, the physical condition and mental attitudes of people on relief and WPA, and so on. I have also done a little investigating for the president. All my reports to Mr. Hopkins have been confidential. They have been read by Mr. Hopkins and Mrs. Roosevelt, and, from time to time, by the president and other people in the Administration.

I wish to leave the Government because I think it is a very bad thing for people in the government service to think they have a so-called "vested interest" in their jobs. Being a friend of Mrs. Roosevelt and therefore—in the attitude of many of my confreres, possibly—in a protected position, although no one who knows either Mrs. Roosevelt or Mr. Hopkins well would believe that, I felt that it would be a good thing for me to set a good example by quitting, now that the election is over. I believe that the field of public relations offers me my best opportunity.

I think I could do my best work for you in publicity or in some sort of "contact" job. Mrs. Roosevelt suggested that I might go out with a small model of the World's Fair and sell the fair to small town commercial clubs, women's clubs, and the like. I don't mind travel. In fact, I love it!

Thank you very much for seeing me yesterday.

Yours very truly,

[November 13, 1936]

THE WHITE HOUSE
Washington

Hick darling, How you do castigate yourself!

The letter to Grover [Whalen] was grand, [I] hope & pray you get it & you've certainly done your best. If you get it, we'll have some fun planning your campaign [to promote the fair]. I think I can help.

Darling, will you never learn that love can't be pigeon holed & perhaps we love people more for their weaknesses than for their best qualities of which you have a lot tho' you forget them when you are down.

A world of love,

E.R.

Just before writing this letter, Lorena learned that she had been hired for the World's Fair job.

November 17th [1936]

10 Mitchell Place
New York City

Dearest:

I *am* pleased, naturally, to have it settled. It takes a big load off my mind. I don't know just what I'm going to do yet, except that I'm to be in the promotion end. I'll probably be doing some traveling, I was told. And I report for work at 9 a.m. on January 4th. I came on home and celebrated before my simple, home-cooked meal, with a whiskey and soda, all by myself.

I must do some packing. My deep gratitude to you for your assistance.

Good night, dear.

H

This letter must have been a painful one for Lorena to receive. The first lady's casual reference to the sapphire and diamond ring that Lorena had given her four years earlier was a poignant reminder of the reduced intensity in the women's relationship.

November 21st [1936]

THE WHITE HOUSE
Washington

Dearest, I thought of you when Madame [Ernestine] Schumann-Heink died. Would you like to wear her ring now or put it into safe keeping? I am careful of it but I never want you to feel you can't do what you want with it.

Ever so much love,
E.R.

Lorena had talked to Eleanor's literary agent about writing a book describing the Depression from her perspective as a relief investigator, drawn partly from the letters she had written to Eleanor. So while the first lady was in Hyde Park, Hick was at the White House reading the letters she had written during the previous three years. Lorena then made her first decision related to preserving the correspondence.

December 6th [1936]

Dearest:

A long, dreary, rainy Sunday. I have spent the whole day in Louis Howe's room, while I plodded through those letters. I should say I am now about half way through. Today I stumbled into a lot of the early letters, written while I was still with the AP. Dear, whatever may have happened since—whatever may happen in the future—I was certainly happy those days, much happier, I believe, than most people ever are in all their lives. You gave me that, and I'm deeply grateful. There were other times, too—many, many of them.

What do you want me to do with these letters when I have finished? Throw them away? In a way, I'd like to keep them, or have them kept somewhere. They constitute a sort of diary, as yours to me probably do, too. They might be of some use when I get around to that biography.[23] What do you think? In a way, I haven't minded reading them so much today, although some of them make me feel a little wistful. I don't suppose anyone can ever stay so happy as I was that first year or so, though. Do you?

Good night, dear. You have been swell to me these last four years, and I love you—now and always.

H

---

[23] Lorena was referring to the biography of Eleanor that she was planning to write.

On the day before Christmas when Franklin Jr. developed a sinus problem so serious that doctors confined him to a Boston hospital for the holidays, Eleanor made plans to go to his bedside. Never eager to be alone, Eleanor called Lorena in New York and asked if her favorite companion might be willing to board the train in New York, ride up to Boston with her, and then turn around and return to New York. So at the last minute, Eleanor and Lorena ended up spending Christmas Eve together on the train.

Christmas night [1936]

Hotel Statler

Boston

Hick dearest, Fjr. enjoyed some of his presents but he didn't get at them till late for the doctors came to fuss with his nose. At 12:30 F. called & Fjr. talked with him & James & Elliott[,] & then he had another hemorrage [sic]. The Dr. says his resistance is low & perhaps he should have a transfusion so they tested both our blood to-day. He asked me to stay till they could see a definite improvement so I think I'm here for quite a time.

I saw all the newspaper men at the hospital & one man said I'd be saved a lot if I had the Associated Press girl along who used to travel with me! I told him you came up with me but had returned to N.Y. Bless you dear for coming up with me, the trip was fun & it was the nicest Xmas present you could have given me tho' I love all those others you did give me. The quilt, underclothes, raincoat, etc. are all a *great* joy & will be *very* useful. You yourself were the grandest present. Thank you ever & ever so much & good night dearest,

E.R.

At the first of the year, Lorena had begun her job with the World's Fair. Her office was in the Empire State Building, and she was living in her midtown apartment. In this letter, Eleanor apologizes for not

calling Lorena as she had promised—and then apologizes again for not being able to meet her in New York in two weeks as they had planned.

[January 13, 1937]

THE WHITE HOUSE
Washington

Dearest, I am so sorry. I wanted to telephone you but Elliott & Ruth came home with colds & he wanted to talk & before all my chores were done it was too late to telephone you for I felt with a cold you would go to bed early. I'll try to do better to-morrow.

I'm sorry dear, but I've given up coming up to N.Y. for the day on the 29th so I won't have even a glimpse of you till early Feb. but things are just too complicated here. I've *got* to go to Arthurdale Sunday night but I don't *have* to go to N.Y. for pleasure.

Had my hair & nails done this morning, a lunch for 35 women, the Egyptian minister. I'm weary & good night, take care of yourself. I love you,

E.R.

The irony of the second paragraph of this letter is striking to anyone familiar with how Eleanor revolutionized the role of first lady.

January 21st [1937]

THE WHITE HOUSE
Washington

Dearest, Here all the excitements [of inauguration activities] are over & we are settling back a bit. I went around & thanked everyone to-day for they were all wonderful & when you think that 710 ate lunch & 2700 had tea & everyone so far tells me things moved smoothly I think everyone deserves a pat on the back. I confess that arrangments [sic] & people bothered me but even more my sense of 4 years more begining [sic] bothered me.

Why can't someone have this job who'd like it & do something worth while with it? I've always been content to hide behind someone else's willingness to take responsibility & work behind them & I'd rather be doing that now, instead I've got to use my opportunities & I am weary just thinking about it! Well, we'll live thro' it!

If you can't make lunch Wed., can you make tea about 5 or 5:30 at the Biltmore [Hotel in Manhattan]?

Good night, bless you & all my love,

E.R.

April 26th [1937]

New York World's Fair

Dearest:

Whew, what a day! There were mountains of mail when I got in this morning. My desk looks a good deal like yours, in Washington. And I've had today about as many interruptions as you have. Joe Baldwin[24] sails for Europe Wednesday. And he shoved everything off on to me today with one big "swoosh." He'll be back June 15th. In the meantime he has no confidence in Joe Cohn[25] so I'm to run the department, but be tactful and let Joe Cohn *think* he's doing it. Which is the common lot of womankind!

I must give myself a manicure and do some sewing.

Good night, dear. I hope the speech goes well tonight.

H

Because of Eleanor's hectic schedule, she was finding it difficult to find time to spend with Lorena, and Lorena continued to insist upon either seeing the first lady alone and away from the White House—or not at

---

[24] Joe Baldwin, head of the promotion department of the World's Fair staff, was Lorena's boss.

[25] Joe Cohn was Joe Baldwin's deputy.

all. In early July, Eleanor had offered to go to New York to spend the last weekend of the month with Hick.

[July 27, 1937]
Val-Kill Cottage

Dearest, You are going to think me an unmitigated ass & I deserve it. I never looked in my engagement book & I discover after all my planning that weeks ago I promised to go to a 3 county meeting in Poughkeepsie & speak at 3 p.m. on Sat. Can you forgive me & wait till Friday the 6th [of August]? I want so much to go & will be disappointed if we can't. May I come to you for a night the end of August if the 6th doesn't work out? Dearest, I know how upsetting my uncertainties have been & this is worst of all & I am so sorry, please try to forgive me.

Much love darling,
E.R.

Lorena and her friend Howard Haycraft—he was twelve years younger than Lorena, and people often mistook him for her son—began renting a small house on Long Island as a weekend getaway. Sometimes they both stayed at the house; other times one of them had it alone and invited a friend along. As Lorena was writing this letter, her favorite high school teacher from Battle Creek, Michigan, was her guest. This was the first time Lorena used the stationery she had printed with "The Little House" across the top, bearing a curious resemblance to "The White House" stationery she had received so often during the previous four years.

August 13th [1937]
The Little House
Moriches, Long Island

My dear:
Alicent [Holt] & I have just arrived out here, at 11:30, and I am weary. She arrived this morning to spend a couple of weeks with me. I don't think I'll ever invite anyone to visit me again. I *think* I want them, but I

loathe it when they get here. Just haven't the time nor the energy—nor the money—any more. And I don't give a damn about anyone. I'm so tired out.

I'm just about asleep. So—good night, dear.

H

August 17th [1937]

Val-Kill Cottage

Hick darling, You remind me so much of myself! You are letting yourself be driven largely by your own attitude & you can't get rested because you feel inwardly irritated all the time! You really care for Allicent [sic] & do try to get some pleasure out of her visit. I think two weeks is rather long but you do get some privacy at the little house. I wish you'd come here & sleep a whole week end, I'd make sure no one disturbed you!

Much love to you dear,

E.R.

Lorena was becoming despondent. In addition to having discovered that she despised public relations work, she also had been told by George Bye that, after she had worked on several sample chapters for her proposed book on the Depression, he did not see a market for it. But the major reason for Hick's melancholy state was her concern about what she viewed as the continued deterioration of her relationship with the first lady.

September 8th [1937]

New York World's Fair

My dearest:

I'm glad we had a chance to talk last night and this morning, dear. Not that we got anywhere much. But somehow we seemed closer. It's this drifting—or seeming to drift—apart that bothers me so. I've tried hard to be perfectly acquiescent this summer—I think the feeling that I had to do most of the trying just got me down and completely discouraged. And I've hated the thought so of seeing you—or trying to see you—when you didn't want to see me. Perhaps I was right. I may have been wrong. I don't know any of the answers.

I guess the only thing I really do know is that I love you, with all my heart. And that it's a Hell of a lot harder to see you unhappy or listless than to be unhappy myself. All of which sounds like perfect twaddle.

Here's for brains that jell, dear. Keep your chin up! I love you very much.

H

[September 9, 1937]

THE WHITE HOUSE
Washington

Darling, I'm glad too we had our talk. You don't realize that I have not been to N.Y. without trying to see you, there is no use in you coming here to be miserable. I could go to you, but there has been a good bit to do here & I didn't realize you felt we were drifting apart. I just take it for granted that *can't* happen!

I'm really not unhappy & listless so don't worry. I think I just get annoyed with life as it is & my inability to change it for the moment!

I must go to bed. Bless you & I love you too,

E.R.

Eleanor again began sending drafts of her articles to Lorena for editing. Asking Lorena for help may have been merely a gesture to make her feel needed, however, as Eleanor had been such a quick study as a writer that she no longer needed Lorena's guidance. All Lorena could offer was praise. In the article that Lorena lauded in this particular letter, the first lady tackled the highly sensitive subject of divorce. She argued that be-fore two people marry they should make sure they share the same inter-

ests. She also stated quite emphatically and—*unbeknownst to most of her readers*—from very personal experience, "Where children are involved, a divorce should be avoided, if possible, because a child has a right to both of its parents." Ladies' Home Journal *published the article in April 1938.*

September 28th [1937]

Dearest:

I've just finished reading your article, and I think it's *swell*—one of the best articles you've ever written on any subject. Gosh, it packs some good hefty wallops, and I wonder how the president liked it. I'm *proud* of you, I am.

It says things and states the case frankly & objectively. Congratulations.

You know I love you, *don't* you?

H

As soon as Harper & Brothers released Eleanor's autobiography, This Is My Story *was a hit with readers and reviewers alike. The* New York Times *called Eleanor's book "vivid, interesting, touched here and there with humor, and arresting in its combination of frankness and charm."*

November 21st [1937]

New York World's Fair

Dearest:

I read the notice in the Times today, and it is marvelous. I'm so pleased and proud. It does look as though at last you are coming into your own. Aren't you pleased? You ought to be. I think the review is very sincere—an honest tribute to a *real job.*

H

Because Lorena had taken a pay cut when she accepted the World's Fair job—from $6,000 a year to $5,200—and also was maintaining both her *apartment in the city and, with Howard Haycraft, her house on Long Island, her finances were tight. So the first lady began giving Hick money as her birthday and Christmas gifts. Most of the checks were for $50 or $100, but some were for as much as $200.*

December 11th [1937]

THE WHITE HOUSE
Washington

Hick darling, I think it may be a help for you to have the enclosed check *now*. If you just come on the 20th & we have a happy evening that is enough [Christmas] present for me & please don't spend money on *things* for me, love means so much more & heaven knows you give me that 365 days in the year.

Much love,
E.R.

After a year on the World's Fair staff, Lorena finally admitted to Eleanor—reluctantly because ER had helped her get the job—that she despised public relations work. Lorena found the resolutely positive writing to be dishonest compared to the newspaper reporting she had loved. In this letter, Hick also alludes to a subject that would reappear more than once in her mind and her correspondence: suicide.

December 28th [1937]

New York World's Fair

Dearest:

It's been a very bad day, and I'm more completely disgusted with this outfit than I've ever been before. I'd quit tonight if I were sure of getting another job right away. But $100-a-week jobs don't grow on every bush these days, so I guess I'd better keep calm. And there is no use in bothering you with all the details.

I'm trying very hard to learn not to take this job seriously. The best way, I guess, is to live my life outside and give as little time and thought to the job as possible. But I loathe living that way. I want to be interested in my job, dammit, and do it as well as I possibly can. Oh, my dear, WHY can't I be better adjusted to life? God knows, I try. But about 90 per cent of the time I'm out of step with life and miserable. I'll not try to step out of it—at least not as long as I have enough to live on in fair comfort. And probably, even if I were broke and hungry, physical cowardice would keep me from finding a way out. But it's been a miserably uncomfortable business, most of it, and I'm tired of it all and bored with past, present, and future.

There, there, Hickok!

I wonder where you are right this minute.

I must powder my nose and get going. Much love, dear.

H

The article Eleanor mentions in this letter was about Washington's cherry blossoms and was published by Reader's Digest *in April—without revision.*

January 6 [1938]

THE WHITE HOUSE

Washington

Hick dearest, I have thought so much of you & your weariness & it seems so hard that life should be so little worth living to you when so many people love & depend on you but I have felt as you do & I keep hoping that someday things will change for you & seem more worthwhile.

I am sending you another article which went out tentatively but may have to be lengthened & revised. I feel you are much too tired to be bothered with this stuff so don't hurry about reading it. When you do[,] be as critical as possible!

I have to go up to N.Y. to-morrow night & I'd like to see you but fear I won't be long enough for even a glimpse. Bless you dear.

I love you,

E.R.

As this letter attests, Hick continued to be frustrated by her job—and continued to express that frustration to ER.

January 7th [1938]

10 Mitchell Place
New York City

Dearest:

I'm sorry I talked to you with such bitterness the other night. It wasn't fair. But—since I did say it—it's true. I've felt this way for nearly a year.

I'm not *entirely* ungrateful [to be alive], dear. I do appreciate the affection and loyalty of my friends. And I try to pay them back in kind. But—oh, I don't know. I'm just tired of it all. It isn't worth the bother. I'll get through this mess, and then there will be another—maybe worse.

Well—I'll try not to talk about it any more. You shouldn't be such a good listener.

The Associated Press called me today wanting to know where you were. I told them I had no idea!

I *would* love to see you tonight. Poor Mrs. Nesbitt.[26] But *not* poor *Mr.* Nesbitt. It's all over for him, and tonight I envy him a little!

Good night, dear, and God bless you!

H

[January 19, 1938]

The White House
Washington

Dearest, I realize how unsatisfactory probably a week end here would be & so we'll try for something else, perhaps part of your vacation?

Of course dear, I never meant to hurt you in any way but that is no excuse for having done it. It won't help you any but I'll never do to anyone else what I did to you. I'm pulling myself back in all my contacts now. I've always done it with the children & why I didn't know I

---

[26] The husband of Henrietta Nesbitt, the head housekeeper at the White House, had died earlier in the week.

couldn't give you (or anyone else who wanted & needed what you did) any real food I can't now understand. Such cruelty & stupidity is unpardonable when you reach my age. Heaven knows I hope in some small & unimportant ways I have made life a little easier for you but that doesn't compensate.

I must say goodnight, bless you dear, & much, much love,

E.R.

April 14th [1938]

The White House
Washington

Dearest, We've just come up from F's speech & I think it was good, if a bit arrogant in spots.[27] He did not stir me but I may have been too tired or perhaps he can't. Another busy day over, starting with [a] bunch of school children at 10:45, then press conference, column, lunch & talk to Congress [members'] wives & from 3:30-6 the strangest mixture of people in a steady stream. Everyone tells me how they feel[,] thinking it will seep through to F.D.R.[,] & of course I never tell him! Dinner on a tray as F. ate in bed & the others working on the speech ate late. At 8:30 spoke at American University & was back here to listen to F. at 10:15!

I wonder what you are doing this week end? I hope you are going to the country for it is beautiful & spring like here.

My hair is so straight that I have to get a permanent to-morrow instead of riding.

Much love dear one,

E.R.

[27] In his "fireside chat" on the radio, FDR took credit for the nation's successful economic recovery, saying that the national income rising from $38 billion in 1932 to $68 billion in 1937 had been entirely due to New Deal programs.

Eleanor wrote the next three letters while she was on a month-long speaking tour in the Midwest.

[October 15, 1938]

Hotel Robidoux
St. Joseph, Missouri

Hick dearest, It was nice to find your letter here & this looks like rather an interesting old place & after lunch we[28] will drive about the town a bit. Lecture to-night on "Peace" is a difficult [topic] in the light of recent events & I'm just going over it to see what I dare to say.

I doubt dear, if I'll ever have the money to travel except on a money making basis such as lecturing or writing & I cannot imagine that you would enjoy it even if I were not the president's wife for one does of necessity so much one does not want to do. We can take short motor trips when I have more time someday & those when I am no longer recognized wherever I go you will enjoy again.

I do hope you are more comfortable to-day. Be careful of yourself & much love,

E.R.

Lorena had been having problems with her teeth. She was making weekly trips to the dentist, who was attempting to save three of her teeth while replacing the rest with an upper plate and a partial lower plate. Lorena was concerned that the dental bills would be so high that she would have to give up her car.

[October 20, 1938]

Hotel Northland
Green Bay, Wisconsin

Hick dearest, Sorry all this [dental work] is going to be costly as well as so painful but it is worth it. Don't neglect the doctor or dentist again

---

[28] Eleanor's secretary Tommy Thompson accompanied the first lady on her speaking tours.

you pay more in the end. Don't worry about the car, we'll manage that for Xmas & birthday, as for Xmas presents I think nice letters are the nicest of all & you write the nicest letters I know! How about keeping Tuesday night, Dec. 20th to celebrate [Christmas] with me?

The speech went well but they robbed the box office while I was speaking. Wisconsin has no state police however so it seems unlikely that they will catch the thieves.

We have to be up & on the train at 7 a.m. so goodnight dear, don't work so hard,

E.R.

Beginning the night of November 9, the Nazis conducted an orgy of violence against German Jews; they burned 191 synagogues, looted or destroyed 7,000 businesses, and subjected thousands of Jews to wanton violence and sadistic torment—killing nearly 100 people. In response to the event that became known as Kristallnacht *(the night of broken glass), the United States ordered its ambassador to Germany, Hugh R. Wilson, to return to Washington.*

November 14th [1938]

Netherland Plaza
Cincinnati

Hick dearest, I was relieved to know the teeth were out & I do hope you will feel much better but I hate to think of all your discomfort.

This German-Jewish business makes me sick & when F.D.R. called to-night I was glad to know Wilson was being recalled & we were protesting.

The speech went well to-night, then a reception was a bit long. We came home & had supper having eschewed dinner.

I've been thinking of your being under a boss you don't like & I hope he will soon be changed or couldn't you be looking for a new job? Business is picking up this might be the time for you to start thinking out something you could build up for the future. Why not go & see Eddie

Roddan[29] in N.Y. & suggest a female side to national publicity they need it to help the states. N.Y. State has had little or no publicity for the women in this campaign.

Much, much love,

E.R.

[November 21, 1938]

Henry Grady Hotel

Atlanta

Hick dearest, Talked to F. about a plan for National Committee publicity. Eddie Roddan, you & a youngster. He's much interested but doubts if Jim [Farley][30] wants a liberal democratic party. I'll talk to Jim soon & let you know how things develop. I'd rather see you in private business & yet this cries to be done & is most interesting.

To-morrow will be busy. I don't suppose I can reach you on Thanksgiving Day by wire so here is my love dear & may you have much to be thankful for,

E.R.

November 22nd [1938]

New York World's Fair

Darling:

You were a peach to talk to the president about that Democratic Committee job. Many, many thanks. No, I don't think Jim is much interested in a *liberal* Democratic party, but let's hope he has the political acumen

---

[29] Eddie Roddan was a former International News Service reporter who was now working at Democratic National Committee headquarters.

[30] Jim Farley was now chairman of the Democratic National Committee.

to keep it more liberal than the Republican party. I think the National Committee job might be interesting.

Worked until 8 tonight, and, since I came home, I've packed. We drive to the country tomorrow night,[31] and I don't expect to be back here until Monday night, although I'll be at the office Friday and Saturday morning.

I have to go to a business dinner the 27th. What about the 28th? We do have the darnedest time getting together.

I have much to be thankful for—a great deal of that "much" being *you*.

Good night and bless you!

H

During a quick trip to New York the day before writing this letter, Eleanor had not found the time to meet with Lorena but had telephoned her.

[January 3, 1939]

THE WHITE HOUSE
Washington

Dearest, It was a flying trip to N.Y. but it was good to hear your voice.

I had my talk with Jim [Farley] to-day & he seemed to take kindly to the idea of using you but said he must talk to Charlie Michelson[32] & see about funds. I said $500 a month expected. I just pray it goes thro' but am far from sure yet!

---

[31] Lorena and Howard Haycraft were spending most weekends at the house they shared on Long Island.

[32] Charlie Michelson was another Democratic National Committee staff member.

I'm playing a rather mean trick to-night, pleaded a headache & sent Mama down to sit as hostess at the Diplomatic dinner! She told everyone at lunch to-day how much she disliked having to sit so far down the table so I thought this was a good way to put her at the top & I'll stay in my room & *really* be able to enjoy the music for a change!

Much, much love dear,
E.R.

January 19th [1939]

New York World's Fair

My dear:

Cold and snowy again this morning. I have a kind of half a case of the grippe, which I am fighting off. I don't feel sick enough to go to bed—and, after all the time I've lost with my teeth, I'd have to be really sick to go to bed.

I probably should not try to keep the Little House and the car on top of my other expenses. My third heavy—and what might be termed, with the others, *luxury*—expense is Prinz. And naturally I simply won't entertain the thought of giving him up. There are limits, after all.

Now of course it would be perfectly reasonable to say that it was silly—insane, really—for a woman of 45, almost 46, without a cent in the world except her salary, without any very promising prospects for a well paid job in the future, etc, etc to try to hang on to these three luxuries. All the sane arguments are on that side, I know. They just can't be answered logically at all. But I'll just have to answer them in my own way. Living—just going on living—simply doesn't mean a God damned thing to me, dear. I'm being perfectly honest when I say I'll be relieved when it's over, provided the actual ending isn't too painful. You are always horrified when I say that I wish it had happened when I had that automobile accident out in Arizona. But I still do. I'd have died happy, as happy as I've ever been in my life, and it would all have been over. But it didn't happen that way, and here I am.

I'm not complaining, dear. Nobody has a perfect time in this life, of course. Lots of other people have had harder times. But in the final analysis each person has to live his life alone and fit himself to it in his own way.

> Much love, dear.
>
> H

[January 31, 1939]

THE WHITE HOUSE
Washington

Dearest, We've just had our last dinner & musicale till spring & then oh! boy, we're going to have 'em every other day!

Now for the interesting news. Charlie Michelson came in to-day & we talked over the plan & he's thrilled with the idea & with having you. Says you are ideal. They don't want to start till April but he would like you to come & see him so I wondered if you'd let me *give* you the trip down & back on March 3d or 4th as a birthday present? It would be fun to have you here!

> Much love dear,
>
> E.R.

By the spring of 1939, Lorena's worklife was busier than ever, as the World's Fair was preparing to open on April 30. Nevertheless, she continued to hate the PR job. Perhaps to boost Lorena's sagging spirits, ER gave her a particularly lavish birthday gift.

March 9th [1939]

New York World's Fair

My dear:

Your "little" gift was at the apartment when I got home last night, and it left me a bit breathless. I'd hardly call a box of lingerie like that a "little" gift. Well, anyway, it's gorgeous stuff, and I love it. Many, many thanks.

I finally brought most of my birthday cake here [to the office] today and passed it around. Not a chance to have anyone in for a party at home, and I was afraid it would just dry up. It certainly was a delicious cake, dear. And thank you again for it.

Much, much love, dear.

H

On the morning that Eleanor wrote this letter, the German army had in-vaded Poland. She was in Hyde Park for the last weekend of the sum-mer.

[September 1, 1939]

Val-Kill Cottage

Dearest, I grieve, but I can't lunch Friday. I may be down [in New York City] Wed. & we might do it that day. I'll let you know.

F.D.R. telephoned at 5 a.m. to tell me about Poland & so I sat with Tommy & listened to Hitler's speech. His voice is to me so unattractive! It all seems so senseless, he must have all [the territory] he wants & so Europe will be a battlefield. I feel deeply discouraged!

I hope you have a peaceful week end & that you get labor day [off] for you deserve it. I'd like to pay *all* your indebtedness & have you pay me as suited you, would you like to do it that way?

Much, much love,

E.R.

At 11 a.m. on the day that Eleanor wrote this letter, Great Britain had declared war; six hours later, France had followed suit. In the fireside chat that FDR delivered in the evening and that Eleanor refers to, the president proposed the sale of arms to Great Britain and France on a cash-and-carry basis. The proposal, which Congress quickly approved, demonstrated FDR's uncanny ability to read the national mood— people wanted to support the Allies but feared American involvement in armed conflict.

[September 3, 1939]
Val-Kill Cottage

Dearest, A cloud seems to hang over everything but somehow I feel more reassured now that it is done. If they had let Hitler repeat his past performances I think we would have felt more uncertain, tho' Lord knows this may mean a Europe in ruins.

We listened to F.D.R. & I thought him restrained & wise in what he said. War must affect us all but there is no use in making people fear our being drawn in till it is necessary & I pray that may never be.

I hope you had a quiet Sunday & feel better dear.

Much, much love,
E.R.

When Eleanor wrote this letter, she was beginning a month-long speaking tour in the Midwest and South. The last sentence is very telling.

[September 23, 1939]
Hotel Woodworth
Robinson, Illinois

Hick dearest, You've asked about questions [being asked by people attending the lectures], they are dull, run about like this: "Do you think we can keep out of war? What can women do to keep us out of war? What can we do to remain neutral?" Last night I had written questions & was asked if I loved my husband, which I did not answer!

E.R.

November 1st [1939]

New York World's Fair

My dear:

It was good to hear your voice this morning. I needed reassurance! I had wakened at 6, moaning and covered with a cold perspiration, dreaming you had died! Second morning in a row. Only yesterday morning it was Prinz—he had been run over by a train. Funny, because I hardly ever dream. I shall feel better after I've heard from you tonight.

It would be so much better, wouldn't it, if I didn't love you so much! It makes it trying for you.

You are very sweet to me always.

H

Lorena was spending her two weeks of annual vacation at her country home.

November 30th [1939]

The Little House
Moriches, Long Island

My dear:

I'm all dressed up in new corduroy breeches and hunting boots ordered with $11 of the money you gave me for my vacation. I paid bills with the rest. I'd been wearing my riding breeches and boots down here, but the woods, especially in wet weather, would soon ruin them utterly. So I'll keep them to dress up in and wear these for rough work. Boots, tan with rubber bottoms, $7. Breeches, dark blue corduroy, $4. Gee, I love clothes like these.

Only three more days of my vacation. Well—it has been a heavenly interlude—something to look back on. I wish you *could* have come down. Well—maybe sometime you won't be so busy in November. Or I'll take my holiday in Summer.

It's sweet of you to invite me down to the Gridiron Widows' party, but I think I'd better sit tight financially. I got my first request for a loan from Ruby this morning.[33] It may be only a short loan, but it means I can't buy a doggoned Christmas present again this year.[34] It wouldn't be only the fare, but I'd have to get my evening things out, have them pressed, etc. So I think I'd better just slip quietly—and inexpensively—out to the country and see Prinz.[35]

Much love.

H

December 1st [1939]

The Little House
Moriches, Long Island

My dear:

Just heard over the radio that you've been given some sort of award as the "leading statesman of the week" for standing by the American Youth Congress.[36] Good for you! I'm darned proud of you and glad somebody had that much sense.

Well, the vacation is about over. These have been two perfect weeks, anyway. I can't ever remember having had a happier time on a vacation—except that time you and I drove around the Gaspé Peninsula. We *did* have a good time on that trip, didn't we?

Much love.

H

---

[33] Ruby and Julian Claff, Lorena's sister and brother-in-law, had both lost their jobs.

[34] Lorena could not afford to buy Christmas gifts in either 1938 or 1939.

[35] Lorena had arranged with neighbors in the country to take care of Prinz during the week so he could get more exercise than he could in the city.

[36] The House Un-American Activities Committee had accused the American Youth Congress of being a Communist-front organization, largely because its youthful members held liberal—sometimes radical—beliefs. Eleanor steadfastly defended the organization.

Despite ER's repeated efforts, Democratic National Committee staff members had still not found the money to create a job for Lorena.

Christmas night 1939

10 Mitchell Place
New York City

My dear:

I just sent you a belated Christmas wire—and I hope it gets there before you've gone to bed! Yours was here when I arrived from the country today, and I *should* have sent one off to you at once. But I *did* have to hustle to get the house in order and dinner ready on time,[37] so I let it slip. And now they've just gone.

It's been a queer Christmas. I haven't been terribly unhappy—I don't get terribly unhappy any more. But just sort of miserable and hang-doggish. Utterly lacking in enthusiasm. And not liking myself. Of course it would be so much better if I had a job I liked. But, oh Lord, how *does* one go about using people & selling oneself. I *know* how to get newspaper jobs. But that was my profession, and I had such confidence in myself. Well—I've got to start doing something unless Jim [Farley] comes through pretty soon.

Got up at 6 this morning, cleaned up this place and cooked a fairly elaborate dinner for Ruby and Julian. I do wish I were fonder of them—it would be so much easier. I got awfully annoyed inside tonight when I discovered *they* had given presents to some people, on money they had borrowed from me—when letting them have it meant that I couldn't get presents for anyone!

Well—to pleasant topics!

The turkey and the plum pudding,[38] darling, are *delicious,* and the turkey so big that I could just get it into my oven and that was all. If it had been an ounce bigger, I'd have had to send it out to be roasted! And *good*—I think it's even better than the one you sent for Thanksgiving. I'll have enough to last me the rest of the week. Ruby indicated that she thought—because I did it last year, I guess—I'd give them what was left,

---

[37] Lorena hosted her sister and brother-in-law for Christmas dinner.
[38] Eleanor had sent both items to Lorena for her dinner.

but I fooled her, although I did weaken and give them some to take home with them. Well—it's a *lovely* turkey, dear, and I wish I could give *you* some of it!

Another very pleasant thing. Julian got a letter telling him to report to the Census people this week for a job.[39] *Darling, if you only knew how grateful I am!* Somehow, just to say "Thank you" seems inadequate!

Good night, dear, and bless you.

H

---

[39] Eleanor, at Lorena's request, had urged Bureau of the Census officials to hire Julian Claff.

Eight

1940–1944

Enemies Abroad;
New "Friends" at Home

During the early 1940s, the most compelling drama playing out in
Eleanor and Lorena's correspondence was the one that reflected events
that were unfolding on the world stage. World War II widened the gulf
between the first lady and Hick, propelling Eleanor into even greater
service to her country as an international ambassador—a voice of stability, morality, and humanity in a chaotic world.

Lorena's life during the early 1940s was blotted with more medical
and financial difficulties. Health issues included more dental problems,
repeated bouts with fatigue, diabetes, a low blood count, menopause,
and heart trouble; economic issues included long periods of unemployment, a salary history that crept downward rather than upward, and the
realities of a job market that was not exactly bursting with opportunities for a middle-aged woman. Lorena was not left entirely on her own,
however, as the first lady repeatedly came to her aid. Eleanor helped by
providing Lorena with a place to live and prodding a potential employer
toward making her a job offer; at other times, ER's generosity came in

the form of hand-me-down dresses, boxes of fresh fruit shipped from Florida, a check to pay for a new set of curtains, and even the services of a maid. What this multitude of contributions added up to was the reality that Lorena, who in previous stages of her life had insisted upon being totally self-sufficient, was gradually but undeniably becoming financially dependent on Eleanor.

One aspect of the relationship that did not waver was Lorena's support and encouragement of Eleanor. "I'd never have believed it possible for a woman to develop after 50 as you have in the last six years," Hick wrote on one occasion, and "I grow prouder of you each year," she said on another. Lorena also continued to proclaim her undying love for the first lady. "You are still the person I love more than anyone else in the world," Hick wrote.

By 1942, however, another woman began gaining prominence in Lorena's life. In fact, Marion Harron—a judge in the United States Tax Court who was ten years younger than Hick—lavished so much attention on Lorena that she was competing with Eleanor as the central figure in Hick's life.

By 1940, a new person also had entered ER's emotional life. Joe Lash, twenty-five years younger than the first lady, was an intense and moody intellectual who shared her progressive social ideals. Eleanor and Joe spent many days together until he was inducted into the army in 1942. Scholars consider their intense relationship to have been that of a mother and her devoted son.

Because of Eleanor's rising stature as a global ambassador combined with Lorena's growing friendship with Marion and Eleanor's involvement with Joe, this period marked a dramatic reduction in the volume of letters they wrote. In 1939, they had written each other a daunting 533 letters; by 1944, that figure had plummeted to fifty.

By the end of January 1940, Lorena's job with the Democratic National Committee had finally been created, with her responsibilities centering on reaching out to disenchanted voters. She would spend half her time in New York and half in Washington. Although Eleanor invited Hick to stay at the White House when she was in Washington, the first lady no longer asked her friend to sleep in the sitting room adjoining her own bedroom. From this point on, Hick would occupy a small bedroom across the hall.

January 29th [1940]

10 Mitchell Place
New York City

Darling:

I think I can stay at the W.H. alright if you want me to, and there is room. I'd like to very much, because it gives me at least a few glimpses of you. But I'm *not* going to hang around the place the way I used to. I shall live, as far as possible, a normal business life, going to the office every morning, putting in a full business day, usually lunching out. It's better so, dear. That business of moping around the W.H.—never again.[1]

Now you are either laughing like Hell or a little bit hurt inside. I hope—and believe—you are laughing, dear.

I'm glad your nose and throat are better, dear, and *please* don't think I'm unappreciative.

You are sweet and thoughtful and generous, and I love you—with all my heart!

H

---

[1] Lorena kept the fact that she lived at the White House a secret, fearing that her bosses at the Democratic National Committee would expect her to produce favors for them if they realized she was living with the first family. So even though Lorena was, in reality, sleeping no more than twenty feet from the president, she pretended that she was living at the Mayflower Hotel on Connecticut Avenue five blocks from the White House. If someone insisted on taking Lorena home after work or dinner, she would direct her escort to the hotel and wave goodbye as she entered the lobby. As soon as the friend was out of sight, Lorena would leave the hotel and walk to the White House.

Never before had an American president served more than eight years in office, but Eleanor was now beginning to face the unpleasant prospect that her husband might break that tradition. The last two words in the first paragraph of this letter aptly summarize Eleanor's attitude toward that prospect.

[February 11, 1940]

Dearest, Your Thursday letter came to-day & that third party business is really bad.[2] Everywhere I go people talk it & to-day Mr. [Bernard] Baruch[3] who came in for an hour seemed won over to the idea that circumstances would close in & make F.D.R. run & win. I groan!

Much love,

E.R.

Lorena was in the Midwest trying to strengthen the grassroots network of Democratic women there.

February 25th [1940]

Commodore Perry Hotel
Toledo, Ohio

My dear:

Spent the entire morning on busses, getting from Columbus to Lima, a distance of about 90 miles. The man I had to see, the Democratic leader up in that neck of the woods, invited me up to his house for dinner. Not a very good dinner, and he talked politics at me right straight through dinner and for a couple of hours afterwards. I felt so sorry for his wife and children. They must have been awfully bored! When I see what some women have to put up with, I certainly can bear my spinsterhood with equanimity.

Much love.

H

---

[2] Ardent conservatives and isolationists were so dissatisfied with both major political parties that they were seriously considering organizing a third party.

[3] Bernard Baruch was an international financier Eleanor had known since her girlhood.

To help ease Lorena's financial worries, the first lady began having her dresses altered to fit Hick.

March 8th [1940]

Hotel Harrison
Indianapolis

My dear:

I'd love the dress, dear, if that's what you had in mind for my birthday. I'd much rather have something like that—that you thought of—than a check.

I didn't write last night because I was too tired. I put in a twelve-hour day—solid, with no break—yesterday, on about five hours' sleep.

Today was a twelve-hour day, too! But I get so interested during the day that I don't even realize that I'm getting tired until I get back to my room at night. The mornings *are* tough. But once up and out, I forget all about being tired.

Darling, I'm sorry, but it's all Third Term! Labor people—even those in the [Paul] McNutt[4] organization here—tell me privately they would much rather have the president run! Nobody says with any real conviction that McNutt could carry even his own state! In Ohio I found not a single person who would give us a chance of carrying the state unless the president runs and they said it wouldn't be a walk-away even for him!

Much love.

H

My measurements: Bust 43
                   waist 40
                   hips 44

---

[4] Paul McNutt from Indiana was hoping to win the Democratic nomination for president.

Just before Eleanor wrote the following letter, the United States had learned that Hitler's armies were simultaneously invading Holland, Luxembourg, Belgium, and France.

[May 11, 1940]

THE WHITE HOUSE
Washington

Hick dearest, The world gets worse & I've about decided short of an army we must do what we can for the Allies. I'm trying to think of something worthwhile I could do for the Red Cross. Talked to F. to-day & see Mr. [Norman] Davis to-morrow.[5]

You will see me at breakfast on Tuesday.

Bless you dear, it will be good to see you,

E.R.

The Republicans had chosen liberal businessman Wendell Willkie as their presidential nominee.

[June 30, 1940]

THE WHITE HOUSE
Washington

Dearest, The papers are discouraging to me since F. told me he really felt Wilkie [sic][6] was a crook or words to that effect. I have a hunch he's going to win, what is yours? The lull in European news makes me dread the storm.

I hope you all have a good time in Chicago.[7] With the state of the world as it is[,] campaigns seem unimportant.

---

[5] Eleanor proposed to Norman Davis, chairman of the American Red Cross, that she go to Europe and help with the refugee relief effort by administering first aid, providing hot meals, and delivering medical supplies in cities that had been bombed. The president rejected his wife's proposal point blank—far too dangerous.

[6] Eleanor consistently misspelled Wendell Willkie's name throughout the campaign, even though Lorena repeatedly spelled the name correctly.

[7] Lorena was planning to attend the Democratic National Convention in Chicago.

Mine was another day spent wondering what men do in their businesses, they are so slow on committees!

Much love,
E.R.

In the "My Day" that appeared the day before Lorena wrote this letter, Eleanor criticized Wendell Willkie's platform as vague. "Sometimes I wonder if we shall ever grow up in our politics and say definite things which mean something," she wrote, "or whether we shall always go on using generalities to which everyone can subscribe, and which mean very little."

July 2nd [1940]

Democratic National Committee

My dear:

No, I don't think Willkie is a crook, but I don't care for the crowd that is backing him. And he is too darned plausible—*too* simple, etc. I think the man is devilishly clever, and that he will beat any Democrat except the president—and very likely the president. We are all having a hard time over at the office, trying not to get a defeatist attitude. I don't know whether Willkie is a fascist or not, but I certainly *do* suspect the crowd behind him. The man is the white hope of the Tories, and, unfortunately, by his charm and his smooth talk, he may win over a lot of women, young people, and even liberals. He may be "der Fuhrer" we've all been expecting!

Oh, you had a *good* column yesterday about Willkie!

A "respectable" Huey Long—that's the way he impresses me!

H

Many delegates to the Democratic convention balked at FDR's choice of liberal Secretary of Agriculture Henry Wallace for vice president, preferring a conservative. Tradition dictated that the president not appear at the convention until after the ticket had been decided, so when the dele-

gates threatened revolt, FDR loyalists turned to Eleanor to restore order to the party. She flew to Chicago and waited at the back of the stage with Lorena until the presiding officer called her to the microphone. The delegates had been loud and raucous, but when they recognized the first lady, they fell silent. She spoke of the grave responsibility of every citizen at this critical point in history. "This is no ordinary time, no time for weighing anything except what we can best do for the country as a whole." When she finished, the organist played "God Bless America"— and the crowd cheered. The delegates then nominated FDR's choice for his running mate.

[July 20, 1940]

Val-Kill Cottage

Dearest, It was so good to see you & I am glad you were satisfied with my job in Chicago. The "few words"[8] must have come over the air well from what people tell me.

I've been like a pea on a hot shovel in recent days. I spoke last night at a meeting of foreign born citizens & to-day at the United Jewish Appeal & both meetings were strangely moving.

So much love,
E.R.

August 8th [1940]

Democratic National Committee

My dear:
The open season on Anna Eleanor Roosevelt is here. "Look" magazine and the Associated Press have both been after me today, wanting to know your plans, whether you are going to be active in the campaign, etc. AP in the person of an old newspaper pal of my Minneapolis Tribune days who phoned from New York, and Ruby Black, who is to write the story for "Look," came in and had a drink with me late this af-

---

[8] Eleanor referred to her speeches with the same casual phrasing that many of the people asking her to give them did when requesting her to say a "few words."

ternoon. Ruby's story is to be about the part, behind-the-scenes or otherwise, you are taking in the campaign. I *could* have given her one or two juicy bits, but refrained. Lord, I hope they don't start pestering me for inside dope on you this Summer! Oh, well—if they do, I'll just be polite and tell 'em nothing.

Congratulations on losing six pounds!

Good night and much love.

H

[August 11, 1940]

Val-Kill Cottage

Dearest,

I'm sorry you are being bothered [by reporters] but I shall be doing little [in the campaign] & the one reason I'm glad to be going down to [Democratic National Committee] headquarters is that I will be seeing you!

I had 800 ladies to tea to-day. It was awful but I think successful!

I have a deep discouragement about the world these days & would like to run away from having to face it. If I feel that way[,] what must other less [economically] secure people feel?

Much love dear,

E.R.

This letter contains Lorena's first mention of Marion Harron. It is unclear exactly when or where Lorena met Marion.

August 21st [1940]

Democratic National Committee

Darling:

The other day, when we were talking about next weekend, I clean forgot that I had invited Dorothy Cruger[9] to the country. Would you give me a

---

[9] Dorothy Cruger was a co-worker of Lorena's at the Democratic National Committee.

rain check? I'm having company over Labor Day, but could go to HP [Hyde Park] the weekend of September 10th or 17th or sometime in October. I realize these may all be impossible for you, and I'm sorry about next weekend. Marion will be here to go down to the country with me the weekends of September 24th and October 1st. She will be hearing cases in NYC that week.

Got settled today in the room I'm to have during the campaign. It's on the nineteenth floor of the Beekman Tower,[10] with a nice breeze and a lovely view of the East River.

I'm terribly sorry about the weekend and hope you will forgive my stupidity.

Good night, dear, and much love.

H

[September 6, 1940]

Val-Kill Cottage

Hick dearest, I've just been notified that on Sunday we have all the exiled Austrians for lunch.[11] I find royalty heavy & boring!

What you need is a maid to take care of you. If you can get one at $15 a week I'd like to give her to you as my Xmas present to move from city to country with you & take care of you. I think you'd find yourself less tired.[12]

I'll be down [to New York City] on Monday but only for a brief time in the morning. I hope you have a good week end but I'd rather have you here when royalty is gone & F. is not up!

A world of love,

E.R.

[10] The Beekman Tower was an office and residential building at 3 Mitchell Place very near Lorena's apartment building.

[11] When the Nazis invaded Austria in March 1938, members of the aristocracy fled.

[12] Lorena took Eleanor up on her offer. Hick insisted that she needed a maid only during the work week, however, and not on the weekends when she was at the Little House.

In her job, Lorena spoke frequently with ordinary people and was convinced—and worried—that the Democrats would lose the upcoming election. Eleanor, as this letter indicates, was less concerned.

[October 22, 1940]

20 East 11 Street
New York City

Hick dearest, Don't worry about Nov. 5th dear, you have done your best for the things you believed in. If the Republicans win[,] it will mean that the majority wanted Wilkie [sic]. We are democrats & believe in the will of the people, don't we?

[Westbrook] Pegler was poisonous to-night.[13] I'll be glad for the kids['] sake when the campaign is over! If F.D.R. wins I'll be glad for him & for the country & if he loses I'll be glad for myself & the kids!

Much love to you dear,

E.R.

On Election Day, FDR won 55 percent of the popular vote—the smallest margin of victory in a presidential election since 1916. Because Lorena had been hired to help the Democrats win, her job ended the day after the election.

November 7th [1940]

10 Mitchell Place
New York City

My dear:
And how do you feel, now that it's over? I hope you don't mind too much. I thought about you a lot the other night, as it became clear that we were winning, and hoped you were not too low in your mind.

---

[13] The *New York World-Telegram* columnist criticized James Roosevelt—Pegler called him "the Eaglet of the New Deal Dynasty"—for using his position as the president's son to gain publicity for the vending machine business he was involved in.

I told Charlie [Michelson][14] that, of course, I'd like to stay on the payroll and land that job as director of the [Democratic National Committee] women's division, but that I didn't want to stay on if, by doing so, I crowded out some of the little people who also need their jobs and didn't have the connections I had. I told him that, if I stayed with the committee, it should be on my record—and not simply because of pressure from you or anybody else. And that is the way I feel about it—badly as I do want to stay.

So, I'm off to the country tomorrow morning, and there I shall stay until I hear from Charlie.

I hope, dear, that you won't mind these next four years too much. And I think you must know how grateful I have been and am for this job I've had with the committee. And I owe that to you.

> Much love.
>
> H

[November 8, 1940]

20 East 11 Street
New York City

Hick dearest, No, I don't look forward to the next four years for I will probably be too old for a new job at the end & I dread getting accustomed to 4 more years of easy living but perhaps I can keep from being too dependant [sic] on it. Anyway what is the use of worrying about tomorrow let alone 4 years from now!

> A world of love dear,
>
> E.R.

[14] Charlie Michelson was an official at the Democratic National Committee.

November 11th [1940]

The Little House
Moriches, Long Island

My dear:

I'm glad you are taking these next four years so philosophically. What do you mean by "easy life"? I don't know anyone in the world who works harder than you do! And I don't believe you'll ever be too old for a job, either. If you were going to get old, you'd be showing signs of it by now. I don't see any. As a matter of fact, I'd never have believed it possible for a woman to develop after 50 as you have in the last six years. My God, you've learned to do, surpassingly well, two of the most difficult things in the world—to write and to speak. I'd not worry about a "life of ease" or getting old if I were you.

When I couldn't sleep the other night, I read Ruby Black's book through.[15] The first part, of course, is just re-hash of your autobiography, and you did that better yourself. But the chapters on your career in the White House are excellent, I think—much better than I could do. My trouble, I suspect, has always been that I've been so much more interested in the *person* than in the *personage*. I resented the personage and fought for years an anguished and losing fight against the development of the *person* into the *personage*. I still prefer the person, but I admire and respect the personage with all my heart!

H

[November 15, 1940]

Stevens Hotel
Chicago

Hick dearest, Hope the [Thanksgiving] turkey will be good & I'll be thinking of you. I'll be at the Big House in Hyde Park.

[15] The United Press reporter's biography of Eleanor, *Eleanor Roosevelt: A Biography,* had been published the previous month.

I wrote Eddie Flynn[16] & have written again to Molly Dewson[17] about the job. She worries as to whether you will have patience to answer endless letters constructively & help endless "little" women to move up one step at [a] time in [the] organization. Also meet the endless visitors & stand constant entertaining & hounding me to entertain those I should. I am writing her that I too think it will be hard for you at first but I can work with you & that seems to be important in their minds for some unknown reason.

Much love dearest,
E.R.

November 18th [1940]

The Little House
Moriches, Long Island

My dear:

I honestly don't think you and Molly [Dewson] have any real cause for worry about my getting bored or impatient with the ladies. What neither of you seems to realize is just how desperate my plight is—and how little I can afford to be choosy! I am 47 years old, my dear, and have reached an age where it is very, very difficult for a woman to get a job.

I have *got* to have a job, my dear—or else! Now if I had any idea of where to look—or what I could do—in private industry, that would be *one* thing. But I haven't. And any job I could get in private industry that would pay me anything like an adequate income would undoubtedly bore me more than the ladies would. At least on that job I'd be in a field that interests me.

I am exceedingly anxious, if possible, to keep the house out here. It's the only thing that deeply matters to me any more. It's the difference between getting some joy out of life and just merely working to keep on existing.

---

[16] Eddie Flynn was a Democratic National Committee official.
[17] Eleanor's friend Molly Dewson had directed the Women's Division of the Democratic National Committee in the past.

It is most generous of you to offer to guarantee the dentist bill for a Christmas present, but I can't let you do this. It will be a whopper, my dear—at least $300, possibly $400 or $500. One nice feature is that this will probably be the last big one I'll ever have. But, entirely apart from not wanting to take advantage of you, I just can't see any sense at all in investing any more money in this old carcass unless I am fairly certain of being able to support it!

Much love, dear, and thanks for your letters.

H

December 10th [1940]

THE WHITE HOUSE
Washington

Hick dear, I've written to Jim [Farley] & ought to get some answer before long. I still hope in the future to get a job where you & Tommy & I could work to-gether but it must be something where age won't put us out!

Much, much love dear,
E.R.

December 27th [1940]

10 Mitchell Place
New York City

Darling:

You *are* so cute and funny! I arrived here today to find the big box of fruit from Florida and a lovely basket of candied fruit from California, with one of your Christmas cards enclosed. Madame—am I never to stop receiving Christmas presents from you? Oh, damn it—what have I ever done to deserve a friend like you! Well, any way, I thank you—for a very great deal of pleasure.

Thanks again, you dear, for all the sweet things you think of and do. And I love you more than I love anyone else in the world except Prinz— who, by the way, discovered your present to him on the window seat in the library Sunday. I wouldn't let him have it until Christmas, but he kept sneaking in there every chance he got the next two days and sniffing it, and, when he was in there with me, he'd lie on the floor and look at it long minutes at a time! You *should* have seen him open it!

Much love—

H

After six months of being unemployed, Lorena was finally hired by the Democratic National Committee. Gladys Tillett from North Carolina would be director of the Women's Division and make most of the public appearances; Lorena would be executive secretary—at a salary of $5,000 a year, less than at either of her two previous jobs—and concentrate on behind-the-scenes activities, such as organizing a Democratic women's conference in Minnesota.

June 3rd [1941]

Hotel Lowry

St. Paul, Minnesota

My dear:

Well—I'm here. Being the first arrival from Washington, I was greeted by a barrage of personal publicity, plus photographers, which I *loathed*. But the conference needs every bit of publicity it can get, and I'll be the only one they have to write about until Ed Flynn arrives tomorrow. Mrs. Tillett gets in Thursday. I'm even going on the radio tomorrow, for the first time in my life. Have to. We are offered the time free, with no one to fill it. Please offer silent prayers that my teeth don't click! One Minneapolis paper wanted to write a story with the lead: "Hick came home today—" I begged them not to do it!

Goodbye for now and much love.

H

[August 4, 1941]
Val-Kill Cottage

Dearest Hick, I'm so glad you want a new suit for Xmas. I'll bring [fabric] samples when I come in on the 20th. I'll be at the White House for breakfast that day.

What worries me however is your ankles swelling, that is bad & would mean a visit to the doctor at once if you had any sense. Will you please go at once & I will gladly pay.

I found Mama in bed with high blood pressure. I think she just missed having a stroke & I fear it means I must be a bit more considerate of her, instead of running away. You know that won't be to my liking!

Much love dear,
E.R.

Sara Delano Roosevelt had died the morning that Eleanor wrote this letter.

[September 7, 1941]
Val-Kill Cottage

Hick dearest, I am so weary I cannot write. I was up most of last night, 1 1/2 hours was the time I spent in bed & I've been seeing relatives all day.

Mama's death was peaceful but putting Hall in the hospital last night was a job & keeping him there is worse.[18] I've got to be at the hospital at 9:30 a.m. & try to use moral suasion.

Devotedly,
E.R.

[18] Like her father, Eleanor's brother Hall suffered from alcoholism and the emotional upheavals that often accompany that disease. On this particular occasion, Hall had collapsed and been taken to Vassar Hospital in Poughkeepsie.

Hall Roosevelt died on September 25, with his sister at his bedside; he was fifty-one. When Lorena wrote this letter, she was in Kansas meeting with Democratic women there.

October 8th [1941]

Dearest:

I was sorry to hear that you were so weary and "indifferent inside." I wonder, though, if fatigue may not have had something to do with your mood. I think Hall's illness and death undoubtedly took more out of you than you realize or would ever admit, even to yourself. And remember—even when you're feeling that way, you do a better job at whatever you're doing than most people do. I meant what I said in the wire I sent you today—I grow prouder of you each year. I know no other woman who could learn to do so many things after 50 and to do them so well as you, Love. You are *so* better than you realize, my dear.

A happy birthday, dear, and you are still the person I love more than anyone else in the world.

H

On the Sunday before Eleanor wrote this letter, Japanese aircraft attacked the United States naval base at Pearl Harbor, propelling America into the war. All four Roosevelt boys quickly donned uniforms—Elliott in the Air Force, James in the Marines, Franklin Jr. and John in the Navy. Immediately after the attack, Eleanor flew to the West Coast to help bolster the civilian morale there.

[December 11, 1941]

Hick dearest, How much has happened since I bid you goodbye!

We had an anxious trip out, fearing the West Coast was being bombed & we had a blackout in Los Angeles last night coming thro' from San Diego. It has been very strenuous but I hope useful & I have learned a great deal.

It seems like a completely changed world.

Devotedly,
E.R.

Eleanor and Lorena spent the evening of December 22 together for their annual pre-Christmas gift exchange. Lorena had vacated her New York apartment and now considered the Little House her primary residence. She stayed at the White House when her job took her to Washington and rented a room in the Beekman Tower when she was in New York.

December 23rd [1941]
Beekman Tower

My dear:

Had the final fitting on my suit this morning, and it is a *beauty*. I think you are going to be very much pleased with it. Ordered my red fox furs out of storage, to be sent to Washington to wear with my new suit. Had lunch with Marion Harron, who was in New York for cases and came bringing me a big box of jam and stuff, although we had agreed not to give each other presents.

Many thanks for last night, dear, and a happy Christmas.

H

When Eleanor wrote this letter, Prime Minister Winston Churchill was meeting with FDR to develop war policy and strategy. In the course of their talks, the two leaders committed themselves to focus on defeating Germany first—an unpopular stand for Roosevelt to take after the surprise Japanese attack on Pearl Harbor.

December 26th [1941]
THE WHITE HOUSE
Washington

Hick darling, I hope you had a happy [Christmas] day & will enjoy to the full the day in the country.

The day went off well here from an official point of view. I've talked much with the P.M. He is a forceful personality but the stress on what the English speaking people can do in the future worries me a little. I don't trust any of us with too much power & I want the other nations in too!

I'm dying to see your suit & the fox furs!

E.R.

The meeting between the president and prime minister that Eleanor refers to in this letter resulted in American forces striking the Japanese at Midway Island, the farthest outpost of the Hawaiian chain. Catching the enemy off guard, the Americans destroyed four Japanese carriers, one heavy cruiser, three battleships, and 372 aircraft; 3,500 Japanese sailors were killed. The Battle of Midway was a turning point in the war.

[June 1942]

THE WHITE HOUSE
Washington

Hick dearest, You are moved into my room just for Wed. night because the King of Greece [George II] & his Chamberlain are using the Lincoln rooms & my sitting room over night.

Last night the P.M.[19] dined at the Embassy so the [Henry and Elinor] Morgenthaus dined with us & it was fun.

To-day Elliott & Ruth talked with me a long time over breakfast & I realized again how much each of my children feel I failed them.

Much love,
E.R.

Eleanor was now renting a seven-room apartment in the Washington Square section of New York City.

July 6th [1942]

The Little House
Moriches, Long Island

Dearest:
Your Saturday letter came this morning, and I was very pleased to get it.

I didn't try to stay at your apartment because I didn't think I ought to

---

[19] British Prime Minister Winston Churchill was staying at the White House to strategize with FDR about the war.

ask you to let me take a stranger there.[20] But it was nice of you to think of it. You are so sweet.

I certainly was amazed at the news about Harry Hopkins.[21] Gosh, I shouldn't think he'd be any bargain as a husband. He looks as though he might die any minute![22] And how awful to take his poor bride to live at the White House. They won't have any life of their own at all, will they? It may have been the president's idea, but I'll bet Harry didn't fight it much. Kitty-kitty![23] And what a Hell of a thing for *me* to be saying.

Much love, dear, and thanks for your letter.

H

Lorena and Marion's favorite activity while at the Little House—they were spending their summer vacation together there—was working in the garden. Digging in the soil helped Lorena forget her medical and financial worries, while giving the serious-minded Marion a break from the highly detailed tax codes that she dealt with each day.

July 7th [1942]

The Little House
Moriches, Long Island

My dear:

Your Sunday letter came today, and I cannot see why you think you've been a failure with your children. You were much better than an average mother, albeit, perhaps, a bit too strict, and they are nice children and a credit to you.

---

[20] Marion Harron had come to New York to spend several days with Lorena.

[21] Hopkins, whose wife Barbara had died four years earlier, had married the beautiful socialite Louise Macy.

[22] Hopkins, at fifty-two, had been rendered gaunt and pallid by the cancer eating away at his stomach.

[23] With the phrase "kitty-kitty," Lorena was acknowledging that she was being catty about Hopkins and his young and beautiful new wife.

Tomorrow I am going to buy the curtain material with the check you gave me for my birthday.

The house is cool and quiet tonight. Marion has gone to bed.

Good night, dear!

H

Lorena disliked living in Washington and avoided staying in the city any more than her work demanded. But when Marion's mother left town on a trip and Lorena had the chance to spend three weeks alone with Marion in the Harron home, she gladly accepted the invitation.

August 10th [1942]

My dear:

Just a note while waiting for Marion to stop by for me to go and do our marketing and then go on out to her house and cook our dinner. It's such fun staying out there with her in Chevy Chase.[24] She has the sweetest little house, most attractively furnished, two cats, and a funny little colored maid who can't cook but who is a marvelous cleaner! Her mother will be away until about September 1st, so I'll be out there a good deal of the time. And it does seem good not to be traveling for a few weeks!

I must run.

Goodbye for now and my love.

H

---

[24] Chevy Chase is an upscale neighborhood in the northwest section of Washington, adjacent to the suburb of Chevy Chase, Maryland.

In response to Eleanor's repeated requests to help with the war effort, FDR sent the first lady on an inspection tour of conditions in England after the German bombing.

[October 23, 1942]

BUCKINGHAM PALACE
London

Hick dearest, This [stationery] is to impress you! Tommy & I have a nice sitting room with a page to take us hither & yon!

We had to stay over in Ireland but they sent a special plane this a.m. & we landed in Bristol. Everything is wonderfully cleaned up but it is easy to see the havoc bombs have brought. The Queen[25] showed me her own destroyed rooms here & all windows are out! It is a curious place but the people give you a sense of unity. I'm anxious to get out among them.

There is some protection but there is a sense of tension.

To-morrow a.m. I have a press conference, then the King & Queen take me to the blitzed east end.

I'll be glad when Buckingham Palace lies behind me & I can get to work!

Much love dear,
E.R.

---

[25] Queen Elizabeth was the wife of King George VI and the mother of today's Queen Elizabeth II.

The press gave extensive coverage to Eleanor's trip to England, including front-page photos and stories in both the Washington Post *and* New York Times.

October 26th [1942]

Democratic National Committee

My dear:

I'm simply delighted with the press you are getting. *Nice* stories! I ran into [Treasury Secretary] Henry [Morgenthau] on the train coming down from New York today, and he, too was so pleased! I judge that you *are* doing a good job, dear. The kind of job you can do better than anyone else I know—and I'm awfully happy about it and so proud of you. The Washington News story today has a lovely bit in it, which I'll clip and enclose.[26]

Much love to you and Tommy, and I'm so glad things seem to be going so well.

H

November 1st [1942]

[Washington]

Darling:

I am thrilled about you—and worried.

Worried over the increased activity of the German bombers over England. Apparently they visited Canterbury right after you were there. No use telling you to be careful—they are probably taking as good care of you as they can, or as you will let them. Anyway it's all on the knees of the Gods. But I can't help worrying.

I'm thrilled because of the job you are doing. More than anyone else in the world, *you* are holding the British and us together right now. And

---

[26] The "bit" included a photo of Eleanor eating a donut with an American soldier and a story about soldiers cheering the first lady because she had not even flinched when an air-raid siren had begun to wail.

in your own straightforward, honest way. Oh, I'm *so* proud of you! Your press over here is wonderful.

Good night, much love, and I'll say a little prayer for your safety—

H

November 5th [1942]

[London]

Dearest Hick, I wish too you could [quit work and] live in the country if you really want to do that but I think you would soon be very weary of doing no work outside a narrow circle.

To-day has been a quiet day in which my only official engagement was a lunch with the [British] Cabinet wives & they are as dull as ours!

Cambridge [University] yesterday was interesting & my first introduction into industrial billeting. The beautiful Colleges seem on the whole to be little hurt [by the bombing].

Our most vivid impression I think is what a blackout of an entire city really means.

You get a curious feeling over here that nothing but people count.

A world of love dear,

E.R.

Upon Eleanor's return from England, she arranged a nationwide hook-up on NBC radio to express her "deep sense of pride and satisfaction" in both the American and British soldiers she had seen.

November 20th [1942]

The Little House

Moriches, Long Island

Dearest:

I just listened to your speech and I think it was *swell*—exactly what I had hoped you would do. You certainly managed to put over a lot of good stuff about the British, but subtly. You put that point over about not complaining in letters to boys in the service superbly.[27] So—congratulations, dear!

I arrived out here late this afternoon and brought Marion Harron, who has been hearing cases in New York, with me. We've had a couple of walks—the second one in the moonlight—a very good dinner, have washed the dishes, and listened to your speech.

It was a *swell* speech, Madame!

Much love—

H

Marion's letters, which Lorena preserved along with her own and ER's, clearly show that Marion had, by the end of 1942, fallen in love with Lorena, although the lack of letters from Lorena make it unclear if she reciprocated those feelings.

December 23rd [1942]

The Little House
Moriches, Long Island

My dear:

A box of very lovely handkerchiefs arrived from you this afternoon—for which, many thanks. The turkey is here, too.

I go down to Washington Sunday afternoon to spend most of the week between Christmas and New Year's with Marion.

Good night, dear. Thanks for everything, and my love always—

H

---

[27] Eleanor had urged mothers and fathers, when writing to their sons overseas, not to complain about gasoline and coffee rationing, as it made the soldiers worry about conditions on the homefront.

Lorena was traveling on Democratic National Committee business in the West.

March 20th [1943]

Hilton Hotel
Albuquerque, New Mexico

My dear:

I should say that the Democratic party out here is definitely *not* in good shape. OPA has done a great deal of harm.[28] And the resentment, among the leaders, seems to be directed against the president. We begin to encounter definite anti-Fourth Term sentiment.

I'm getting very clothes-conscious! I'm having three of the dresses you gave me fixed so I can wear them—a very good looking black one with accordion pleated panels (remember it?), a black evening gown, and that gorgeous white and gold evening gown. They are all going to be *very* good looking. You'll be surprised to learn that I can wear the white and gold dress without alteration—except for shortening![29]

I must go. Much love, dear—

H

July 3rd [1943]

Democratic National Committee

My dear:

Well, the thing I've dreaded for a long time has finally happened. Dear old Prinz died Wednesday afternoon. The vet wrote that his hind legs gave out entirely, and that he became paralyzed. I don't know whether he put him out or not. I think I'd rather not know. I had instructed him to do it if the time ever came when he thought Prinz was suffering, but

---

[28] The Office of Price Administration was a new federal agency designed to prevent profiteering and unjustified price increases.

[29] Hick was not the only career woman who was becoming clothes conscious. At Lorena's urging, Marion began having her business suits made by the same New York tailor who made many of Eleanor's clothes. Lorena also persuaded Marion to let Eleanor's hairdresser give the judge a less severe coiffure.

asked him to wait, if possible, until I could get there. I thought I might be able to reassure him a little, as I used to do when they gave him injections to prevent distemper and rabies. Probably he was so far gone, though, if they did give him a hypodermic, that he didn't realize it. Annie [Ross][30] had them wrap him in my old raincoat and bury him down in the West lot—a place he loved above all others, because we used to start our walks there. Well, he was a good dog, and he lived a long and honorable life. When so many women are suffering so much greater losses these days, I probably have no right to mourn over the death of a dog. But you can't lose an old, loyal, and very dear friend like Prinz without feeling lonely and a bit desolate. I think I shall miss him all the rest of my life.

And my love to you, always.

H

In the fall of 1943, FDR sent Eleanor to the South Pacific to boost the spirits of American troops stationed there. It was to be such a grueling trip—26,000 miles—that the first lady decided not to travel with her faithful secretary Tommy Thompson. While Eleanor was on the other side of the globe, Lorena and Marion were growing closer. Marion visited Lorena so often while she was living at the White House that the guards at the gate recognized the judge's car and waved her through without checking her identification.

Auckland [New Zealand]
September 1st [1943]

Hick dearest, Well, the trip is nearly half over. The people here are kind & they like F.D.R. & our Marines have won all their hearts. So they are very nice to me. I make so many speeches daily that I shall soon be talked out.

These boys break your heart, they're so young & so tired. Malaria is almost as bad as bullets. They are hardly out of [the] hospital before

---

[30] Annie Ross was Lorena's neighbor who had taken care of Prinz during the week when Lorena was not at the Little House.

they are at the Red Cross Clubs & dances & they laugh at everything. I take my hat off to this young generation & I hope we don't let them down. I've talked to every kind of group, from hospital patients, high ranking officers & the people of New Zealand.

> Much love dearest,
> E.R.

> September 12th [1943]
> [Australia]

Hick dearest, The terrain in which these boys fight is unfamiliar & unbelievably difficult. I do camps, hospitals, Red Cross services day & evening & see men who have either been into New Guinea & come out with a shadow on their faces but a grim hatred of the Japs or new men going in to something they know nothing about & are ill prepared for. I've only done 2 radio talks, one in New Zealand & one in Australia. There have been several short "few words" daily to very varied audiences. I begin to think this job has been a good one as far as these countries are concerned[,] but for our own F. should have insisted that I go to Guadalcanal or not sent me.[31]

My love to you dear. I think of you & your love for travel & wonder if you would have enjoyed this trip.

> Devotedly,
> E.R.

Eleanor returned to the United States the day that Lorena wrote this letter. In the column that Lorena mentions, Eleanor praised the bravery of

---

[31] FDR had written General Douglas MacArthur and Admiral William Halsey that his wife was "anxious" to visit the battlefront on the island of Guadalcanal, but he left the final decision in the hands of the military leaders. They initially refused her request, but after the first lady's tireless visits to hospitals and Red Cross clubs boosted troop morale beyond anyone's expectations, Admiral Halsey reversed his position and allowed her to travel to Guadalcanal. During that visit, ER spent an evening with Joe Lash, whose being stationed on the island was part of her eagerness for wanting to visit it.

American soldiers. "*I have seen many a boy hospitalized because he went back for a buddy who was wounded,*" she wrote. "*When you try to tell them of your admiration for their courage, they seem embarrassed.*"

September 24th [1943]
[The White House]

Oh, darling—I'm glad you're home!

My phone at the office rang about 2 o'clock—*our* time—yesterday afternoon, and it was Tommy.

"I talked to her!" she said. "I talked to her. I was crying, and I couldn't think of anything to say."

Dear Tommy! I felt like crying, too! What a relief!

Your wire was here when I came in last night, and it was wonderful to have it.

Gosh—I can hardly believe you're *really* back!

Your column yesterday was one of the best you've ever written. I caught Leone Crowlie[32]—whose 19-year-old boy is somewhere in the Mediterranean theater—reading it last night, with tears rolling down her cheeks.

All my love—
H

In 1943, for the first time, Eleanor and Lorena did not spend an evening together to exchange gifts and celebrate the Christmas holiday. Eleanor was at the White House; Lorena was at her Little House.

[December 25, 1943]
The Little House
Moriches, Long Island

My dear:

I can't let Christmas go by without telling you how very grateful I was for all the things you do all the year round to make life easy and com-

---

[32] Leone Crowlie was a co-worker of Lorena's at the Democratic National Committee.

fortable and happy for me. I think sometimes that all of us—those who love you and those whom you love—may take you too much for granted. But when we stop to think—we don't.

Merry Christmas, dear, and God bless you—

H

Although Eleanor and Lorena could not find an evening to spend together during the holiday season, not so Lorena and Marion. On December 10, they spent the night together at the Hay-Adams Hotel a block north of the White House. The next day, Marion sent Lorena a postcard with a photo of the hotel on the front, penciling in an arrow that pointed to a room on the sixth floor. On the back of the card, Marion wrote the suggestive message, "X marks the spot."[33]

In one of Marion's ardent love letters, she wrote, "I hope 1944 will be a good year for you, darling, and I hope the Gods will give us many happy hours. Dearest Hick—I love you very much."[34] *Meanwhile, Eleanor was bound for the Caribbean and South America to boost troop morale and to inspect military bases there.*

March 7th [1944]
[The White House]

My dear:

The beautiful material and your very generous [birthday] check were here when I came in just now. I don't think it should cost seventy-five dollars to have that dress made, dear. I'm going to put the money into a bond now. I'll have the dress made in the Fall, and I think I should return to you the balance.

Well—I'm 51 years old today. Sometimes I *feel* 101!

---

[33] Marion to Lorena, 11 December 1943.
[34] Marion to Lorena, 5 January 1944.

I, too, have thought a lot about you starting out over the [Caribbean] route we covered ten years ago this Spring. Can you believe it was *ten* years ago? I find it difficult. Yet so much has happened. And we are both older and, in *my* case, I hope, wiser. Well—it was a beautiful trip, dear. But I wish I had been more mature, more stable.

Good night, dear. My love and my thanks for your generosity.

H

March 9th [1944]

La Fortaleza
San Juan, Puerto Rico

Hick dearest, I have thought of you so much ever since I arrived.

The wind blows all the time so it is cool & really very beautiful. One does feel farther away from the war here. The problems are as bad as ever for the people & wages don't sound very high.

Much love dear,
E.R.

March 17th [1944]
[The White House]

My dear:

Your very interesting letter of March 13th [from Brazil] was here when I came in a few minutes ago. I'm looking forward with interest to your return and the stories you'll have to tell. I'm glad you're having a comfortable trip. Gosh, I'd like to go to South America sometime.

I suppose those boys do want to go home. But how about the boys in the Pacific, which must be infinitely less comfortable. Or in Italy. Sometimes I think *no* one really appreciates what those kids are going through. Except a few people, like you, who have been out there. We were talking about it at dinner tonight—Marion and I—the seeming lack of understanding and awareness of people here at home. We were wondering if so much drama, on so large a scale, hasn't stultified us.

The news on the diplomatic front has me down. "Sphere of influence"—power politics—I'm uneasy.

Must go to bed. Thanks for your letter, dear. And my love to Tommy and you—

H

It was in the paper about Elliott and Ruth [divorcing] yesterday. I'm awfully sorry, dear. I wish she'd had the sense and wisdom to wait until the war is over. After all, she's no child.

H

Eleanor returned from South America in late March and by early summer had escaped the Washington heat for a visit to Val-Kill.

July 7th [1944]

Val-Kill Cottage

Dearest Hick, Being here gives one a very remote feeling about all the problems of the world.

Elliott is apparently on the way to matrimony again but I've had no word from him anymore than I had from Ruth about her marriage.[35] I think he [Ruth's new husband] has a cruel face which does not seem to promise happiness for her or for the children.

[35] Almost immediately after Elliott and Ruth divorced, they both remarried.

I hope you had a satisfactory time in N.Y. & that now you & Marion Harron will enjoy every moment of this holiday.

Devotedly,

E.R.

Lorena was in Chicago for the Democratic National Convention, which would nominate FDR for a fourth term. The Republicans nominated New York City Mayor Thomas E. Dewey.

July 12th [1944]

Blackstone Hotel

Chicago

Dearest:

I didn't know that Ruth had married again. I can't help thinking she did it out of pique, and that she will be sorry. Foolish little idiot!

It struck me tonight that in my discussion with you on the telephone today I hadn't even let on that I was aware of the president's statement that he would run! Well, for your sake and his, I hate to see him do it. If it were not for this war and all the problems that go with it, I'd not be a party to it. I'm not a Fourth-Termer, under normal conditions. But there's no one else I'd trust now. But it's awfully tough on you—and him.

Next time we're both in New York, let's have lunch or dinner and have Tommy along, and I'll fill you in on the convention. I'd love to spend a weekend with you at your place or mine. If it isn't convenient for you to leave Hyde Park, I'll go up there.

Darling—all my thanks for everything. I love you with all my heart.

H

Lorena had been planning a visit to Val-Kill. But when FDR decided to bring Winston Churchill back to Hyde Park after their meeting in Quebec to discuss war strategy, Eleanor had to inform Lorena that the president's plans pre-empted hers. Allied forces were, by this point in the

war, confident of victory. American and British leaders were now strug-
gling to devise a plan to prevent Germany from starting yet another war
in the future.

September 12th [1944]
The Citadel
Quebec

Hick dearest, F.D.R. thinks we'll bring the Churchill party back getting to Hyde Park Sat. or Sunday so unless you want to come anyway & take your chances, which of course I'd be delighted to have you do, you had better wait & come on the 30th when I know I'll be in the cottage. I won't be in N.Y. either next week as I hoped[,] but I will be there from the 25th-29th. Perhaps either the 26th or 27th you would dine & go to the play with us? Tommy will be there too.

I don't know what work goes on here[36] but we talk much at meals. These people are all nice people & in some ways that is discouraging because [if] they've not found the answers, how can we hope that we'll find them in the future.

Do you want a new skirt & long coat for Xmas, it seems to me about time? If you don't want that, what are your wishes Madame?

Devotedly,
E.R.

September 14th [1944]
Beekman Tower

My dear:
I received both your letter and your wire today. And so I'll go up to Hyde Park Saturday.[37] It will be good to see you.

---

[36] When foreign leaders were in attendance, FDR did not include Eleanor in policy-making sessions.

[37] Lorena opted to visit Hyde Park despite the commotion that FDR and Churchill's presence would bring. In the end, Lorena enjoyed meeting the prime minister, later considering it one of the highlights of her life.

No, I don't think I'll need a skirt and coat this year. If my plans work out as I hope they will, I'll be spending a good share of next year down in the country. You see—I realize that I'll have to work the rest of my life. I'm tired—a kind of cumulative fatigue that has been building up for a couple of years. I believe that a good long rest and change would probably prolong my working life by several years. So I'm going to take it. Six months anyway. Longer if I can swing it financially. As a matter of fact, I now have enough ahead to keep me going for a year, maybe—down there. I don't know just when I'll leave the committee. If we win, I probably should stay and help through the inauguration business. If we lose, they'd probably appreciate it if I removed myself from the payroll as soon as possible. Marion thinks I ought to resign January 1st.[38]

I'd love to have dinner with you and Tommy either on the 26th or the 27th. We can fix the day this weekend.

Good night, dear. It will be good to see you.

H

September 21st [1944]

Val-Kill Cottage

Dearest Hick, Your letter came on Monday & I think I would resign [from the Democratic National Committee job] Jan. 1st if you really feel completely exhausted. I doubt however whether you will need or want more than 3 months rest & I'd try to get the future job lined up before you leave. Since you don't want a suit for Xmas why not let me just fill your stocking with silly things & give you a check toward the vacation?

I loved having you here for the week end.

Much, much love,
E.R.

[38] Marion was trying to persuade Lorena to leave her job so the two women could set up housekeeping together in Washington.

FDR's margin of victory was even less than it had been four years ear-
lier—only 54 percent of the popular vote.

November 10th [1944]

The Little House
Moriches, Long Island

My dear:

Well—are you glad the darned old campaign is over? I'll bet you are.
And so am I! It was, beyond any doubt, the meanest campaign since
1928—and I think it was meaner than that one. God, it would have
been awful, had [Thomas E.] Dewey been elected.

I have a seat back on the Congressional [train] Saturday, the 25th, to
spend the weekend with Marion, in her new apartment.[39]

I'll phone the White House and see if you are there. I'll be in Washington until just before Christmas. Back here for the holidays and in
Washington during all of January. After that, my plans are uncertain.[40]

Darling, I don't like to think about the next four years for you. Rotten luck—but, my God, we couldn't let that little man with the mus-
tache be president! Not *now*.

H

Eleanor had invited Lorena and Marion to dine at the White House,
and the first lady also had persuaded Lorena to make an appointment
with a Washington doctor for a comprehensive physical examination.

November 20th [1944]

The Little House
Moriches, Long Island

Darling:

It was sweet of you to offer to go to the doctor with me, and I do appreciate it a lot.

[39] In hopes of persuading Lorena to live with her, Marion had moved out of her mother's
house in Chevy Chase and was renting an apartment in downtown Washington.

[40] Lorena had agreed to move in with Marion on a trial basis for one month, with the possibility of making the arrangement permanent.

I think we are now witnessing the twilight of the Democratic party. The Democratic party didn't elect the president—this year nor four years ago. He did it himself—as Charlie Michelson remarked several times during the recent campaign, *in spite* of the Democratic National Committee.

Marion and I would love to have dinner with you Sunday night. And I think I'll stay there that night if it's alright. I want to get some clothes—I left my winter things there.

I love you!

H

Eleanor's reference in this letter to feeling like Elliott's new wife was nothing more than "a passing house guest" speaks to the first lady's increasing frustration with her children's marital instability. The five Roosevelt children eventually would rack up a total of nineteen marriages among them—a startlingly high figure for an upperclass family of the era.[41]

December 21st [1944]

THE WHITE HOUSE
Washington

Hick dearest, I hope this will reach you before Xmas. I shall think of you in the little house & hope that the day will be very happy & that the coming year will bring you much happiness.

Let me know about the doctor. I really want to hear all details & I hope you have all the necessary tests.

Elliott's new wife [Faye Emerson] is pretty, quiet. She seems capable but I don't feel that she is more than a passing house guest! I hope I've behaved well!

Much, much love dear,

E.R.

---

[41] Franklin Jr. and Elliott led the pack with five marriages apiece, followed by James with four, Anna with three, and John with two.

December 23rd [1944]

The Little House
Moriches, Long Island

Darling:

Were you *ever* right! It seems I have a blood sugar of 272, which is pretty high, considering the fact that normal is under 100.

I'm on a very strict sugar-free diet over the holidays and am to have another blood sugar before I go back to Washington on the 2nd.

Mostly my trouble, he says, is fatigue. He says my heart sounds like "a tired old man." I have orders to sleep nine or ten hours every night and to relax and not push myself at all when I feel tired. He enthusiastically approves of my taking a long rest and wants me to get away as soon as I can. There is evidence of infection in my septum—probably sinus. And I have a low blood count, though not dangerously low.

I'm apparently going through the menopause with a minimum amount of trouble. He didn't even recommend shots for that!

Darling—thanks for making me go to the doctor. He says you probably saved my life.

A Merry Christmas to you. And all my love.

H

Nine

1945–1962

Living in Two Different Worlds

After Franklin's presidency had kept Eleanor in the bright glare of the national spotlight for twelve years, his death in early 1945 finally offered her the opportunity to leave public life and design the private life that she had, for so many years, said that she wanted—and that Lorena had dreamed of. And then, just four months after FDR's death, Hick ended her relationship with Marion Harron. But instead of Eleanor and Lorena creating a life together in that little cottage that Eleanor had written of so longingly a dozen years earlier, the first lady's sense of duty propelled her to still greater heights. Even though she told Lorena "I'm going to be no leader of thought or action but a homebody," ER did not scale back her activity. In fact, she soon became not *merely* first lady of the United States but—as President Truman so aptly dubbed her—first lady of the world.

As Eleanor traversed the globe, she continued to write to Lorena, but the lengthy letters from past years gave way to brief notes scribbled on postcards—from Paris and Rome, Hong Kong and Karachi. It is unclear, by this point, how much of Eleanor's sustained contact with Lorena, still plagued by poor health and financial worries, was driven by genuine love and how much by loyalty and the first lady's legendary sense of duty.

This final period of correspondence was dominated by Eleanor's letters, with only a handful from Lorena. Perhaps the most telling passage came in a letter the first lady wrote in 1955—"Of course you will forget the sad times at the end & eventually think only of the pleasant memories. Life is like that, with ends that have to be forgotten."

[March 7, 1945]
Val-Kill Cottage

Hick dearest, I hope you have a happy birthday. This little check brings you my love & the hope that you will use it for some little thing you want.

I wish I could be with you.

All my love,
E.R.

After the month-long trial living arrangement with Marion in January 1945, Hick opted not to move in permanently but to live in the Little House by herself. So in March, Lorena left her job at the Democratic National Committee—as well as Washington.

March 21st [1945]
Democratic National Committee

Dearest:

The goodbyes have all been said, and presently I shall be on my way out of Washington with two orchids pinned to my shoulder—and wishing that I could live up to the nice things that have been said to me these last few days. With you as an example, I tried awfully hard to do a good job, and, most of the time, I think I honestly did give the best that was in me. But many times I was irritable and impatient and intolerant. One of the qualities I love most in you is your tolerance, and yet I can be so *in*tolerant if people do not live up to my standards—which have been mostly set by you. It's all very mixed up—and inconsistent and makes me very much dissatisfied with myself. And also makes me feel awkward and inadequate when people say nice things to me—even though I love to hear them and even though, especially now, they mean a lot to me.

I wish I had the words to tell you how grateful I am for your many kindnesses these last four years—and especially for letting me stay at the White House. It did two wonderful things—kept me near you and made it possible for me to hang on to my Little House, which is so infinitely precious to me. I shall miss you. Yet I shall feel that you are near. After all these years, we could never drift very far apart. You are a very wonderful friend, my dear.

Goodbye and God bless you.

H

Easter Sunday
[April 1, 1945]

THE WHITE HOUSE
Washington

Dearest Hick, It has been a lovely day & everything is so lovely. I hope it is begining [sic] to bloom with you too.

We've had a busy time. I left F.D.R. at Hyde Park on Tuesday a.m. & put in a busy day in N.Y. speaking far too often! Got in here Wednesday a.m. & F.D.R. arrived Thursday a.m. & left in the p.m. for Warm Springs.

Much much love dear,
E.R.

On the afternoon of April 12, the president suffered a cerebral hemorrhage while vacationing in Warm Springs—Lucy Mercer Rutherford was with him. Eleanor, who was in Washington, flew to Georgia but did not arrive until after her husband had died. When Lorena heard that the president was dead, she sent a telegram to Warm Springs, offering to fly to Eleanor immediately. Eleanor then telephoned Lorena on Long Island, suggesting instead that they meet at Eleanor's apartment in New York the next week, as soon as she vacated the White House.

April 13th [1945]

The Little House
Moriches, Long Island

Dearest:

It seems like only a few minutes ago when I was writing you, yesterday, a letter about housekeeping and gardening and feeling, although I did not mention it, very complacent about the progress of the war.[1] I guess I never realized what implicit faith I had in him [FDR] until now—since he has gone.

It was wonderful and reassuring to hear your voice this morning. No use burdening you with *my* bewilderment and terror. After all, I guess I only felt like millions of other people in the world. And they'll all be telling *you!* You are like that—people instinctively run to you for comfort, even when *you* are in trouble yourself. And I guess I'm like all the rest.

For you and your future I have no worries at all—although I *do* hope you will take at least a few weeks off this Spring and Summer to rest. You will find your place—a very active and important place, I feel sure—and fill it superbly. I'd like to hope that it may be something in which I can help you if only indirectly, from the sidelines. In a way, you know, you are going to be more your own agent, freer to act, than you've ever been before. Only, for goodness' sakes, do take care of yourself and keep strong and well. We've seen one magnificent constitution break and go down under overwork and strain.

God, he used to be so strong, so vital, so full of energy! I'm glad I didn't see much of him at the last. I want to remember him as I knew him and saw him so often in the thirties. I'll never forget his warm, firm handclasp—the handshake he had, not for the receiving line, but for his *friends*. The last time I shook hands with him—last September—I was shocked to find that his hand felt soft and sort of flabby, like the hand of an old man. How much better for him to go quickly this way. He would have so bitterly resented the kind of disintegration that comes with old age. I shall go into New York next Thursday afternoon and have my blood sugar [check-up] Friday morning. I'll see the doctor Saturday morning, and from then on—and as long as we both shall live—I shall be yours to command.

Dear one, I love you with all my heart—

H

---

[1] The fighting in Europe was almost at an end. Hitler would commit suicide on April 30, and Germany would surrender on May 8.

Franklin's funeral was conducted in the East Room of the White House on April 14, opening with the hymn "Faith of Our Fathers" and ending with the powerful line from FDR's first inaugural address: "The only thing we have to fear is fear itself." That night, the funeral train carried the coffin to Hyde Park for burial. Several reporters who covered both the funeral and the graveside service noted that at all times Eleanor's eyes remained dry.

April 16th [1945]

The White House
Washington

Hick dearest, Three letters from you in two days & I love them. I don't wonder you felt panicky [upon hearing that FDR had died], we all did I think.

I am so glad you will be in N.Y. on Friday. Take the guest room & have Marion Harron whenever you like. She wrote me such a sweet note & I'll be happy to see her.

Life is so busy that I have no time to think! I was offered two jobs to-day one paid & one unpaid but I'm not deciding on anything till later in the summer.

Much love dear & thanks,

E.R.

Mrs. [Bess] Truman toured the W.H. this morning & I liked her—

April 16th [1945]
night

The White House
Washington

Hick dearest, I loved hearing your voice at Warm Springs & I've felt you near in thought every day. When these busy weeks are over, the business settled & the children all busy with their own lives again you will come & be with me a while, won't you? Be sure to go to the apartment when you wish as I'll be there this Sat. & Sunday & there is room anyway.

I'm too weary to do more than say I love you—

E.R.

During this busy and emotionally draining period immediately after Franklin's death, ER wrote Lorena four letters in four days. This particular letter was written on stationery bordered in black.

April 18th [1945]

Hick dearest, Your Monday note came last night & I love hearing of your doings & feeling that you are thinking of me.

I'll be out easily Friday night.[2] The Trumans are more than kind. The office people have to take a bit longer.

I'm begining [sic] to sleep better though not too long as yet.

I'm going to have the newspaper girls at four to-morrow to say good-bye. Others drop in & consume time but all are kind & many feel lost. All my love,

E.R.

Eleanor supervised the packing of a thousand boxes—they filled twenty army trucks—of the belongings that the Roosevelts had accumulated in twelve years of living in the White House. Despite this enormous task, Eleanor made sure that one special item found its way to the Little House. That item was a blue Staffordshire cup that Lorena had drunk her coffee from while living at the White House. After leaving Washington, Eleanor would spend a weekend with Lorena at the New York apartment before going to the Val-Kill cottage, which would become her home. She gave the Springwood mansion to the government as a public museum.

April 19th [1945]

THE WHITE HOUSE
Washington

Hick dearest, The Trumans have just been to lunch & nearly all that I can do is done. The upstairs looks desolate & I will be glad to leave to-morrow. It is empty & without purpose to be here now.

---

[2] Eleanor had promised Bess Truman that she would vacate the White House on April 20— only eight days after FDR had died.

To-morrow the Cabinet comes at 11. At 3 the Secretary of State etc., at 3:30 office staff, at 4:30 household & garage staff, at 5:30 I leave for the 6 p.m. train & so endeth a period. Franklin's death ended a period in history & now in its wake those of us who laid in his shadow have to start again under our own momentum & wonder what we can achieve. I hope you & I will be working to-gether but as I don't intend to take on anything new till all the business of the Estate is over, you may be at new work before I am.

I may be a bit weary when we get home to-morrow but I'm so glad you will be at the apartment.[3]

Much love dear,
E.R.

Howard Haycraft had married and moved to a new house, leaving the Little House on Long Island all to Lorena.

May 5th [1945]

THE LITTLE HOUSE
Moriches, Long Island

Darling:

It's 11:45 a.m. Mr. Choate[4] has had his run for the day—an hour in the woods.

I transplanted twenty-nine plants this forenoon. It's a perfectly beautiful day, and working in the garden was simply *heavenly*. Do you ever work in yours at Hyde Park? It's so much more fun than just having someone do it for you. You get so fond of things you plant and raise yourself. It's like a child, I suppose, or a dog—the more you do for it, the more you love it!

---

[3] When Eleanor arrived at her Washington Square apartment the next night, Lorena was busy arranging the numerous boxes of flowers that had been sent there.

[4] Mr. Choate was the English setter that Eleanor gave Lorena after Prinz died.

Marion sent me a clipping about Franklin, Jr., being recommended for the Legion of Merit. I'm so pleased! Have you heard from him and John yet?[5]

I had a note from Mrs. Truman today, acknowledging my note to her. Pretty stilted and formal.

I must write to Marion and then get to bed. Tomorrow is wash day.

Much, much love—always—

H

It was wonderful of you to have the paper sent to me.[6] I *devour* the whole thing each day! Bless you!

H

The physical problems that Lorena describes in this letter reached a cri-sis stage in the early summer when she collapsed in a diabetic coma. The doctor said she could no longer control her blood-sugar level through diet but needed insulin daily. So Lorena learned to give herself injec-tions, a procedure she continued every day for the remaining twenty-three years of her life.

May 19th [1945]

The Little House
Moriches, Long Island

Dearest:

I'm so glad you have Fala.[7] He's a dear dog, and he ought to be a lot of fun for you.

I've been feeling rather miserable for several days. Intestinal troubles. During the night last night I was so sick that I really got a little fright-ened. So today I've been on starvation rations—dry toast, tea, a little

---

[5] Franklin Jr. and John had both been at the front when their father died and had not been able to return for his funeral.

[6] Eleanor had given Lorena a subscription to the *New York World-Telegram.*

[7] After FDR died, Eleanor took the president's Scottish terrier to live with her.

scalded milk—and I've been taking soda bi-carbonate to get rid of the gas.

I'll be at the apartment around 6:30 Thursday, and it will be wonderful to see you, dear.[8]

My love to Tommy and Fala and you—

H

This letter contains the first reference to Eleanor hiring Lorena to help organize her private papers for preservation at the Franklin D. Roosevelt Library. ER continued to pay Lorena for this work for the next ten years.

July 29th [1945]

Val-Kill Cottage

Hick dearest, Here is the first salary check. Every third month, I'll have to withold [sic] 10% for the internal revenue which will mean you will only get $35 that month.

I'll be glad when Marion gets to you. I hope you have a good time.[9]

Much love dear,

E.R.

This letter contains Lorena's last reference to Marion Harron. Although Hick did not relate the details of their fiery break-up to Eleanor, Marion "got sore" because Lorena continued to refuse to move in with her in Washington. It is unclear if Lorena mentioned to Marion that Moriches was only two hours from Hyde Park where Eleanor was now living, while Washington was eight hours away. Lorena may not have told

---

[8] Lorena was meeting Eleanor at the Washington Square apartment.
[9] Marion Harron was coming to the Little House to spend her two-week summer vacation with Lorena.

Eleanor the details of the argument because she did not want ER to feel responsible for the break-up.

August 30th [1945]

The Little House
Moriches, Long Island

Dearest:

Marion has gone, after a pretty stormy visit. The child is not very well, and she is in a nervous and emotional state very similar to mine at her age. I really think that change of life—I don't know how to spell the other word for it—must start, for spinsters, when they are about 40, and that the worst years are from 40 to 45. At least, that was my experience,[10] and Marion seems to be going through the same thing. I feel terribly sorry for her, but there isn't much I can do except tell her that I probably understand a lot better than she thinks I do! And that she will feel better when she gets to be 50! Of course it makes her very explosive. She got sore at me and packed up to leave. Thank God I'm as placid these days as a cow! Poor child—I wish I could help her. She really behaves a lot better than I did, as I look back to those years, and she is a very dear, warm, generous person, and I'm terribly fond of her.

I must run. You're a darling, and I love you very, very, VERY much.

H

September 1st [1945]

29 Washington Square West
New York City

Hick dearest, I can well imagine what a time you've had with Marion but it was bound to happen & at least you know time makes a difference. I gather your health is fine or you wouldn't have stayed placid!

I beautified myself all morning! Had my first facial & didn't think much of it & won't bother again!

---

[10] Lorena was forty-one when she had her emotional outburst during the Yosemite trip.

My dear, I feel more of an old lady than at 50 but I've learned to hide it better! I have more limitations but I know them & accept them! I'm going to be no leader of thought or action but a homebody in the near future & able to enjoy my friends.

I love you dearly too.

Devotedly,

E.R.

After a year of receiving no income except from Eleanor, Lorena began writing speeches parttime for the New York Democratic State Committee. Eleanor had begun a new job, too, as President Harry Truman had persuaded her to become a member of the American delegation to the United Nations that began meeting in London in January. She was the only woman in the delegation.

April 1 [1946]

29 Washington Square West

New York City

Hick dearest, I'm thrilled about your job. It is just right & I think you'll make a great success & carry it easily.

Could you manage to spend 2 days here reading a pile of stuff? It is so heavy to send. I only want you to look thro' & read what you think I should know or mark what you think I must read in full.

Much, much love & congratulations,

E.R.

By 1946, Eleanor was serving not only as an American delegate to the United Nations but also as chair of the organization's Human Rights Commission. During the next two years, she would lead the commis-

*sion's monumental task of defining the human rights of the citizens of
the world.*

August 8th [1947]

Campobello Island

New Brunswick, Canada

Dearest Hick, It was good to get your letter for I feel as though ages had
gone by since our last meeting.

They have put off the Human Rights Commission meeting till after
the close of the General Assembly in Nov. in Geneva. The assembly begins the 16th & briefing comes before so I'll be in town from the 8th or
9th except for week ends.

I think the book has got on well.[11] I hope you liked the changed
copy.[12]

Much, much love,

E.R.

*By early 1948, the Human Rights Commission was nearing completion
of a Universal Declaration of Human Rights that the members would
take before the General Assembly for approval. The assembly would be
meeting in Paris, and the American delegation crossed the Atlantic on
the luxury liner* Queen Elizabeth. *Meanwhile, Lorena was attempting,
with Tommy's help, to write a biography of Eleanor. The former first
lady hoped that the royalties would provide a steady income for Lorena*

---

[11] Eleanor was writing the second volume of her autobiography, covering the years 1920 to 1945.

[12] In the first draft of her autobiography, Eleanor had written that she had given Lorena a private interview on Inauguration Day in 1933, adding: "Later I came to realize that in the White House one must not play favorites." When Lorena read the draft, her pride was hurt. "I didn't get that story because I was anybody's pet reporter," she wrote Tommy Thompson. "In those days I was somebody in my own right. I was just about the top gal reporter in the country." Eleanor then rephrased the statement to read: "Soon after the inauguration ceremonies Lorena Hickok, to whom I had promised an interview, came up to my sitting room. Both my husband and Louis Howe had agreed to the interview because she was the outstanding woman reporter for the Associated Press and they both had known her and recognized her ability." See Lorena to Tommy Thompson, 23 July 1947, Eleanor Roosevelt Papers; Roosevelt, *This I Remember,* 78.

and Tommy for the future. Lorena and Tommy's book venture ulti-mately failed, however, as they were unable to find a publisher for it.

March 30th [1948]

Cunard White Star
RMS "Queen Elizabeth"

Dearest Hick, I'm thrilled that you've begun to write & that you find it easy. I'd rather have you two dissect me than anyone else in the world & I'll feel so much more secure feeling that you both have a little security!

We are most luxurious & Tommy is a good sailor too, much better than I am really. I never *want* to do anything or to be nice to anyone on ship board & about all I can manage is 2 meals a day!

I like flying better because it is over more quickly! We've had one fairly sunny day, otherwise fog & rain but not very cold. Lots of love to you dear.

Devotedly,
E.R.

It was widely predicted that President Truman would be defeated by Republican Thomas E. Dewey in the 1948 election. Eleanor was reluc-tant to become an active Truman supporter, however, because she felt that delegates to the United Nations should refrain from political activ-ities.

November 1st [1948]

Hotel de Crillon
Paris

Hick dearest, It was wonderful to get your letter of the 25th.

Ed Flynn[13] telephoned me that he had some hopes [of the Democrats winning] in N.Y. state & asked me to make a short broadcast which I did rather against my better judgment!

---

[13] Ed Flynn was an official of the Democratic National Committee.

From this distance the campaign doesn't seem to be going well. [Alben] Barkley[14] certainly hasn't been much help he is not colorful & has got little popular appeal. Truman had done much by himself in the campaign in spite of a few mistakes. Dewey will win I think but should Truman win the task of keeping him up to his progressive statements [he made during the campaign] will be quite a task!

Tommy sends love & so does your ever devoted E.R.

Lorena, now that her Eleanor biography had failed, was attempting to write her own autobiography, emphasizing her work as a pioneer woman journalist in the early 1900s. She recently had written Eleanor that she was not confident, however, that there would be a market for the book.

November 28th [1948]

Hotel de Crillon

Paris

Hick dearest, Don't get an inferiority complex about your book, you've got lots to tell that will help the young gal who wants to go into the newspaper business! It will be very interesting much more interesting than Bess'.[15]

I didn't think Mr. Truman could be re-elected & now that he is I have a horrible sense of responsibility.[16] He made so many promises which can only be carried out if he gets good people around him & that he hasn't done successfully as yet!

Anna & Buzz & Johnny[17] will all be with me for Xmas which is going to be wonderful. I hope it would mean John Sr. would come too but that I haven't any sense about.[18]

---

[14] Alben Barkley of Kentucky, the Senate majority leader, was the Democratic candidate for vice president.
[15] Associated Press reporter Bess Furman was writing her autobiographical *Washington By-Line.*
[16] Eleanor had publicly endorsed Truman.
[17] Johnny was Anna and John Boettiger's son.
[18] In 1946, John Boettiger had purchased a newspaper in Phoenix, Arizona, but by this point both the newspaper and the Boettiger marriage were failing.

The work [of the Human Rights Commission] is hard now & high tension but it is coming to an end.[19]

A world of love dear,
E.R.

Lorena was suffering from a major new health concern. Many mornings she awakened to find that she could not see out of either eye. Although the total blindness ended by midday, her left eye was growing progressively weaker.

August 28th [1950]

Val-Kill Cottage

Hick dearest, I am so sorry about your eyes. This is serious for you and I know you worry.

We [Eleanor and Tommy] just can't come to you for a night as we are engulfed in work. I know you can't come here and I also know that you should enjoy your little house as long as you can swing the expense and are comfortable there[,] but when you want to come up here for a short or a long time just let me know. Meantime let's meet in N.Y. Could we have lunch to-gether on Wednesday? I'll try to come anywhere convenient for you and bring Tommy. She will phone you to-morrow.

All my love,
E.R.

Even though when the United Nations delegates met in Europe they were housed in the most elegant of hotels, Eleanor preferred the casual style of Val-Kill where she lived between sessions. She decorated the cottage with overstuffed easy chairs and hundreds of photographs— Lorena's photo was prominently displayed on the mantle in the living

---

[19] On December 10, 1948, the United Nations General Assembly accepted the Universal Declaration of Human Rights that Eleanor had been the leading force in creating.

room. In the fall of 1950, Lorena's part-time work at the New York De-
mocratic State Committee ended.

November 9th [1950]

Val-Kill Cottage

Dearest Hick, Tommy told me last night about the Committee but I think dear this may not be all black. You need a rest [and] then you need to get at writing. I can lend you what little you'll need these next weeks & before you know it you'll find ways of making money. Have you ever thought of trying to get a course in journalism [to teach] at Vassar or Bard [College], or trying to do some features for the Poughkeepsie paper?

All my love,
E.R.

After Lorena had failed to land either an agent or a publisher for her au-
tobiography, the first lady had arranged for her to meet with Nannine
Joseph, Eleanor's new literary agent.

December 7th, 1951

Hotel de Crillon
Paris

Hick dearest, Your letter sounds a bit low but I'm glad you will see Nannine. Good luck, I'll keep my fingers crossed for you![20]

This means I hope you can come to me [at Val-Kill] for Xmas. I'll let you know when I get in but it won't be before Xmas eve I fear in the morning as I can't leave here till the 22d.

---

[20] The publisher that Nannine Joseph persuaded to look at Lorena's autobiography rejected it, saying the four sample chapters that Lorena had written "lacked the breath of life."

I'm sure the Democratic party has been in power too long but the alternative of [Robert] Taft[21] is even worse!

The [United Nations] work is heavy now so this is just a line to send you love from Tommy & me.

Devotedly,
E.R.

This letter contains Eleanor's first reference to another way that she helped Lorena financially. The book project ultimately evolved into a series of profiles of women political figures titled Ladies of Courage.

July 26th [1952]

Val-Kill Cottage

Dearest Hick, Harper's [publishing house] wants a primer for women on politics. I can't do it alone, but if you'll do it, I'll help & work with you & both our names can go on as co-authors. Please consider it, it is needed, but I can't give the time to consultation with them, research & basic writing. I'll discuss [the content] with you & write some parts & go over all of it & we'll have fun I hope. They'll give you an advance.

Thanks again & write soon,

E.R.

After President Eisenhower was elected in November, the new Republican administration replaced Eleanor and the other American delegates to the United Nations. Eleanor then began dividing her time between living at Val-Kill and traveling around the world to visit people she had worked with at the United Nations. Her first venture was a trip around the world, including stops in Beirut, Damascus, Tel Aviv, Karachi, and New Delhi. She then returned to Hyde Park. During this same period,

---

[21] Conservative Robert Taft of Ohio was a serious contender for the 1952 Republican presidential nomination, although moderate Dwight Eisenhower ultimately became the nominee.

Lorena was at the Little House, desperately short on money and writing furiously on the book about women in politics.

December 26th [1952]

Val-Kill Cottage

Hick dearest, I'm sad you can't come up but I understand how rushed you are.

We had a nice Xmas & I missed you.

My love always,

E.R.

In early April, Tommy Thompson died at age sixty-six of a brain hemorrhage. She had served Eleanor for thirty years.

April 19th [1953]

Val-Kill Cottage

Hick dearest, How sweet of you to write & how nice to get it to-day before going off. You will miss Tommy, as we all will daily for she did so much for those she loved. Nevertheless we will all be happier for her constant memory.

I'll try to get my interviews for the [*Ladies of Courage*] book to Nannine [Joseph] before I leave.[22]

My dear love & thanks again.

Devotedly,

E.R.

Eleanor had begun giving speeches on behalf of the American Association for the United Nations, an organization dedicated to building pub-

---

[22] Japanese officials had asked ER to make a series of speeches in their country to encourage Japanese women to enter public life.

lic support for world peace and cooperation. She had just returned from speaking in Hong Kong, Athens, and Zagreb.

August 19th [1953]

Val-Kill Cottage

Hick dearest, At last to-night I've finished reading your material [for *Ladies of Courage*] & it is simply swell I think. Much more interesting than I thought it could possibly be made.

All my love & your work is fine,

E.R.

October 26th [1953]

Val-Kill Cottage

Dearest Hick, I'm sending as my usual Xmas gift the money for your coal[23] as you must want to put it in soon.

I do hope the eyes are holding up & the work [on *Ladies of Courage*] is nearly finished. Anna & Jim [Halsted][24] will be here the 5th & 6th & 8th & 9th & she may stay on a few days.

Traveling pretty steadily but here in snatches.

All my love dear,

E.R.

Besides providing financial support, ER also attempted to use her influence, as she repeatedly had in the past, to secure a job for Hick. This

---

[23] Heating the Little House during the winter had become Lorena's biggest expense.

[24] Anna and John Boettiger had divorced in 1949, and she married Dr. James Halsted in 1953.

time, Eleanor asked New York Governor Averell Harriman, a fellow Democrat, if he might have a position for a writer. Harriman reviewed Lorena's credentials and interviewed her, but he did not hire her. Meanwhile, Eleanor was traveling in Europe, sending the following message on a postcard from the Grand Hotel Flora in Rome.

March 12 [1955]

Dearest Hick, Good trip so far, tho' rain & sleet this p.m. Stay well & love, E.R.

Eleanor and Lorena both were listed as authors of Ladies of Courage *when it was published, but Eleanor gave all the royalties to Lorena. When Eleanor came to New York City, she stayed at an apartment she was renting on the Upper East Side.*

May 19th [1955]

55 East 74th Street
New York City

Dearest Hick, Here's a little check Nannine [Joseph] sent me but I don't want it for you did *all* the work on the book so use it for odds & ends. Let me know if you are really short of money.

I'm sorry about these attacks & anxious to hear what the doctor found after your hospital check up. Do let me know.[25]

---

[25] The doctor diagnosed the recurring pain in Lorena's legs as arthritis, which became increasingly severe in the next few years.

Have you got the money for coal or do you want it for Xmas & how much?

Much, much love,

E.R.

Eleanor was traveling on a speaking tour—she gave an average of 150 lectures a year—in California. While on the trip, Eleanor received a telephone call from Lorena's landlady, who explained just how destitute Lorena had become. Several months behind on her rent and with nothing but rejections in response to her attempts to publish books on her own, Lorena was living solely on the money Eleanor sent her. After the phone call, the first lady dispatched her chauffeur, Tubby Curnan, to Long Island to move Lorena to the Val-Kill cottage. Lorena never saw her beloved Little House again.

August 9th [1955]

Rolling Rock Ranch

Hick dearest, Of course you will forget the sad times at the end & eventually think only of the pleasant memories. Life is like that, with ends that have to be forgotten.

The future is what I am thinking about & please let me know what you plan.

I have been riding again & thought of you & the Yosemite [vacation] many times. It is beautiful country with lovely mountain trails. We leave here Friday at 6:30 a.m.

Much love dear,

E.R.

Nannine Joseph persuaded Lorena to try a new approach in her publishing efforts, suggesting that her simple reportorial style was well suited to books for young adults. Lorena did not initially embrace the idea, but then she thought of a subject she was sure would be an inspiration to juvenile readers: Helen Keller. No one had written such a book

before because the woman who had triumphed over blindness and deaf-
ness had refused to give any author a private interview; when Eleanor
personally asked Keller to spend a day with Lorena, however, Keller
agreed.

October 8th [1957]

55 East 74th Street
New York City

Dearest Hick, Your letter came in record time & I was happy to hear.
You were sweet to think so far ahead & I've made no plans for I don't
intend to celebrate till I'm 75.[26]
What a lot you've had to learn about the blind!
I'm in a mad rush but it will end someday.
Much, much love & thanks again,

E.R.

Lorena living at Val-Kill worked fine when Eleanor was traveling. But
when ER was at the cottage, there was so much activity that Lorena be-
came agitated and could not concentrate on her writing. The situation
was so reminiscent of Eleanor's days in the White House that in late
1957 Lorena decided to rent her own apartment in the village of Hyde
Park three miles from Val-Kill, paying her rent with the $4,000 in roy-
alties from Ladies of Courage.

December 18th [1957]

55 East 74th Street
New York City

Dearest Hick, I'll go to you from the train Saturday & we can go & see
the apartment & then perhaps you will come back & lunch with me?
I hope you will take it as I feel you will be better off in the village. I
think I can find enough furniture & buy essential kitchen things if an ice
box & stove are in [the apartment already]? Anyway it is worth considering carefully.

[26] Eleanor's seventy-third birthday was only three days away.

Hope your eyes & nerves improve.
Much love dear & I'll see you Sat.

Devotedly,
E.R.

When Eleanor wrote this letter, she was visiting the Brussels World's Fair and planning a trip to the Soviet Union. Lorena's biography of Helen Keller had been published, and she was busy revising her biography of Eleanor to tailor it toward a young audience.

September 6th, 1958

Metropole Hotel
Brussels

Dearest Hick, How goes it with you? The fair is interesting & fun & this city itself is attractive. My columns are full of the fair because I thought no one had told us much about it. I'm so far ahead with the columns that I don't think I'll have to write any at all when I'm in Russia.

My love to you & good luck with whatever you are writing.

Devotedly,
E.R.

During 1960, people close to Eleanor noticed that she was tiring more quickly, and a trip to the doctor led to a diagnosis of aplastic anemia, also known as bone-marrow failure, and an order for Eleanor to rest more. It surprised no one when she ignored the doctor's directive. Early the next year, Eleanor attended John F. Kennedy's inauguration in Washington and then flew to Arizona for a series of lectures.

January 23d, 1961

Arizona Inn
Tucson, Arizona

Dearest Hick, Here we are. Yesterday we had sun but to-day it is rainy & not at all like summer.

The snow last Thursday really played havoc with Washington. Traffic was snarled, cars ran out of gas or their radiators gave out, & they were abandoned in mid street adding to the chaos. I tried to get to the gala performance[27] but sat 4 hours in traffic & when a break came I went home! Inauguration day itself was cold & beautiful & the ceremonies impressive. I thought the speech magnificent, didn't you? I have reread it twice.[28]

I'll see you the 30th if all goes well & the weather plays no tricks.

> Much love dear,
> E.R.

Eleanor was planning a reunion for the women who had covered her White House press conferences thirty years earlier. Of course she included on her invitation list the woman who had suggested the historic sessions that had been such a success—and yet had not been repeated by any of the first ladies since then.

> January 4, 1962

> 55 East 74th Street
> New York City

Dearest Hick, On February 3rd I plan to have the dinner for all the newspaper women and I wonder if you could come down and spend that night with me? Tubby [Curnan] could bring you down and take you back.

I would plan on having dinner at 7:30, and I look forward to hearing that you will come.

> Much love,
> E.R.

---

[27] The Inaugural Gala at the National Guard Armory included readings by actor Sir Laurence Olivier and musical numbers by singer Frank Sinatra.

[28] A single line in Kennedy's speech became the hallmark of his administration: "Ask not what your country can do for you; ask what *you* can do for your *country.*"

In the summer of 1962, Eleanor's doctor feared that her anemia was on the verge of causing internal bleeding, so he gave her steroids to prevent the bleeding. Unfortunately, the steroids reactivated an old tuberculosis lesion that dated back to 1919. Because of Eleanor's failing health, she had to dictate this letter to a secretary, who then typed it for ER's signature.

September 14, 1962

55 East 74th Street
New York City

Dearest Hick, I was glad to get your letter and I do hope the blood sugar levelled off a little bit lower and you don't have to take more Insulin. I am happy if talking to Walter Reuther was helpful.[29] I'll be back on Monday.

Love,
E.R.

The tuberculosis that spread rapidly through Eleanor's body resisted all treatment. The final item in Eleanor and Lorena's correspondence was sent by the Roosevelt family on the day after Eleanor died, at the age of seventy-eight.

---

[29] Eleanor had arranged for Lorena to interview labor leader Walter Reuther, the subject of Hick's next juvenile biography.

[November 8, 1962]

WESTERN UNION

[to]   MISS LORENA HICKOK
       HYDE PARK NY

THE FAMILY OF MRS FRANKLIN D ROOSEVELT INVITE YOU TO THE
CHURCH SERVICE TO BE HELD AT ST JAMES EPISCOPAL CHURCH HYDE
PARK NY SATURDAY NOVEMBER IOTH AT 2:OO PM AND TO THE INTER-
MENT SERVICE IN THE ROSE GARDEN FRANKLIN D ROOSEVELT LIBRARY
HYDE PARK IMMEDIATELY FOLLOWING - PLEASE PRESENT THIS TELEGRAM
FOR ADMISSION

EPILOGUE

The Long Way Home

Lorena chose not to attend Eleanor's funeral. She had always hated sharing the first lady with a crowd, and this was no exception—particularly when the event was televised and the crowd included such luminaries as President Kennedy, Vice President Johnson, and former Presidents Truman and Eisenhower. Only after all the other mourners had departed did Lorena craft her own private—almost eccentric—farewell.[1]

Her first step was to enlist the aid of the rector of St. James Episcopal Church. The courtly, white-haired Reverend Gordon Kidd already knew Lorena because Eleanor had asked him, from time to time as she was

---

[1] The description of Lorena's life after Eleanor died is based on interviews with people who knew Lorena during this period. Those people are Gloria Kidd Gordon, the daughter of the Reverend Gordon Kidd; John Gordon, Gloria Kidd Gordon's husband and Lorena's landlord for ten years; Eileen DeVries, who did secretarial work for Lorena; Sandra DeVries, who walked Lorena's dog; and Hitze DeVries, Eileen and Sandra DeVries's father, who often talked with Lorena and who, along with his wife, Patricia, had Lorena to dinner at the DeVries home. The interviews were conducted in Hyde Park during August 1997.

preparing to depart on a trip, to look in on Lorena while she was away. He agreed to drive Lorena to Eleanor's grave so she could place some flowers there and say her personal goodbye. It had struck him a bit odd, however, that she insisted the visit be after dark, so no one would see her. Regardless, on the appointed night he dutifully picked up Lorena at her apartment and drove her through the gates at the Roosevelt property—the guard, recognizing Father Kidd, waved them through—and as close to the rose garden as his car was allowed. Then they began walking the several hundred feet remaining on their nocturnal pilgrimage. Overweight and hampered by both her arthritis and the intensity of her emotions, Lorena was breathing so heavily that she had to pause more than once before finally being forced to give up altogether. Then she quietly handed the cluster of goldenrod and other wild flowers to Father Kidd—it was too dark for him to see if there were tears in her eyes, but he suspected there were—so he could carry the humble bouquet the final distance and deposit it at the foot of the white marble slab.

Lorena's failure to complete that final tribute to Eleanor was only the first of many disappointments that would define the last years of her life. Earlier it seemed that Eleanor had succeeded in placing Lorena on a financially rewarding course as an author of biographies for juvenile readers. The first lady had not only connected Lorena with her own New York literary agent, Nannine Joseph, but also had arranged Lorena's crucial interview with Helen Keller that had virtually guaranteed the success of that first biography. By the time Eleanor had died, Lorena already had churned out four more biographies aimed at the same youthful audience—two on Franklin, one on Eleanor, and one on Anne Sullivan Macy, Keller's teacher. It was only after Eleanor's death that it became clear, however, that such biographies with their narrowly defined audience did not produce significant royalties. Nor did *Reluctant First Lady,* which focused on Eleanor's life from 1928 to 1933, sell more than a few hundred copies. In addition, Lorena's failing eyesight impeded her writing, preventing her from completing the biography of labor leader Walter Reuther. Still, the royalties from the Helen Keller biography and *Ladies of Courage* paid the modest rent on Lorena's two-room apartment and the dollar or two a week she gave neighborhood children to go to the grocery store for her and to walk her dog Jenny, the miniature Shetland sheepdog that had been one of Eleanor's last gifts.

Those children provided Lorena with her only human contact on many days, as she became increasingly reclusive. She wore no makeup and kept her hair cut short (she cut it herself), and she wore the same khaki trousers and men's shirt a week straight. Never a religious person, she repeatedly turned down the offers from St. James parishioners to take her to church; on the rare occasion that she joined one of the families in the neighborhood for supper, she seemed to do so not because she was eager but because she felt obligated—if she didn't accept an invitation once in a while, maybe the parents wouldn't let their children walk Jenny.

The other invitations Lorena found onerous were those from Ray Corry, director of the Franklin D. Roosevelt Library. The first friend had given a few of Eleanor's letters to the library in 1958, stipulating that they could not be opened until ten years after her own death. After that initial deposit, Corry was relentless in his effort to obtain as much of the correspondence as possible. Corry continually wooed Lorena with elaborate dinners, complete with cocktails and wine, at his home. He told her it was her obligation to history that the letters be preserved, but she found the evenings with Corry burdensome—she preferred staying at home and listening to the Metropolitan Opera on the radio.

By the mid-1960s, Lorena was almost totally blind. Her arthritis became so bad that she was barely able to walk on her own and finally had to resort to a cane, then a walker, and finally a wheelchair. Lorena's tobacco addiction gave her a hacking cough, and yet she persisted in smoking a pack of Camels a day even into her mid-seventies. Then, in the spring of 1968, Lorena's doctor told her that the numbness in her toes was a result of her daily doses of insulin and that it would be necessary for him to amputate at least one of her legs, possibly both. Lorena admitted herself to the hospital in Rhinebeck, half an hour north of Hyde Park, in April, and she made it through the first of the two operations in fairly good shape. But not the second. She died on May 1, 1968, at the age of seventy-five, outliving Eleanor by five and a half years. Patricia DeVries, the member of St. James parish who was with Lorena when she died, recalled that she was delirious at the end, talking incoherently about friends and friendships from the distant past. Not once either during those final hours or during her final years, the people who knew Lorena said, did she express any resentment toward Eleanor Roosevelt.

Hick had spent a good deal of time during her final years typing and retyping her will, even though her monetary worth was minimal. She had taken great pride in maintaining a $1,000 balance at Farmers-Mattewan National Bank so she would be able to return to the Roosevelt family the exact same amount that the first lady's will had given her. In those final difficult years, however, the vicissitudes of life had forced Lorena to dip into the account from time to time. When her will was probated, only $700 remained to be divided equally among the children of Eleanor Seagraves, the little girl Lorena had known during the White House years as "Sisty."[2]

Lorena was even more deliberate in her efforts to ensure that the most precious of her gifts from Eleanor be returned to the Roosevelt family. Most of the items went to Eleanor Seagraves. First on the list was Jenny, the sweet little dog that had kept Lorena company to the end. Then came several pieces of furniture from the Val-Kill factory—a walnut desk and chair, a maple daybed, a mirror with a maple frame. Next came Lorena's collection of the books Eleanor had written and numerous photographs of the first lady taken at various times during the previous thirty years, each signed "Dearest Hick, with all my love, E.R." Then came the hemstitched napkins and a table runner that the first lady had somehow found time to make, embroidering Lorena's initials into the fine linen fabric, while living at the White House. Then three final items that Lorena bequeathed to Eleanor Seagraves's children—her typewriter to Nicholas, her tape recorder to David, and the blue Staffordshire cup from the White House years to Eleanor Seagraves's only daughter, Eleanor.

Eleanor Seagraves, now in her early seventies, lives in Washington, D.C. Although she never saw Lorena after the first lady died in 1962, Seagraves still has clear—and fond—memories of going on picnics in Hyde Park with her grandmother, her children, and Lorena. "She was very crippled up—had diabetes really bad—and she was penniless, but she was always in high spirits when my grandmother was around. And Lorena always fawned over my children." Seagraves also speaks fondly

---

[2] File 59691, Surrogate's Court, Dutchess County Courthouse, Poughkeepsie, New York.

of Eleanor and Lorena's relationship. "They came from very different social strata, and that somehow freed both of them up to talk about the unhappiness of their lives and to share a very special closeness." When asked about the nature of that closeness, Seagraves does not hesitate. Having been with both women numerous times between 1933 and 1962, she has come to her own conclusions about the relationship. "Lorena was very much in love with my grandmother, but Lorena was also a very emotional woman—and she went overboard. My grandmother was always bound by a sense of duty, and she felt a very strong sense of gratitude and appreciation for what Lorena had given her—in working with the media and in her emotional life as well." Did Eleanor Seagraves ever detect any bitterness on Lorena's part because of the downward turn in her career, at least partly because of her relationship with the first lady? "Absolutely not. I never sensed any resentment whatsoever from Lorena toward my grandmother. Lorena loved my grandmother totally and unconditionally—with all her heart. That love never faltered." Does Seagraves believe Lorena and her grandmother's relationship included a sexual dimension? "Certainly my grandmother loved Lorena—there is no question about that. But by the time they met, my grandmother had consciously forsaken sex of any kind. Oh, yes, she had participated in sexual activity earlier in her life, in the early years of her marriage. But she had been betrayed. By the time my grandmother met Lorena, she had become entirely asexual."[3]

While Lorena devoted a great deal of time during her final years to making sure that the first lady's granddaughter and great-grandchildren inherited her rather meager worldly possessions, she did not spend as much time considering the disposition of her bodily remains. And that lack of attention, unfortunately, placed a poignantly sad ending to Lorena's life. Father Kidd did as Lorena had requested, arranging for her cremation at Dapson Funeral Home in Rhinebeck and conducting a simple service, with only himself and the undertaker present, at the cremation chapel. But in the note Lorena had typed and attached to her will, she had failed to indicate exactly who should be responsible for the final detail—"The disposal of my ashes is immaterial, although, if it can be done, I should like to have them dug into the soil around growing

[3] Author's interview with Eleanor Seagraves, 24 October 1997, in Washington, D.C.

trees, which may benefit from whatever chemicals the ashes contain." With no one specifically named to take that final step, the director of the funeral home placed Lorena's cremated remains on a storage shelf with other unclaimed ashes. Not so much as a granite headstone or bronze marker—and certainly no white marble slab—was erected to the memory of Lorena Hickok.

Acknowledgments

In an effort to minimize my disruptions of Eleanor and Lorena's intimate conversation, I opted not to insert citations for the various sources that I used to identify references in the letters and to fill in the gaps between those letters. I certainly am indebted, however, to the dedicated historians who have previously examined the lives of these two women and, therefore, helped me to craft the headnotes, footnotes, and narrative sections of this book. Among the authors I turned to most often were Blanche Wiesen Cook, Doris Faber, and Joseph P. Lash. I sincerely thank them for their fine scholarship.

I also want to acknowledge the assistance provided by my research apprentice, Laura Pohl, who helped me decipher many of the letters contained in this book. Laura's energy and can-do attitude—not to mention her youthful eyes—were a godsend.

With regard to the overall content and direction of this project, I want to thank Bruce Nichols, my talented and insightful editor at The Free Press. Bruce envisioned what this book could be and then steadfastly shepherded it from concept to completion, all the while providing me with support and reassurance.

I also want to thank Kyle Rose for his careful reading of a draft version of the manuscript. One of the greatest benefits of being a professor is the pleasure I receive from watching former students grow and succeed. Kyle is one of those students whose evolution has brought me a great deal of joy.

At American University, my gratitude goes to the Senate Research Committee and Dean of Academic Affairs Ivy Broder for providing me with a university research grant. The financial assistance was beneficial; the knowledge that my colleagues supported me was priceless.

On my own faculty in the School of Communication, I want to express my deep appreciation to Dean Sanford J. Ungar. His wise counsel and unwavering support on this book project, as on my various other undertakings during the past dozen years, have been invaluable. Without Sandy, my achievements would have ended long ago.

Finally, I want to acknowledge the central role that Tom Grooms and my children, Matt and Kate, play in every aspect of both my professional and my personal life—indeed, in my very being. I am very proud of them and who they are. Without them, my life would be as empty as Eleanor knew, in March 1933, that hers would have been without Lorena.

Index